# SUPERCONNECT

# SUPERCONNECT

Harnessing the Power of Networks
and the Strength of Weak Links

RICHARD KOCH
GREG LOCKWOOD

**Property of
Baker College
of Allen Park**

W. W. Norton & Company
New York • London

For information about permission to reproduce selections from this book,
write to Permissions, W. W. Norton & Company, Inc.,
500 Fifth Avenue, New York, NY 10110

For information about special discounts for bulk purchases, please contact
W. W. Norton Special Sales at specialsales@wwnorton.com or 800-233-4830

Manufacturing by Courier Westford
Production manager: Julia Druskin

Library of Congress Cataloging-in-Publication Data

Koch, Richard, 1950–
Superconnect : harnessing the power of networks and the strength of weak links /
Richard Koch, Greg Lockwood.—1st American ed.
p. cm.
"Originally published in Great Britain under the title Superconnect:
The Power of Networks and the Strength of Weak Links."
Includes bibliographical references and index.
ISBN 978-0-393-07160-3 (hbk.)
1. Social networks. 2. Success. I. Lockwood, Greg. II. Title.
HM741.K67 2010
302.3—dc22

2010017950

W. W. Norton & Company, Inc.
500 Fifth Avenue, New York, N.Y. 10110
www.wwnorton.com

W. W. Norton & Company Ltd.
Castle House, 75/76 Wells Street, London W1T 3QT

1 2 3 4 5 6 7 8 9 0

*This book is dedicated to Christina and Zoe,*
*and to Matthew and Tocker*

We keep passing unseen through little moments of other people's lives.

*Robert M. Pirsig,*
*Zen and the Art of Motorcycle Maintenance*

# Contents

# Authors' Note

The authors decided that it was too confusing for us both to use 'I' in recounting stories in our lives. As Greg is far more modest than Richard, he used 'I' less. We therefore decided that 'I' would mean Richard. Where there is a story involving Greg, he is introduced by Richard.

# Preface

This book should never have happened. If it wasn't for the most bizarre and twisted sequence of events involving a diverse array of people it wouldn't have. Let us explain. If some-one we, the authors, had wanted to impress – a publisher, say, or a book reviewer – had asked us how it had emerged, we could have come up with all kinds of things to establish our credentials for writing it. But they would have been only a small part of the story of how it came about, and not the interesting bit either. The truth is much more human and fascinating – and it also gets to the heart of the book and shows how networks *really* work.

Greg has always been fascinated by 'network theory' – the findings of sociologists, mathematicians and physicists, which seemed to translate to the real world of links between people. Early in his professional life at *Auto Trader* magazine in Canada he got to see an extraordinary network of buyers and sellers in operation. Later, when he became a venture capitalist – someone who invests in new or young companies, hoping that some of them will become very valuable – he applied what he'd learned. He invested in businesses that could benefit from the way net-works behave, and this approach yielded some notable successes.

Richard came from a different slant. For twenty years, he was a 'strategy consultant', using economic analysis to help firms become more profitable than their rivals. He ended up co-founding LEK, the fastest-growing 'strategy boutique' of the

1980s, with offices in the US, Europe and Asia. He also wrote books on business strategy, and in particular championed the 'star business' idea, which stated that the most valuable venture was nearly always a 'star', defined as the biggest firm in a high-growth market. In the 1990s and 2000s, Richard successfully invested the money he had made as a management consultant in a series of star ventures. He also read everything available about networks, feeling intuitively that they were another reason for business success, and might also help explain why some people's careers took off while equally intelligent and qualified people often languished.

So, there were good reasons why Greg and Richard might want to write a book together about networks. But the problem with all such 'formal' explanations is that they ignore the human events and coincidences that took place before that book could ever see the light of day. The most obvious of these is that, prior to 2001, Richard and Greg were not aware of each other's existence. And it is absolutely certain that this book would not have been written if we had not met.

When asked how *that* happened, we can give a one-word answer, but behind it lie a large number of unlikely events which together add up to extreme implausibility. That one-word reason is 'Betfair'. This venture was founded in 2000 on a shoestring and has since become the world's largest 'betting exchange', worth around two billion dollars.

Now for the more complete answer. On Richard's side, he was contacted one day in 2000 by a friend of a friend of someone called Robert Markwick. Robert and Richard did not know each other. But Robert knew Jeremy Black, whose brother Andrew was trying to raise money to get his invention – an online betting exchange which linked gamblers to other gamblers so that they could make and take opposite sides of a bet – off the ground. So Richard heard of this fledgling company, Betfair, at four removes from its founders, and did not know the

three closest links to the company at all. In deciding to invest in
Betfair, Richard relied heavily on advice from Patrick Weaver, a
racing journalist, whom he had met by chance at a party near
Santa Anita racecourse in California. If Richard had not met
Patrick, and if Patrick had not given a favourable verdict on
Betfair, Richard might not have invested in the company.

Meanwhile, Greg heard about another investment opportunity, in a similar betting exchange called Flutter, also launched in
2000, this time by two former management consultants from
California. One of them, Josh, had met a guy called Tim Levene
while working in Sydney, Australia, who much later joined him
in the Flutter start-up in London. Tim told the story of this
start-up to Jason Katz, a long-time buddy in the banking world.
Jason knew Greg, and that Greg was interested in investing in
online businesses, so he told him about Flutter. Greg suspected
that Flutter could be a business benefiting from a network, like
*Auto Trader* all those years before. So he invested.

By early 2001, therefore, Richard and Greg had become
shareholders in similar businesses, both based in London. But
they still didn't know each other. However, they had unwittingly
taken a step closer to meeting when they agreed to go on the
boards of directors of Betfair and Flutter respectively. But the
ventures were rivals, and didn't talk to each other. Then, to cut
a long story short, a merger between Flutter and Betfair was
mooted. And after protracted negotiations – which nearly broke
down at several points – the two firms joined forces. Greg joined
Richard on the enlarged Betfair board.

That is how, one muggy day in spring 2001, in a tiny,
crowded space in Parsons Green, south-west London, which
Betfair humorously called its 'boardroom', we eventually got
acquainted. We also came to see that the firm's success stemmed
largely from the network of gamblers it assembled. As Betfair's
network became much stronger than that of any rival
exchange – particularly once Flutter had joined forces – serious

gamblers gravitated to it. The chances of getting their bet 'matched' by someone taking the opposite view was much better on a larger exchange than a smaller one. As more and more gamblers joined the Betfair site, it grew to become twenty or thirty times bigger than any other exchange. It became what we have come to term a superconnector.

So how did *Superconnect* the book arise? It came about because Greg suggested the idea to Richard. Richard had put him on an email list consisting of a diverse set of friends and acquaintances he used to test out his new book ideas, and Greg spontaneously replied, 'These are all OK, but there's something interesting to be written around six degrees of separation and network effects.' Richard loved the suggestion and asked Greg to collaborate on the book.

Again, it took a combination of experience to tackle it with confidence. Greg was sure of the subject matter, and Richard was the author of a string of successful books about business, ideas and careers. But even then, this book would not have reached its current form but for a book agent in Oxford called Sally Holloway, who forced Richard and Greg to write a decent proposal that led to an auction in which three leading New York publishers participated. Richard had only come across Sally because a former colleague had suggested they meet.

So the way the authors met and the way the book originated each comprised a series of human contacts, long chains of personal links that became fully apparent only in retrospect. If any one of the links had not existed, we would not have worked at Betfair, we would not have met, we would not have written this book. In the pages that follow, we will present dozens of stories – and a lot of scientific evidence – that indicate that our experience, while unique, is also routine. In other words, the improbable is the rule! If you look backwards at any key event in your life, the chances are that it shouldn't have happened how it did.

★

This was an unusual book to write. Sometimes it felt that as we wrote it we were exploring the truly unusual – cutting-edge insights into the way the human world works. As one of those involved puts it, 'Network science is *the* science of the twenty-first century.' At other times it was as if we were merely distilling the wisdom of grandmothers, dispensed for free at every kitchen table. The territory is so familiar to everyone – the relationships we have and the groups we belong to – that anyone can have an opinion on it. And grandmothers have lived a long time and generally learned a thing or two. But grandmothers are not usually adept at science, and there is a true subtlety about the material we uncovered – those things we live with every day and think we know, yet may know the least – that no grandmother of our acquaintance has been able to put into words.

For instance, it wasn't immediately evident how one of the core findings of the book – that the friendly acquaintances and distant contacts we often forget about lead to knowledge, opportunity and innovation that make life much more exciting and fulfilling – came into play. Nor that our strong relationships with people and groups – those we depend on the most – can actually hold us back. But we found that putting these things together unlocked a powerful new perspective on social and career mobility.

Coming as even more of a surprise to us was the realisation that the network of relationships between people and groups that makes up society is shaped mostly by superconnectors – a rare group of people and businesses who are disproportionately connected. These people and businesses are the bridges to distant and different parts of society that make our world smaller, and its vast richness accessible. And in the business world they are the increasingly dominant crossroads that hold far-reaching implications for market structure, strategy and industrial policy.

An array of scientists – including sociologists, psychologists, physicists, mathematicians and computer experts – have recently made some dramatic advances in understanding how networks behave. As authors we see our job as explaining their discoveries, and placing them in a human, social and practical context that will help you to understand how to shape your own networks, and decide which ones to play in and which to avoid.

However, the more we thought about the science of networks, the more we found it describes and informs a variety of important but disparate aspects of our world – innovation, poverty, the interrelationship of ideas and the nature of society itself. And as our world becomes increasingly connected through technology, these network effects grow ever more pronounced.

So, this book covers a lot of scientific ground, yet it also relates directly to people's personal lives. Have you ever asked yourself how anything important in your life happens? If you look back on any turning-point, you'll uncover a chain of human contacts – as we did – who played a critical role in what happened to you. This book is about how those contacts operate, and how to increase the chances of happy outcomes in our personal life, career or business.

But, of course, all of our lives have to consist of key events. The world may not be predictable, but its unpredictability is, and this is shaped by networks. Once you grasp this point, and the fact that the world is unpredictable in a beautiful and ordered way, you can begin to shift the odds against opportunity and even happiness in your favour.

Networks behave in predictable and characteristic ways that we humans are not programmed to understand or appreciate. And they typically create few winners. So if we want to lead lives full of opportunity, we had better learn how to play by their rules.

## CHAPTER ONE

# AUTHORS OF OUR OWN SUCCESS?

*Charlie Chaplin, Marlon Brando, James Dean,*
*and the unsettling discovery that outside forces*
*may determine success*

> Maximise the serendipity around you.
> *Nassim Nicholas Taleb*

## Hollywood, 1936

If you wanted to protest against the dehumanising effects of the Industrial Revolution by projecting a single striking picture of its oppression, how would you do it? In the movie *Modern Times*, Charlie Chaplin came up with a timeless image – he placed himself within a great revolving cog, as if inside a giant clock, part of a great mechanised factory, and showed himself buffeted by the wheel's endless revolutions.

Although it was a new and powerful portrayal, Chaplin stood – or rather, lay – in a great tradition of the 'romantic' railing against industry and its enslaving machines, stretching back to William Blake's 'dark Satanic mills'. Writers such as Blake contrasted the smelly, sordid slums of Manchester with the contented cows and peasants painted a few years earlier by Thomas Gainsborough against a bucolic background of haystacks, green fields and gently rippling rivers.

But the romantics were better at poetry and painting than they were at history. The truth was that very few British agricultural workers in the eighteenth century enjoyed much freedom or what we would today call 'job satisfaction'; theirs was a hard life in which they did what they were told, rarely had enough to eat, and faced famine and starvation at regular intervals. That was why so many people fled their rural slums to find work in the cities. Nobody forced them to go. They went in droves because, however awful life was in the mill towns, it was a great deal better than in the countryside. Karl Marx knew this – he said that industrialisation rescued workers from 'the idiocy of rural life'.

Even so, Chaplin's fate in 1936 was essentially the same as that of a mill worker in 1836, or a peasant in 1736, or at any earlier time in human history. The ordinary person – a category which includes the huge majority of humans since time began – had a horrid, tedious, unsatisfying existence, with precious little say in how to run his or her life.

This is very different from our experience today – so when did the big change occur? Some say the Beatles reflected this change in society, but the landscape had actually shifted a decade before they arrived on the scene, with Hollywood marking and magnifying the upheaval. In 1953 Marlon Brando played motorbike rebel Johnny Strabler in *The Wild One*, and throughout America movie audiences were electrified by the young star's raw charisma and assertiveness. Mothers, intoxicated and paralysed by Brando's animal magnetism, let their small children run up and down the aisles, shouting, 'Vroom-vroom!' Two years later, *Rebel without a Cause* introduced James Dean as high school gang leader Jim Stark, portraying a teenage world of knife fights, drag racing, stolen cars and death by speeding. The picture indelibly presented young people at the centre of their own universe, existentially responsible for their own destiny, heroically deciding how to live . . . and how to die.

This really was something novel – individualistic youth culture. And it happened not just in America, but in Britain and Europe; and it cropped up in music, plays and books as well as films. The Beats of the 1950s – with their poetry, long hair and propensity to drop out, go on the road and experiment with drugs – prefigured the hippies and punks of later decades. John Osborne's ferocious 1956 play *Look Back in Anger* transformed English and American theatre, introducing the foul-mouthed working-class antihero, the 'angry young man'. Colin Wilson's book *The Outsider* came out in the same year, highlighting the impact on society of many influential outsiders, including Albert Camus, Ernest Hemingway, Franz Kafka and Jean-Paul Sartre.

The golden age of youthful individualism came to full fruition in the sixties, with psychedelic drugs, music and lifestyles, student revolts, and rejection of authority in every part of life. That spirit of personal liberation was eventually transmuted by baby boomers not just into new creative spheres but into business, which became much more radical, decentralised, individualised and personally rewarding. The grey-suited, white-shirted, conformist 'organisation man' gave way to colourful semi-hippy entrepreneurs, doing their own thing, running their own show. Steve Jobs and Steve Wozniak founded Apple Computer and launched the Macintosh during a famous advertising slot in the 1984 Baseball World Series, in which the new computer was touted as the rebel alternative to Big Brother IBM. This was an explicit reference to George Orwell's *1984*, in which Big Brother, the dictator modelled on Stalin, crushed the spirit of Winston Smith, the ordinary citizen whose sole crime was to explore his individuality. Steve Wozniak later used the fortune he made from Apple to subsidise his favourite rock bands, before starting another high-tech venture.

Individualism – painful and pointless as it could often be – replaced the image of the hapless victim crushed by the heartless organisation. Since then the view that everyone can take charge of their life, realising their own success and happiness, has had a good run, becoming pretty universal. Don't you feel that you have a self, that you have inner depths, in almost the same way that you have arms and legs? Don't you feel that your personality can be developed in any way that you choose, that you can rise above whatever your parents achieved or strike out on new, personal paths? In our society, 'I did it my way' is not just a line from a song but the title of endless autobiographies, because we feel an automatic identification with the individualist, the maverick, the rebel. Everything has become personalised – we have personal computers, personal trainers, personal iPods. This is a universe away from Chaplin's revolving wheel, and the fate of humanity generally down the ages.

But here's the thing. Just as control by society was replaced by control by the self, another huge change is coming – indeed, it is already here, but we are only beginning to appreciate it. Consider this for a moment – when youth culture catapulted around the world, often in highly subversive ways and without the help of official media, how did the same dirty jokes and sexual lore suddenly turn up everywhere, decades before the Internet had been invented? How, in 1968, did identikit student revolts spread from California to Paris to Tokyo and, in paler imitations, to thousands of other campuses within a matter of days? The following year, how was it that several hundred thousand young people suddenly converged on the muddy fields of Woodstock, in the middle of nowhere, when there was no advertising, no promotion, no television coverage? What is the paradox of identical individualism, of feeling pressured to do your own thing, of 'groupthink' masquerading as personal discovery? How do fads – from hula-hoops to hoodies – explode and then fade away?

The search for individual expression is genuine enough, but it takes place within groups and it is spread by networks. And, in many ways, networks are the antithesis of the lone individual. Even when they are spontaneous and anarchic in origin, networks favour big concentrations and bind people together in ways that no individual intended or can control. The World Wide Web may be democratic and open to all, but a few websites get the lion's share of its traffic, and a very small number of people get most of the financial rewards, usually to their immense surprise. Nobody intended that to happen; and nobody can prevent it. It's just the strange way of networks.

So it's pretty clear that complete individualism is something of a delusion. It's important, it's valid, it's liberating and it's changed the world – mainly, in our opinion, for the better. But it's not the full picture. It's not a reliable guide to how the world works. To understand our world, we need a new way of thinking – which is what this book aims to provide.

This time the academics – a new type of scientist – have already done the heavy lifting for us. Now we should follow them into a world where our individual efforts are only part of the picture, a place where our success and happiness are determined by far more than our own talents and achievements. This is still a world of individuals, but it's also a world of networks – the hidden background that shapes our lives. It's a strange land, puzzling and confounding, but it's also very exciting. Whereas the heroic individualism of Dean and Brando gives us the illusion of determining our fate, the new territory we're about to explore shows the strings that are tugging us this way and that. By understanding the real nature of our world, by cooperating with the network forces around us and harnessing them to our ends, we can swap the delusion that we can control the world as individuals for the reality of creation, in collaboration with other people. When we understand our century's network society properly, we can run our lives slightly differently and benefit enormously. For example, we'll see that maintaining a large circle of casual acquaintances who come from different backgrounds with contrasting attitudes and lifestyles, or who live a long way from us, can provide knowledge and insights that have the potential to change our lives. We'll also see how vital it is to choose the people we collaborate with much more carefully than most of us do. And once we understand the insidious way that groups can operate, we'll be much more cautious about thinking in the same way as our colleagues, or about staying in an organisation (or a relationship) that makes us unhappy.

So the new perspective comes from thinking about networks. But what does 'network' mean?

A network is a set of interconnected people or things that can communicate with each other, share information and achieve results that would not be possible if the network did not exist. Networks confer benefits – as well as costs and obligations – on members; meanwhile, non-members are excluded. Every part (or member) of the network is connected to all the other parts.

It helps to visualise a transport network that you know – the New York Subway, the London Tube, the Paris Metro, a train network, or an airline network. The stations or airports are the 'members', the fixed parts of the system, and they are all connected to each other by railway lines and trains, or flight paths and aircraft. On all underground systems, you can travel from any station to any other station – unless the destination is closed and therefore isolated from the links.

In network language, the people or things – such as stations – that are connected are called 'nodes', and the network consists of the nodes and the connections (or 'links') between them. Picture a necklace of precious stones – the jewels are the nodes and the string comprises the links. Or a telephone network – the individual phones are the nodes and the telephone lines or fibre-optic cables are the links.

The links between nodes in the system can be communications

technology or social connections. Think, for example, of a group of friends who all know one another – they constitute a network, and they all share certain values or a common identity. Now imagine that these friends are all together, perhaps at a classical music concert, in a much bigger crowd. A stranger in the crowd has no barrier of technology or physical distance stopping her from talking to one or all of the group, but another type of barrier – a social barrier – is likely to prevent her from doing so because she is not a member of the network of friends. She cannot presume that she will share the champagne and smoked salmon, or the conversation.

Now consider any type of organisation – a corner shop, a hairdressing salon, a new venture, a medium-sized corporation, a gang of drug traffickers, a football team, the United Nations, Google, or the place where you work. They are all networks, with their own rules and values and ways of communicating. If you are inside the network, you give and receive in ways that those outside the network do not. If you are an employee of Exxon, for example, you can call up a fellow employee on the other side of the planet and expect some degree of cooperation, even if you have never met the person, because you are members of the same network.

The links between non-human networks are mainly technological, but those between human networks are mainly psychic or social. Yet, one of the fascinating things about networks, as we will see, is that they behave in their own characteristic ways, which are similar whether the network is human, man-made or natural, and whatever the nature of the connections linking the nodes.

When people are linked together in networks, it can make a big difference – a transcendent, sometimes bizarre difference – to them as individuals, and to their happiness and opportunities. Participation in networks has to change each one of us, because the network gives power to (or removes it from) the individual;

and the network has its own logic and rules, its own ways of operating, that have nothing whatsoever to do with the individual attributes of the people trapped within or liberated by it.

We recognise this easily in romantic and other two-person relationships. A successful relationship enriches our life in wonderful and often unpredictable ways: we find and define ourselves by the relationship and are transformed by it; we become positive and creative. A destructive relationship operates in a similar but opposite way: we become embittered, constrained, limited, negative, fearful. A two-person relationship is nothing more or less than a miniature network. Unless we're hermits, we live our lives in a large number of different networks, and the more people there are in a network the less likely we are to understand what is really going on, or appreciate the subtle but potent ways in which our fate is affected, happily or miserably, by the dynamics of the network.

Let's be a bit more precise about the components of the networks we shall explore. From the individual's perspective, there are three crucial ingredients of networks – two types of quite distinct links to other individuals or groups, and the groups ('hubs') in which we participate. These three network elements have been around in some form or another since our ancestors skulked around in caves, but their relative importance has shifted dramatically in recent decades, as have the means to benefit from them.

The first network element to appear on the planet comprised *strong links*. These are the strong relationships we have with individuals around us – typically the friends, family and workmates we see most days. These are the most permanent or long-lasting relationships we have, and the least changed in nature since Adam and Eve walked together in the cool of the morning, before that pesky serpent started to make life trickier and more interesting.

Strong links are essential for our emotional wellbeing; people who lack them are sad. So we all need strong links . . . but they are not enough on their own! And they can even be dangerous if we rely on them too much. They often give us a very poor return on our emotional and practical energy. Sociologists have proved that those people who are exclusively or largely reliant on strong links tend to be isolated, deprived of much valuable information, and unable to improve their lives. Poor communities everywhere rely on strong links far more than rich or middle-income communities do.

The second element, whose power has become apparent only in recent decades, consists of *weak links*. Forget about the common interpretation of the 'weakest link', because in the network world weak links are marvellous and among the most powerful and creative forces. These are the links we have with people who are more acquaintances than friends; although, to be effective, we must be on friendly terms with them. We see these people occasionally or rarely – they are friends of friends, our more distant or reclusive neighbours, people from the past who used to be among our strong links but with whom we have now almost completely lost touch, as well as strangers and acquaintances we happen to meet, or could meet, every day. They are the people who occupy the background of our lives.

The intriguing thing about weak links – some of them, anyway – is that the relationship with them demands little time or effort, yet it can deliver enormous dividends, sometimes in the form of casual information that can change our lives. As we'll show, the right type of information at critical junctures can determine how much we thrive or reach our potential. Random encounters, often with people we barely know or have just met, are frequently responsible for our biggest breaks or our greatest happiness. In these pages you'll find many such stories. Adrian Beecroft, one of the most accomplished venture capitalists in Europe, tells how his first, crucial break came from a casual contact at his local cricket club. Robin Field, a turnaround specialist, got the job that made his career through someone he knew only because the fellow had run off with his girlfriend. Chicago publicist Jane Graham met her romantic partner through an email from a former colleague. A huge number of such potentially serendipitous contacts present themselves to all of us all the time – yet we ignore the vast majority of them.

The third network element consists of *hubs*. We can visualise a hub as the junction of many weak and strong links. Human hubs comprise groups of people collaborating for some common purpose, including families, businesses, social circles, schools, churches, clubs and nations. We can think of life as an adventure where some of the most important decisions we make are which hubs to join or start. With whom should we collaborate for important purposes in our life, even if the objective is sometimes just to have fun?

With one important exception – the family we inherit of parents, siblings and others – we can choose which groups to cultivate and influence. For most of us, the mark we make in life and our degree of fulfilment depend to a large extent on the hubs we select and how adept we are at changing from one to another. Unlike Chaplin's picture of life as something that happens to us, unlike the vast majority of people in history, those of us alive today and fortunate enough to live in wealthy countries will participate in many hubs during our lives; and, unlike most of our forebears, we have the privilege of being able to chop and change hubs, or start new ones of our own.

Yet few of us pick our hubs and the roles we play in them with much care; and few of us understand the strange and sometimes sinister ways in which hubs behave. Groups, whether large or small, are far more than the sum of the people in them; they have lives and characters of their own, and they follow peculiar scientific laws. If we want to get the most out of our hubs and therefore our time on earth, we have to treat hubs as experimental stages in our lives. We must progressively learn, by trial and error, which type of hub is best for us and for which type we are best. And we must be willing to move from one hub to the next before we really want to.

One final question in this chapter, which brings us back to Marlon Brando and James Dean: do you believe that, by and large, you determine your own success?

That was our view until recently. People who attain a degree of success nearly always believe it is due to their innate ability. But is this right? Do you have a niggling feeling that luck or some kind of sixth sense makes some people ultra-successful? What is so special about the rich and famous?

F. Scott Fitzgerald got it exactly right. 'The rich', he wrote, 'are different. They have more money.' That is the only difference. Wealthy or famous people are not more intelligent than a lot of other people who aren't so lucky. Some high achievers might be highly determined and work very hard – but lots of other people who never get there are too.

In 2000, two physicists at the University of Paris, Jean-Philippe Bouchard and Marc Mézard, constructed a set of equations for a network of a thousand people and ran a whole series of simulations. Each person in their model was allocated a random amount of money within a narrow range at the start, and everyone was endowed with equal money-making skills so that differences would arise randomly, from luck rather than skill. Surely, in this egalitarian world, big differences in wealth would not arise? Wrong! Whenever the model was left to run for a long time, a small proportion of people ended up with most of the wealth, precisely in line with the 80/20 principle, which says that around 80 per cent of results (in this case, wealth) will end up with 20 per cent of the participants (in this case, people).[1] Now, the physicists' results were almost identical to the unequal patterns of wealth we observe in real life throughout the world. Their work suggested that the rich could benefit from a non-meritocratic process. We'll see later that this is consistent with the tendency of networks to concentrate around only a few hubs – as scientists have observed in all manner of social and economic networks, and to reward those who are already ahead of the game.

In a curious way, then, the process contains a lot of luck for individuals, and there's a great deal of randomness, yet predictable patterns also emerge.

Come back to the question. Why them – the rich, the successful – and not you? If it's not intelligence, or dedication, or rare skills, what exactly is it? It could be pure luck, but it isn't – which is just as well, for that wouldn't be a very helpful conclusion, as it wouldn't allow us to do anything differently. To jump ahead, it turns out that the very high performers in life, whether they excel in making money or in more difficult and useful pursuits, have a few tricks up their sleeves that are all related to networks. They achieve by instinct, without thinking about the network effects that are driving them forward. Yet those instincts follow a common pattern, which has everything to do with networks. If we understand how networks work, we stand a much better chance of achieving their sort of results.

Besides the healthy desire to get ahead, there are other reasons for exploring the hidden forces ruling our lives – it's interesting, it's fun, and it puts us in the charmed position of understanding more about what's going on in our lives and why. In Chapter Two, we begin by looking at how easy or hard it is for us to connect with any other person or group in the world.

CHAPTER TWO

# DO YOU LIVE IN A SMALL WORLD?

*The small world – reality or urban myth?*

Everything is linked together ... beings are
connected with each other by a chain of which ...
some parts are continuous, though in the greater
number of points the continuity escapes us ... the
art of the philosopher consists in adding new links
to the separated parts, in order to reduce the
distance between them as much as possible.
 *Denis Diderot (1713–84) in the* Encyclopédie

To demonstrate that people on Earth are much
closer than ever, a member of the group suggested a
test. He bet that we could name any person amongst
Earth's one and a half billion inhabitants, and
through at most five acquaintances, one of whom he
knew personally, he could link to the target person.
 *Frigyes Karinthy (1887–1938)*

Have you heard of 'six degrees of separation'? In 1990 the
idea burst on to the public stage, quite literally, with John
Guare's eponymous play, which three years later transmuted into
a Hollywood movie. The idea had originated in a short story

called 'Chain Links', written in 1929 by Frigyes Karinthy, now largely forgotten but then an acclaimed novelist (at least in Hungary). You'll see from the epigraph above the basic idea – anyone can reach anyone else in the world through a short chain of acquaintances, five or six hops from the start of the chain: A to B, whom A knows, to C, whom B knows, and so on to the target F or G.

Somehow Karinthy's idea reached Jane Jacobs, the great chronicler of American cities,[2] who tells that when she first moved to New York, in the early 1930s, she and her sister played a similar game called Messages:

> The idea was to pick two wildly dissimilar individuals – say a head hunter in the Solomon Islands and a cobbler in Rock Island, Illinois – and assume that one had to get a message to the other by word of mouth . . . The one who could make the shortest plausible chain of messengers won. The head hunter would speak to the head man of the village, who would speak to the trader who came to buy copra, who would speak to the Australian patrol officer when he came through . . . Down at the other end, the cobbler would hear from his priest, who got it from the mayor, who got it from a state senator . . . We soon had these close-to-home messengers down to a routine for almost everybody we could dream up.

Do you think six degrees of separation is roughly right? Or just wishful thinking?

It's quite an important question. Another way of putting it is: do you live in a small world or a big world? A small world in this case means one where you can easily connect to anyone you desire. It doesn't mean that your world is provincial or limited; quite the opposite. A big world implies one where communication falters or dies, a world of separate groups, defeated by distance or social barriers. If you believe there are only six degrees of separation between very different people in different countries, you vote for the small world. A small world would be comforting – the idea that we are all linked intimately to everyone else.

But is it true? It took a maverick social psychologist called Stanley Milgram to conduct the first scientific test, back in 1967, of whether we live in a small or a big world. It should be pointed out here that Milgram was one of the most interesting and controversial figures ever to grace American academic life. Before he dreamed up his small world study, he was already quite famous – or rather notorious – as the American professor who electrocuted his students. Well, almost. In a series of gripping experiments at Yale University in 1961–2, Milgram got white-coated experimenters to take charge of volunteers in 'a study of memory and learning'. Some of the volunteers took the role of 'teacher', who would help the 'learner', who was strapped into a chair. If the learner couldn't remember the right answer, the teacher was supposed to administer a small electric shock. Moreover, the teacher was told to ratchet up the voltage if the learner continued to give the wrong answer, until they screamed out in agony.

Now, the learners were really actors and there was no electricity. But the teachers didn't know that. The point of the experiment was to see how far they would go in administering pain when instructed to do so by the white-coated psychologists who represented 'authority'. The answer, in many cases, was disturbing. Most of the teachers dispensed what they thought were ever greater electric shocks, and a substantial proportion continued to the highest level, which was marked 'danger', despite the anguished cries of the learners. In his 1974 book *Obedience to Authority*, Milgram explicitly compared the behaviour of the Yale students to that of Nazi concentration camp guards.

We'll come back to this experiment later, but for now take it as a glimpse into the fertile mind of the man who went on to investigate the idea of the small world. Reporting his results in a fascinating article in the first ever issue of *Psychology Today*, he starts with a story:

> Fred Jones of Peoria, sitting in a sidewalk café in Tunis, and needing a light for his cigarette, asks the man at the next table for a match. They fall into conversation; the stranger is an Englishman who, it turns out, spent several months in Detroit studying the operation of an interchangeable-bottlecap factory.
>
> 'I know it's a foolish question,' says Jones, 'but did you ever by any chance run into a fellow named Ben Arkadian? He's an old friend of mine, manages a chain of supermarkets in Detroit . . .'
>
> 'Arkadian, Arkadian,' the Englishman mutters. 'Why, upon my soul, I believe I do! Small chap, very energetic, raised merry hell with the factory over a shipment of defective bottlecaps.'
>
> 'No kidding!' Jones exclaims in amazement.
>
> 'Good Lord, it's a small world, isn't it?'[3]

We might quibble that the story is clearly fictitious and the dialogue stilted – an Englishman abroad in 1967 was unlikely to have said 'upon my soul', a phrase more redolent of the novels of Evelyn Waugh. No matter. The reader is drawn in and Milgram goes on to explain exactly what he's trying to test: whether the world really is 'large' or 'small'. If it truly is a small world, then Jane Jacob's Messenger game would work with a relatively small number of personal links. The small-world view sees acquaintances as stepping stones or connecting links to any person or group we want to reach. In a later article, Milgram and a collaborator amplified this view eloquently: 'The phrase "small world" suggests that social networks are in some sense tightly woven, full of unexpected strands linking individuals far removed from one another in physical or social space.'[4]

By contrast, a large world would mean that there are mainly unbridgeable gaps between people, with everyone pretty much confined to their own social or local existence. These diverse groups will never meet because they don't intersect. A message will stay trapped within the group, like a fly in a corked bottle, and will never be able to jump out, because nobody is a member of two such groups; there is no common link.

To determine which view was correct, Milgram had the bright idea of selecting participants from two cities – Wichita, Kansas, and Omaha, Nebraska – and seeing if they could pass a folder on to someone they knew on a first-name basis, who would then mail it to someone they knew, and so on until it reached a 'target person'. In the Kansas study the target was the wife of a divinity school student in Cambridge, Massachusetts; in the Nebraska study it was a stockbroker in Boston. Each of the intermediaries in the chain would endeavour to get the folder as close as possible to the target via people they knew personally. Milgram reasoned that if the process worked at all it would provide evidence of a small world; then, the fewer the links, the more the small-world thesis would be upheld. Along the way, since the identities of the intermediaries were tracked, a great deal would be learned about how networks operated.

The first completed chain came in the Kansas study, as Milgram explained:

> four days after the folders were sent . . . an instructor at the Episcopal Theological Seminary approached our target person on the street. 'Alice,' he said, thrusting a brown folder towards her, 'this is for you' . . . [W]e found to our pleasant surprise that the document had started with a wheat farmer in Kansas. He had passed it on to an Episcopalian minister in his home town, who sent it to the minister who taught in Cambridge, who gave it to the target person.

So just two intermediate links had been necessary, making this one of the shortest chains to be completed.

The Omaha test produced a more typical result. Here, a widowed supermarket clerk passed the folder to a friend who was a painter in Council Bluffs, Iowa. He sent it on to a publisher in Belmont, Massachusetts, who forwarded it to a tanner in Sharon, the suburb of Boston where the target stockbroker lived. The tanner then gave it to a sheet-metal worker, also in Sharon, who handed it to his dentist, who passed it to a printer, who gave it to a clothes retailer, all still in Sharon, who finally delivered it to the stockbroker. So this time there were seven intermediaries, not counting either the starting or the target person.

In the *Psychology Today* article, Milgram gives data on the Nebraska study. One hundred and sixty chains were started and forty-four were completed. The number of intermediaries in the completed chains varied between two and ten. He also mentions another twenty chains completed in an auxiliary study, originating in the Boston area, also targeted at the local stockbroker. Combining the studies, the average number of links in the sixty-four completed chains was five intermediaries. Though Milgram never mentions 'six degrees of separation', his experiment appears to be a remarkable vindication of the idea, at least for the United States, if not for the whole world.

Small world proven? An open and shut case? Milgram clearly thought so. And commentators took him at his word, with no lingering doubts about either this or his earlier 'electrocution' experiment. Until, that is, another psychologist, Judith Kleinfeld, came on the scene in 2002. The story goes that she was impressed with the experiment and wanted her students to replicate it using email, but as she investigated Milgram's working papers she became increasingly disturbed that he had drawn unwarranted conclusions. 'Milgram's findings', she wrote, 'have slipped away from their scientific moorings, and sailed into the world of imagination. The idea of six degrees of separation may, in fact, be plain wrong – the academic equivalent of an urban myth.'[5] This is as close as the genteel world of academia comes to crying, 'Fraud!'

Kleinfeld made some disconcerting discoveries in Milgram's papers:

> Very few of his folders reached their targets. In his first, unpublished, study, only three of 60 letters – five percent – made it. Even in Milgram's published studies, less than 30 percent of folders got through . . .
>
> Perhaps people didn't bother sending the letters on. That was Milgram's explanation. But that seems unlikely. The folder was not a simple chain letter, but an official-looking document with heavy blue binding and a gold logo. If the subjects knew how to reach the targets, they probably would have.

Kleinfeld also scrutinised Milgram's samples. In the Nebraska survey, only half of the almost two hundred 'starters' were randomly selected. The others were stock investors, which gave them a natural affinity with the target, the Boston stockbroker. And of the ninety-six folders that started their journey with people who had been randomly selected and so met Milgram's condition of social and physical distance, only eighteen reached the broker!

Kleinfeld concluded that the evidence was inconclusive – maybe we live in a small world; maybe we don't.

So who was right – Milgram or Kleinfeld? New evidence arrived shortly after Kleinfeld penned her critique. Professor Duncan Watts and colleagues did what Kleinfeld had originally intended to do – they organised a massive email exercise to retest the small-world hypothesis. Volunteers registered online and were randomly allocated one of eighteen targets in thirteen countries. The targets included a professor at an Ivy League university, an archivist in Estonia, a consultant in India and a policeman in Australia.[6] Participants were simply asked to send the message to an acquaintance who was 'closer' to the target than they were.

On the whole, the results vindicated Milgram and the small-world thesis. An impressive total of 24,163 message chains were started, and while a mere 384 were completed (a success rate of only 1.6 per cent), the average completed chain length – 4.05 intermediaries – was short. The researchers looked hard at why there were so many incomplete chains. They concluded that chains were aborted not because it was too difficult to find the targets, or because the appropriate links didn't exist, but because of individual apathy or disinclination to participate. One reason for this conclusion was direct research: recipients who did not forward the message after a week were asked why they had not participated. 'Less than 0.3 per cent of those contacted claimed that they could not think of an appropriate recipient, suggesting that lack of interest or incentive, not difficulty, was the main reason for chain termination.'

The other intriguing finding was that one of the eighteen targets – the Ivy League professor – received nearly half of all the completed chains. Now, 85 per cent of senders were college educated and more than half were American, so it seems likely that most senders anticipated little difficulty in reaching him. The researchers believed that the professor's 'true' accessibility was 'little different from that of other targets', but the *belief* that he could be reached encouraged the participants to proceed. 'Network structure', they concluded, 'is not everything' – the motivation of the people in the network matters as well. If someone believed that the target could be reached, he could be.

So, Watts and his colleagues largely validated the small-world idea. Above all, his retest lets us stop worrying about Milgram's low response rates. In fact, in comparison with Watts' study, Milgram's response rate was quite high; and to expect unpaid volunteers to be highly motivated to complete each chain is unrealistic. In any case, an incomplete chain didn't prove that the linkage doesn't exist, just that it wasn't found or used.

As for Milgram's sample sizes, we've looked at all the evidence again and concluded they were satisfactory – there were sixty-four completed chains, with an average length of 5.2 intermediaries. The Watts study corroborates this: 384 completed chains, with a similar number of intermediaries in the US, and slightly more, around seven, for international chains.[7]

Then researchers found the easy way to generate large samples. In 2008 the Microsoft Messenger project was completed by Eric Horvitz and Jure Leskovec. They had the benefit of a vast database of personal conversations – all 30 billion Microsoft instant-message communications sent between 180 million people for the month of June 2006, comprising about half of all the world's instant-messaging traffic at that time. With a complete map of senders and recipients, the researchers were able to calculate the 'degrees of separation' for all 180 million people.

What do you think the average degrees of separation were? The magic number six crops up again – to be precise, 6.6.

'To me, it was pretty shocking,' says Horvitz. 'What we're seeing suggests there may be a social connectivity constant for humanity. People have had this suspicion that we are really close. But we are showing on a very large scale that this idea goes beyond folklore.'

But there was a kicker in the results, showing that not everyone is that well connected. While nearly four out of five pairs of people in the database could be connected in seven or fewer hops, at the other extreme there were some pairs requiring twenty-nine hops to connect. So most of the 180 million people sending instant messages live in a small world, but more than a fifth of them do not. Some poor souls manage the amazing feat of being connected to the Internet and instant-messaging, yet significantly isolated from other inhabitants of cyberspace.

So what? If we live in a small world, what does that mean, and how can we benefit from it?

It's important to be realistic about what a small world does and does not imply. We may all be a few short hops from our president or prime minister, but that doesn't mean he's about to invite us round for tea. As Stanley Milgram said in his article, five sounds like a small number, but in this experiment that's misleading. It really means 'five circles of acquaintances' apart. Almost all Americans were probably only a few removes from Nelson Rockefeller, but very few integrated their lives with his. 'Even in a small world,' Milgram said, 'geographical and social differences are still important.'

As we'll see later, many people remain relatively isolated – through geographical remoteness, poverty or lack of social connections.

Or simply by not feeling part of a small world. In a very real sense, the world is small if we think it is. In Watts' email experiment, the college professor received such a large proportion of completed chains principally because people felt they could link to him. We will try to connect if we believe our efforts will be successful. And this is a virtuous circle, because they are likely to be successful if we try to connect. It's easier than we think to reach almost anyone; the main barrier is in our heads.

Why is it better to live in a small, more connected world? Consider two extreme scenarios. In one, you are a hermit. In the other, you know everyone else in the world. Which life is likely to be richer, more interesting, with more opportunity?

A historical perspective helps. Imagine spending your entire life in a cave, knowing only a few fellow cave people. There could be millions of other caves and tens of millions of other people around the planet, but they are completely irrelevant if you cannot reach them. No contact, no trade, no sharing of knowledge, no friends from beyond your own cave. A large, unknowable and forbidding world outside. And inside? Isolated. Poor. Dangerous.

Now, envision new communications technology connecting the cave people – roads, explorers, merchants, boats, bicycles, cars, trains, planes, telephones, fax machines, inter-cave video-conferencing, cave cyberspace. A small world. Connected. Specialised. Interdependent. Infinitely richer in every way.

Something like that happened over time. Only three thousand years ago, it was impossible to travel any great distance, except at huge inconvenience, expense and danger. As a result, you would have met very few people in your lifetime. Then the Greeks and the Romans spread knowledge, built new cities, traded, increased shipping, constructed roads, and eventually instituted a common religion throughout the Mediterranean and most of the known world. Two steps forward.

In the third century AD, however, the Roman Empire started to collapse. One step back. In the Dark Ages, many towns and cities in Europe lost touch with each other. Communication ceased. Then, thanks to Muslim invaders and scholars, Greek knowledge was rediscovered and networks were forged anew – roads, churches, monasteries, universities, merchants, explorers, artists and architects, even intercontinental voyages, conquest and emigration. Three steps forward. The world became more connected, at first for tiny groups of the elite such as royal families, aristocrats, church leaders and other intellectuals, merchants and financiers; later for industrialists and eventually for ordinary people. At every stage, the people who were best connected, who had privileged access to useful information of all types, had richer, fuller and more useful lives.

We are the lucky beneficiaries of that history. Now the world is smaller, our opportunities are greater.

But Milgram told us something else that's very important. At any point in time, some people are better connected than others. *Much* better connected. So their world is much smaller.

Of the sixty-four folders that reached the Boston stockbroker, nearly half came through three final 'funnels'. Sixteen reached the broker through a Mr Jacobs, a clothes retailer in Sharon. Milgram says that the broker was shocked that Jacobs was by far the most important link to him. We can almost see the broker's nose wrinkling at the social importance of a mere shopkeeper (maybe he was Jewish and gay to boot, if the illustration in Milgram's article is anything to go by). Perhaps the broker took some comfort from the fact that ten folders reached him from one of his colleagues, Mr Jones, and another five from Mr Brown, a fellow broker. Milgram dubs these three key funnels 'sociometric stars' – people who make the world much smaller. He notes that the stars often operate on different dimensions – for instance, geographical in the case of Jacobs, the social focus of Sharon, and professional for Jones and Brown.

One great theme of this book is that there are always a few people who command hugely greater social sway than most of us. These are the 'superconnectors' we celebrate. They are in a privileged position. Being more connected, they have greater and earlier access to potentially valuable information. The identity of the superconnectors may surprise us – as the significance of the shopkeeper shocked the stockbroker – but they are today's elite, the most connected members of our society.

So that is the point of the small world. We all benefit from being more connected than earlier generations. Furthermore, for most of us, there is an underlying structure of interrelationships so that a vast number of people and all the knowledge and possibilities they possess lie just beyond our immediate horizons. Meanwhile, some people – the superconnectors – benefit, and spread benefits, more than the rest of us.

*More* connections, however, are less important than the *right* connections. Which brings us to an even more striking and useful discovery than the small world – the strength of weak links.

CHAPTER THREE

# THE STRENGTH
# OF WEAK LINKS

*When acquaintances are more
useful than friends*

It is hardly possible to overrate the value . . . of
placing human beings in contact with persons
dissimilar to themselves, with modes of thought
and action unlike those with which they are
familiar.

*John Stuart Mill (1806–73)[8]*

Robin Field was thirty-seven and conscious that he hadn't
quite reached the point where he wanted to be. He'd done
all the right things: a great opening job with Jardine Matheson &
Co. in the Far East; a stint at INSEAD business school in France;
some success as a manager in LEK, the consulting firm where I
was a partner. I had immense confidence in Robin and together
we founded Strategy Ventures, to buy into underperforming
firms and turn them around. But we couldn't find the right
target, and we were running out of time and money. Robin's goal
of becoming financially independent seemed to be receding.

Yet he did make it. Within a year, we had injected new
money and management into Filofax, the personal organiser

company. It cost very little; the company was bleeding cash and heading for bankruptcy. Within two years, Robin had turned it around. When we sold it, revenues, profits and cash flow had never been higher – investors made seven times their money. Robin had established a reputation as a turnaround expert and made the money necessary for independence. Filofax changed his life, enabling him to combine a few enjoyable business projects with his passion for sailing.

How did this life-changing event happen? Through a chapter of accidents and the most tenuous connections with people neither Robin nor I knew at all well. When I told Robin I was writing a book about getting valuable information from 'weak links' – acquaintances of one kind or another – he said right away, 'Then you'll be writing about Filofax, of course.'

'Er, perhaps,' I said, as I'd forgotten how the company had come into our lives. 'Remind me how it all started.'

Easier said than done. 'Well,' he said, making five syllables out of the word and clearly playing for time, 'there was this Scottish accountant called . . . What *was* his name?'

It took us five minutes to dredge up the name of Sandy Black.

'I knew Sandy slightly,' Robin continued, 'having met him through 3i [a private equity group]. I had tried to sell him some consulting work. He wasn't interested in that but he did invite me to lunch. Just as we were finishing he happened to mention that Mintel [a market research outfit] was up for sale. You remember – Sandy introduced us to Peter Kraushar, who ran Mintel. Peter in turn introduced us to that curly-haired fellow, Steve Souhami, who ran Mintel's consulting arm. One of Steve's clients was David Collischon, the chairman of Filofax. Steve then introduced you to David. That's how it all happened.

'Think about the odds against all that happening,' Robin concluded. 'It made all the difference to my life. But what if I hadn't vaguely known Sandy? What if he hadn't had a lunch cancellation and invited me instead? What if he hadn't mentioned Mintel, which wasn't at all important to him? What if he hadn't introduced us to Peter, or Peter hadn't put us on to Steve? What if Steve's consulting company hadn't worked for David Collischon, and you hadn't been introduced to him? The odds against all those connections working out must have been thousands to one. And none of those people along the way started as close friends or indeed anything more than casual acquaintances.'

If you haven't yet discovered the power of weak links, probably the most overlooked network element, you should. Let's look at how the idea of weak links arose, and why network scientists think they are so important.

## Cambridge, Massachusetts, 1969

After graduating with a history degree from Princeton in 1965, Mark Granovetter turned to sociology. We find him working on his Ph.D. at Harvard. He's putting the finishing touches to a highly readable paper and he is particularly pleased with the title, 'The Strength of Weak Ties'. He is less pleased, a few months later, to have his paper rejected for publication.

It would be another four years before the paper made it into print.[9] But Granovetter had the last laugh. Many experts consider the concept of 'weak ties' one of the most insightful ever to arise in sociology, and, now as a venerable professor at Stanford, Granovetter is laden with honorary degrees.

He had the idea of contrasting the effectiveness of 'strong ties' – those with close friends and family – with 'weak ties', that is, more casual, sporadic, unplanned and fleeting contacts. His central insight – that weak ties or links are often much more valuable than strong ties – was initially puzzling. Granovetter said that the people with whom we spend little time can frequently be far more useful to us than those we see every day, those with whom we have intimate and intense relationships, those who actively try to help us. He also argued that weak ties between acquaintances or strangers are more important to society than the strong ties of friendship. How could this be?

Put simply, his argument is as follows. Our close friends tend to be similar to us and mainly move in the same social circles. Close friends operate in a dense network, what Granovetter called a 'closely knit clump of social structure', where most people know each other and share the same information. The individual also has a range of acquaintances, few of whom know each other. Each acquaintance is enmeshed in a clump of friends who share information. The weak tie between the individual and his acquaintance 'therefore, becomes not merely a trivial acquaintance tie but rather a crucial bridge between the two densely knit clumps of close friends . . . It follows, then, that individuals with few weak ties will be deprived of information from distant parts of the social system and will be confined to the provincial news and views of their close friends.'[10]

If information is to move from one group to another that is far away, either socially or physically, then the only way is through *bridges* – links between two different people, two different worlds, links that, by definition, are weak rather than strong. As Granovetter wrote in his original paper, 'this means that whatever is to be diffused can reach a larger number of people, and traverse greater social distance, when passed through weak ties rather than strong'[11]. If weak links are removed – the bridges, as it were, are blown up – then this would harm the spread of information more than if strong links were dissolved. If the bridges did not exist, new ideas would be stunted or spread slowly, science would be handicapped, and social divisions would be perpetuated.

To get useful new ideas or information, we must go beyond our immediate circle and make contact with distant parts of the social system. The only way to do that is through weak ties, and in particular weak ties that 'bridge' the gap between one hub and another.

The essence of Granovetter's insight is the value of socially diverse links, between people who don't know each other well. If you think about it for a few minutes, the theory becomes unanswerable. If weak links did not exist, we would still be living in small tribes like our ancient ancestors, totally cut off from one another, and with only a few close family members and neighbours to help us eke out our miserable existence. Weak links connect otherwise isolated hubs or individuals, creating a tissue of interconnections which bind together society.

Granovetter then looked at something that interests almost everyone – how to get a job. He asked managers, technicians and other professionals who had changed jobs recently how they had heard about their new positions. It turned out that personal contacts were paramount in connecting people with jobs. More jobs were found in this way than through direct formal application, and the best jobs – those enjoying and commanding the most pay and prestige – generally came through personal contacts.[12] Job-seekers using weak links were also much less likely to have been unemployed between jobs.

We might expect friends and family to be more important than casual acquaintances in helping us secure a better job, but we would likely be wrong. Granovetter learned that only one in six of the networkers found their job through family or friends; the rest utilised acquaintances – current or former work contacts – whom they met only occasionally or rarely.

Granovetter was particularly struck by the fact that more than a quarter of all jobs were secured through contacts who were hardly ever seen:

In many cases, the contact was only marginally included in the current network of contacts, such as an old college friend or a former workmate or employer, with whom sporadic contact had been maintained. Usually such ties had not even been very strong when first forged. For work-related ties, respondents almost invariably said that they never saw the person in a non-work context. Chance meetings or mutual friends operated to reactivate such ties. It is remarkable that people receive crucial information from individuals whose very existence they have forgotten.[13]

How can this be, when family and friends are so much easier to use and have a greater motivation to help the job-seeker? Granovetter explains the apparent paradox in terms of the superior information available to distant contacts: acquaintances may move in different circles and therefore have job information that we do not possess. The best way to get a new job is when you are not looking for one, but stumble across it through a distant acquaintance, someone from a different world. Granovetter says our chance of making a major occupational change – jumping from one job world to another – is roughly proportional to the number of contacts we have in different worlds.

He quotes the example of 'David M', who became manager of the food concession at the Brooklyn Dodgers' ballpark, worked his way through a local college, went into marketing, and after a few years opened a restaurant on the Massachusetts North Shore. Five years later, a customer noticed David M's name on the liquor licence over the entrance, and asked if he was the same David he'd been at college with twenty-seven years before; they had known each other by sight, but had not been close. They got talking, and thereafter the friend often came back to dine there. He was in charge of a big, privately run social welfare programme in the state, and thought that David M could run one of his schemes, retraining handicapped workers, despite David's lack of any qualifications or experience in that field. After several months of discussions, David accepted the job, in which he subsequently performed strongly.

★

It seems that, for finding a job and for other ways of gaining satisfaction in life, the more networks we can tap, even very loosely, the more likely we are to get what we want. And sometimes the network, unlikely as it may seem, lies right under our nose.

Elon and Kimbal Musk, two would-be entrepreneurs in Silicon Valley, were ready to roll after they set up Zip2, a Web technology company. 'We had a good story, a good product, a good team. Everything was in place,' Kimbal said. There was just one small hitch – they couldn't raise any money. None of the venture capitalists they approached were interested.

OK, they said to each other, if venture capitalists can't see it, we'll try to raise money from angel investors – wealthy private individuals. Surely they could find a computer enthusiast to put up the cash. But after months of trying, they got nowhere. They were about to give up when their landlady asked if something was wrong. The boys explained their predicament, expecting no more than tea and sympathy.

But the landlady gave them something better. She introduced them to a rich friend, who agreed to invest. It was enough to get the business going. However, months later, they were still chasing venture capitalists for proper funding. No dice.

Then one of their casual salespeople, paid by commission only, learned that the firm needed money and introduced a venture capitalist acquaintance. Shortly after, Zip2 had millions of dollars of development funding, and the venture took off.

Kimbal Musk understood the moral of this story better than anyone: 'Some of the people you think will not be able to help you in any way know people who can help you in ways you cannot believe.'[14]

Have you ever stopped to wonder how teenagers and even younger children all over the world somehow manage to gain access to the latest pop-culture knowledge, sexual lore and aggressive humour? Today's easy answer is the Internet. But this happened before cyberspace even existed. Back in 1979, sociologists Gary Fine and Sherryl Kleinman found exactly the same phenomenon and asked how it was that huge numbers of children who'd never met each other gained a common set of attitudes and knowledge across the United States and the world. They found the answer in weak links:

> [The] speed at which children's lore is spread across great distances suggests the role of weak ties. In addition to the school peer group, children who have been geographically mobile may maintain friendships over many miles. The childhood pastime of having pen pals is an example . . . Likewise . . . distant cousins . . . can provide a mechanism by which cultural traditions breach geographical chasms.[15]

Clearly, in the Internet age, these weak links are even easier to forge – current obsessions spread almost instantly and youth culture everywhere has become more homogeneous. The same is true of ethnic, gay, feminist and many other subcultures.

Researchers have also found that weak ties exert more power than strong ties in the most unexpected places. Picture a kibbutz. You might expect the strong chain of command to exert greater influence than more informal and casual connections. Yet sociologist Gabriel Weimann found the reverse. He refuted the conventional view that discipline in a kibbutz is essentially a matter of strong ties, showing that weak ties were more important; and he discovered that widely shared gossip acted as a deterrent to maverick behaviour and was far more effective than face-to-face feedback.[16]

The theory of weak links can be traced back at least 160 years, to the Victorian intellectual John Stuart Mill. As quoted at the head of this chapter, he wrote in 1848 that it was immensely valuable for people to meet 'persons dissimilar to themselves, with modes of thought and action unlike those with which they are familiar'. He was thinking primarily of contact with foreigners, arising from the dramatic increase in international trade the world was experiencing at the time he was writing. In fact, he greeted the expansion of trade with all the enthusiasm (and naivety) of contemporary advocates of globalisation:

> Commerce is now what war once was, the principal source of this contact [with dissimilar people]. It is commerce which is rapidly rendering war obsolete by strengthening and multiplying the personal interests [what we call weak links and their benefits] which are in natural opposition to it . . . [The] rapid increase of international trade . . . [is] the principal guarantee of the peace of the world.

American sociologist Rose Coser, over a century later, developed Mill's insight about the value of meeting diverse people. In 1975, long before 'emotional intelligence' became all the rage, she contrasted people deeply enmeshed in a community of strong links with those who have a wide range of weak links. She observed that people whose links are mainly strong 'may never become aware of the fact that their lives do not actually depend on what happens within the group but on forces far beyond their perception and hence beyond their control'. The strong links 'may prevent individuals from articulating their roles in relation to the complexities of the outside world. Indeed, there may be a distinct weakness in strong ties.'[17]

By contrast, people with a variety of weak ties were likely to exhibit greater individualism. Having to deal with fundamentally different worlds, Coser said, demands 'the ability to put oneself in imagination in the position of each role partner in relations to all others, including oneself'. Weak links, therefore, could become a 'seedbed of individual autonomy'. Empathy creates 'intellectual flexibility and self-direction' – it enables us to select from a broad repertoire of responses in different circumstances.

Paradoxically, Coser said, we find our own direction and unique inner depths when we deal with people whose expectations and opinions are different from our own. Have you ever had the experience of saying something you don't really believe, or withholding your true opinion, in order to get on with someone whose views you know are different? According to Coser, this is no bad thing. It enables us to communicate with the other person, and it does us good, too. In confronting someone whose world-view clashes with our own, we become more aware of what our attitudes and views really are. We begin to realise how many of our own notions are thoughtlessly inherited from our parents or our friends. We sort out those things we really do believe in from those we don't, which allows us to become aware of our inner core, defining who we really are. Conversely, people who don't mix in different worlds might end up simply replicating the personalities of others in their family, community and circle of friends.

We 'centre' and deepen our personality by developing a range of bridges into other worlds. Emotional intelligence, in other words, can be deliberately cultivated through weak links.

Remember Stanley Milgram's small-world experiments from Chapter Two? Do you think that the most successful chains – those that were completed and the shortest ones – were made up mainly of strong links (friends and family) or of casual acquaintances (weak links)? Time and again researchers have found that, when it comes to communicating from one person to a target in a different world, weak links far outperform strong ones.[18]

Why does this matter? Well, it reveals that we tend to overuse our family and friends, and underuse people we don't know particularly well. This is an understandable reflex action, and we all suffer from it. Of course, it's easier to ask a favour of a close friend rather than someone we've just met. Yet, if getting a document closer to a distant target is anything to go by, the people we know less well will achieve better results than those we know intimately.

At first sight this seems strange: our friends are more motivated to help us, yet they perform worse. But it's a real 'light bulb' moment when you realise what this means. Let's say that, for the sake of argument, friends want to help us three times as much as acquaintances do. And let's observe – using the small-world experiments as a guide – that acquaintances are three times more effective than friends when helping us with a difficult task. *In that scenario, acquaintances are nine times better than friends at providing the connections we need or giving us useful information.* Of course, 'nine times' is only a guess – it might be five times, or ten, or twenty. But even this rough estimate brings home how much better acquaintances are at getting us 'distant' information. And the great thing about acquaintances is that we have so many more of them than friends. Somewhere out there, an acquaintance will be able to provide the missing intelligence that we need – even if it's someone whose existence we've forgotten! The power of the periphery is enormous, so the larger our periphery – the wider the range of diverse worlds we can enter – the greater will be our potential insight.

Why are we so biased towards seeking help that is near at hand rather than far away? The biologist E. O. Wilson supplies a plausible and intriguing reason:

The human brain evidently evolved to commit itself emotionally only to a small piece of geography, a limited band of kinsmen, and two or three generations into the future . . . We are innately inclined to ignore any distant possibility not yet requiring examination . . . It is a part of our hard-wired Paleolithic heritage. For hundreds of millennia, those who worked for short-term gain within a small circle of relatives and friends lived longer and left more offspring.[19]

So, in today's small world, we are naturally inclined to behave in a way that diminishes opportunity. When we try to dragoon our friends into helping us, we will often pick people who might be willing but are not best suited for the job. Conversely, if we sift through all our contacts and tap people with different knowledge, we will usually find someone more appropriate. Who is more likely to tell you about a fantastic new holiday destination – your best friend (whose preferred locations you may already have tried) or an intrepid traveller you fall into conversation with on a train? Most of us have far more weak ties than strong ones. We usually have a huge dormant network of contacts, past and present – sociologists estimate that most of us know between five hundred and three thousand people by name. So we can deliberately cultivate many more weak links, windows into new worlds, with little effort. And though the great majority of our casual acquaintances will not uplift our lives, a few just might – and often when we least expect it.

Is your world ordered, random or small?

When we are growing up, our world is ordered. At least until we're teenagers, our world comprises mainly strong links – parents and friends. We live in a *structured* world, with few casual acquaintances. We are well connected to the people around us, and largely isolated from the rest of the world.

My world remained structured until I was seventeen. Until then, the influences in my life were nearly all strong links – my family and friends from school and the neighbourhood. After I finished school, like many adolescents at the time, I took four months out to go hitch-hiking around Europe. I wanted to go with my best friend Ray, who'd done it before, but he wisely deflected me, saying he'd seen too many friends who'd travelled together and ended up not speaking to each other. So I went on my own.

The trip was a complete contrast to my previous, structured

world. To survive, I had to meet dozens of strangers each day, take the initiative, mix with a motley crew of truck drivers, locals and fellow travellers. This was a truly *random* world. Each day I set out, I didn't know where I'd end up, or with whom. I met grizzled Spanish peasants; Italian wide boys; stoned German hippies whose driving was scary; Greeks who told me how much they loved America and Britain; three Australian girls who'd been driving a Mini for two years through endless countries, consuming enough culture and pizza to last a lifetime; an Eastern European refugee who wanted to move to Britain; a Muslim travelling salesman in what was then Yugoslavia; sly American gay men who gave me a lift and asked if I'd been troubled by 'queers'; and an amorous French lady of a certain age who lived in a huge villa on the Riviera. All the people I met were weak links, strung out in an endless chain, whose structure was tenuous and temporary in the extreme. For sure, it was a network; but for four months hubs and strong links were conspicuous by their total absence.

Soon after, I went to university. Here my life was neither structured nor random, but the best of both worlds. I had very strong links to a small number of people – friends, tutors, lovers – and my life and work with them were rather organised. But I also met a huge number of casual acquaintances, and kept up weak relationships with dozens or perhaps even hundreds of them. I was on the fringe of many disparate groups – poker players, Marxists, Tories, tennis players, student politicians, pot smokers, ravers, debaters, drinkers, serious historians, music lovers, and those who lived by our college head's famous dictum that 'fornication is for the afternoon'. University was a *small* world – I belonged to very few close clusters, and beyond these friends had a very wide range of weak links to different groups.

Within the space of a year I'd moved from a structured world, to a random one, to a small one. These three types of network – pretty much – were later described and analysed by physicists

Duncan Watts and Steven Strogatz from Cornell University. Of course, they didn't know about my early life and they wouldn't have cared a hoot. But their findings have an uncanny and intriguing affinity to my three network types.

Doing pioneering research starting in 1996, Watts and Strogatz used computer modelling to explore the relationships between different types of networks.[20] To simplify, suppose they started with a world of a thousand nodes – think for the moment of these nodes as people – arranged and connected to represent a highly structured and clustered large world. You could do this by setting out the nodes in a large circle with each connected only to its five closest neighbours to the right, and the same to the left, making five thousand connections in total.[21] They called this a *regular* network and it corresponds closely to what I've called my *structured* network. The regular network was highly clustered, since each node was connected only to its closest ten neighbours, not to any distant nodes. In such a configuration each node is a high number of links away, on average, from the other 999 nodes – resulting in a high number of degrees of separation. Watts and Strogatz had modelled a classic, ordered, structured, clustered world where strong links mattered most, similar to the world in which we all grew up.

The researchers then constructed the opposite, *random* network. Imagine again setting up a thousand nodes in a circle with five thousand connections, but this time with the connections picked at random, cutting across the circle in any direction, and as a result links between neighbouring nodes much less frequent. In other words, the local clustering would be poor: there would be no well-connected groups of nodes next to each other. Also in contrast to regular networks, Watts and Strogatz found that all the nodes in random networks were much better connected on average – not to any local group (unless by chance, which almost never happened), but to any of the other 999 individual nodes through a small number of intermediaries. Each node could typically reach any other node through a small number of steps – and this results in a very low number of degrees of separation. With a bit of poetic licence, this is similar to my random backpacking days – no clusters, but a terrific range of random connections.

Finally, the physicists started with regular networks – where the nodes were isolated from all but immediate neighbours – and then added random links between the nodes. They were looking for the precise moment when the regular networks turned into random ones – they wanted to know how many links it would take. But what they actually produced – and very quickly – was a third type of network with the best of both worlds. Recall, the regular networks we started with had five thousand connections. If this is rewired by adding fifty new random connections – increasing the total number of connections by a mere 1 per cent, this turns out to be enough to make all the nodes well connected to one another on average. In this respect, the new network is as good as the random one. In the regular network the average number of hops necessary to link any two nodes is fifty; by adding just 1 per cent of random connections the hops necessary (the degrees of separation) plummets to seven. (Moreover, in later research Watts and Strogatz found that, regardless of the size of the network, adding just *five* links at random to a regular network halves the degrees of separation.) Yet, in all cases, the new networks retain the advantage of being highly clustered.

Watts and Strogatz called this new type of network – with high clustering *and* great connections between the nodes – a *small world*. It corresponds to my days at university, where I had the benefit of tight clustering – close friends and well-organised work – and wide connections to disparate, distant groups. Network scientists have since been surprised at the sheer frequency with which these small world networks seem to occur – whether in nature or man-made, ranging from molecules in a cell to routers on the Internet – where networks appear to have been naturally or consciously organised to combine the advantage of tight clustering with ease of connection between all nodes in the network.

So, if your world is largely structured – you rely mainly on strong links in a big world – it is relatively easy to turn it into a small world by adding some random connections, some weak links to groups that are a long way from your own. You can keep all the advantages of structure, all the huge human benefits of close, intimate relationships, all the rewards of specialised groups – all the strengths of strong links – while also gaining access to the new knowledge and insight that come from random connections to other realms. Even better, you don't need to add many weak links – provided they are clearly to social worlds that are different from your own – to transform your personal network and vastly increase the useful, practical information to which you are exposed.

It's true the other way round as well. If your strength is an awesome array of weak links, but you lack purpose, commitment and the mutual support of close friends or a small group, then you can turn your random world into a small world. You can keep the effective bridges to many disparate groups and individuals – your random weak links – while layering on the benefits of joining a small and cosy cluster.

In other words, there is no trade-off between strong links and weak links. We can enjoy the benefits of both. The small world rejoices in both. We can be rooted *and* restless, organised *and* disorganised, disciplined *and* open-minded, committed *and* experimental. True, in terms of achieving practical results, strong links on their own may be weak, and weak links may be strong; but in terms of a rich and fulfilled life, both together are infinitely better. We just need a separate strategy for each, a different mentality for friends and acquaintances, a clear distinction in our minds between the roles the two types of link involve. We need not struggle to turn acquaintances into friends, unless we really want to; and we should not expect our friends to bring us the breadth of information and practical benefits that are a doddle for a wide range of acquaintances. Deep friendship and love are their own rewards; while everyone else in the world is there for our amusement, enlightenment, instruction and mutual help.

One final, central point from Watts and Strogatz's research: they highlighted the asymmetry in small world systems – in all cases, a few random weak links brought about the small world. Not all links were equal. The really valuable links, those doing the heavy lifting for connecting all the nodes, were between distant groups. And their pioneering efforts formed the foundation on which others built – most notably, Barabási and Albert, who demonstrated that some nodes are vastly more connected than all the others, including connections to many far-away nodes. This conclusion which we explore later leads back to Stanley Milgram's phenomenal insight in identifying 'sociometric stars', the superconnectors who make the world small. In both human and non-human small worlds, some very popular hubs bring the world closer for everyone or everything else.

As vital as these superconnectors are, there are very few of them. This explains why we are so surprised every time we experience the small world. We don't see the whole picture, only our own part of the network, and our few strong links. We are scarcely conscious of the extent of our own hidden network, the latent weak links, and are unaware of all the connections they have that can work wonders for us. And we are similarly unaware of the superconnectors and the sterling work they do for everyone. Beyond our sight, but not beyond our reach, the superconnectors have the potential to provide innumerable shortcuts.

Weak links unite humanity. They stop the world splitting into mutually uncomprehending small tribes. They bind together society and the whole globe. They provide the information and social lubrication without which the modern world would quickly seize up and disappear. Weak links are the essential complement to strong links and tight local clusters. The diversity and different roles of weak links, strong links and hubs give coherence and power to networks and enable us – individually and collectively – to achieve our potential.

Any network is made much more valuable when the number of connections increases. Bob Metcalfe, a computer-networking expert, came up with 'Metcalfe's Law', which states that the value of a network roughly equals the number of users squared. One phone is useless because you can't call anyone. Two phones aren't much better. According to Metcalfe, it's only when most people have a phone – or an email address – that the network can change society.

Now, there's an important implication here for weak links. As networks grow, the proportion of weak links to strong links increases, as unconnected or poorly connected hubs are linked to each other. And even a small number of weak links increases the density of connection dramatically. It follows that, for society and our own lives, weak links drive the exponential increase in the value of our networks.

This is both curious and wonderful, because weak links – to casual acquaintances, former friends and colleagues, and new people we meet every day – are also the easiest network elements to form and maintain. Weak links are the lightest, most ethereal, least structured form of network connection. They traverse enormous social, mental and physical distances in a single bound. They enable you to enlarge your effective network and bring into your world a huge array of potentially beneficial contacts and insights that would otherwise not be available to you. Frequently, weak links are the most neglected, underdeveloped and undervalued parts of our lives.

Typically, we are unaware of, or forget, how important weak links are to us: they could be the person who introduced us to our spouse, job or fantastic new hobby; or, more often, the person who introduced us to someone who introduced us to someone else who led us to our piece of good fortune. We are likely to forget who these links were, because they are usually in the background, pop up momentarily to be useful, then quickly fade from our minds. It is only in retrospect that we can truly appreciate how important they were. Yet, if we cultivate a mixed bunch of weak links, and are always open to their help, we will have much more 'luck.'

How do we use weak links in practice? If we know specifically what we want from a contact, then a phone call or even an email may suffice. But the essence of weak links is that they are most useful when we least expect them to be. Such serendipity nearly always arises from personal meetings. In fact, it often flows from helping the person, without conscious intention, by something you say. Then, as if by magic, the favour is returned by something they say. How this happens is a mystery. The richness, intensity and sheer unpredictability of a personal meeting, when for a few minutes everything else goes out of our heads and we focus warmly on another human being, cannot be replicated through a video conference, still less by a phone call, and less again via email, which in our opinion should never be a medium for emotion (because it will invariably be misunderstood). Face to face, weak links can be incredibly strong and even change the direction of our lives. Virtual links might be efficient, but they almost never have this strength because they lack subtlety and texture.

We'll see that successful people are great users and generators of weak links. People who thrive have a knack of moving in a variety of circles and are receptive to the implications of distant practices, scraps of information and insights for their own world. They still have their anchors, strong personal relationships that give meaning to their lives, but they also invest time and energy in cultivating and maintaining a large number of weak links. In short, they are superconnectors, and we are about to meet several of them. These are people who have based their success, usually without realising it, on weak links. And they'll provide many practical ideas for how we might do the same.

## CHAPTER FOUR

# THE SUPERCONNECTORS

*Who are the superconnectors, why do they
matter, and what is their secret?*

For each possible realm of activity . . . there is
likely to emerge a sociometric star.

*Stanley Milgram*[22]

If you were a distinguished mathematician in the second half of
the twentieth century, you'd probably have had a knock on
your front door at some point. You'd be greeted by a gaunt,
grey-haired man wearing spectacles and a rumpled suit.
Clutching a suitcase containing most of his worldly goods, this
academic vagabond would have stepped confidently into your
space and announced himself with the words, 'My brain is open.'

This was good news. You were being invited to collaborate
with the world's greatest serial mathematician. True, you'd have
to put him up in the spare room, and work round the clock, as
he fuelled himself with endless cups of strong coffee and amphet-
amines. Such were the modest requirements of Paul Erdös, a
Hungarian who took his doctorate at Manchester University, and
became a professor at Princeton at the age of twenty-five.
Eventually he abandoned his home and spent the rest of his life
travelling from campus to campus, from collaborators' homes to

scientific conferences, searching out the most interesting problems and colleagues.

By the time he died in 1996, Erdös had become the most prolific author – or usually co-author – of mathematical articles in history. He ended up with 1475 articles to his name, and had 511 different collaborators. His contributions spanned many fields, including number theory, combinatorics, probability, set theory, mathematical analysis, and even the beginnings of the network science that lies at the root of this book. He won many prizes, but perhaps the legacy he would have valued most was the game mathematicians began to play. 'What is your Erdös number?' they would demand of each other. If you had published with Erdös it was 1; if you'd published with someone who'd published with Erdös, it was 2; and so on. As mathematicians are wont to do, someone eventually worked out the Erdös numbers for everyone in the *Math Reviews* database. The median Erdös number was 5 and the mean 4.7 – truly a mathematical small world. Everyone was joined to everyone else through this single, remarkable man, a superconnector who used a large and fluid network to advance human knowledge.

After selling his small software and media ventures, Andreas Meyer took a sabbatical to travel the world. He recorded his sights and experiences with a camera, and so became interested in photography. The creative and reflective part of this hobby was enjoyable, but it was the social part – meeting people to explore a mutual passion – that was the real draw for him. Andreas began to see photography primarily as a means to express and satisfy one's social nature, and he's stayed remarkably true to this vision through the years. He's made many great friends and a large number of friendly acquaintances through his pastime, but, more unusually, he has also devised a way to create many thousands of friendships for others.

As the Internet boomed in the late 1990s, Andreas was well

placed to understand and experiment with it. He'd been an early fan of the Web, and he knew how to write computer code. In 2000 he returned to Cologne, Germany, from his travels. Thinking about what to do next, he looked no further than his new hobby. Could he create a truly vibrant social community around photography?

He set up a website called Fotocommunity, a place where keen amateurs could exhibit their best photos alongside those of other serious photographers. The site was designed to promote the sharing of criticism, encouragement and advice between members. The number of photos one could exhibit was limited to make the act of doing so scarce and valuable. Members were encouraged to contact each other, explore the entire body of someone's work, choose and show favourites, and nominate and vote the very best into a special gallery. Most importantly, face-to-face meetings such as workshops, regular get-togethers and photo-expeditions were organised through the site's public calendar.

Photographers really got behind the idea, and the site grew steadily. Volunteers stepped forward to help new members acclimatise, to flag up offensive material, and to help with customer service. There was a sense that the community itself truly owned and operated the site. A quality ethos arose, helped by the limitation on entries, which promoted the best. There was a tremendous amount of critiquing – an average of ten comments per photo – so it didn't become a repository for holiday snaps; and members strove to earn kudos within the community through peer review and having their work elevated to the top gallery.

Then something unusual happened, particularly for the Web that we've come to know as the land of free service. The site had initially supported itself with advertising, but when the Internet bubble burst revenues dried up and the site began losing money. To save the business, Andreas asked members to pay if they wanted to submit a greater number of photos for review. Heavy users did just that, and this has been the company's profitable revenue model ever since.

Today, Fotocommunity forms part of the bedrock of the German photographic community. If you want to associate with serious photographers, you go to this website, because that's where they all are. It's in the top 200 German sites by traffic, with 400,000 users per month and 5 million viewers. But Andreas is most proud of the beauty of the 3 million reviewed pictures, the 3000 real-world get-togethers that are arranged by the site each year, and the wonderful connections he has forged for himself and like enthusiasts.

You'll find Peter Harding forty miles south-west of London, off the A30 arterial road, down a narrow country lane that leads to a jumble of old farm buildings. On a sunny day, as you cross into the shade, you become aware of a chaotic landscape, thick with dust and cobwebs. Ahead of you are disembowelled engines, pyres of desiccated rubber strips and faded chrome, and the exoskeletal remains of ancient vehicles, like hollow skins shed by long-forgotten mechanised beasts. A fluorescent glow beckons you into a cavernous barn, which is just a little tidier. Your eye is drawn to a gleaming metallic shape, sinuous and stream-lined. It seems strangely foreign, exotic and compelling. This is a 1957 Aurelia B20, built by Lancia, once the grande dame of the Italian car industry. Lancia, whose glory has long since faded, designed and made some of the most elegant GT cars of the mid-twentieth century.

Peter formerly ran an air-freight business, but a quarter-century ago he quit to pursue his passion. After taking three years to restore his own Aurelia, he knew that working with these cars would make him happy for the rest of his life. Although he had no formal engineering or mechanical training, he set up shop in the barn and found customers almost immediately. He has been busy ever since. The hours and the demands of the cars' owners can be unpredictable, the work is dirty by nature, and the barn is freezing in winter, but Peter doesn't care.

There are perhaps seventy B20s in England, and Peter maintains more than forty of them. His customers come from all walks of life and have become his friends. They often tour with him in France or Italy. He introduces them to each other, and they introduce each other to him. He also connects a lot of things related to the cars – buyers with sellers, auctioneers and dealers with both, owners with suppliers of parts. He doesn't advertise or have a website, just an answering machine beside the kettle in his office. But if you happen to buy one of these cars, need one fixed or maintained, or are just interested in them, at some point you'll find yourself going off the A30 down the narrow lane.

Peter is a specialist superconnector, fitting together all the pieces of the world around this particular car. Because he dominates this network, he connects everyone and everything in it. People find out about Peter and seek him out, which is what Greg did.

As Greg was leaving after one visit, maybe because of his North American accent, Peter asked him, 'Do you know this Jay Leno fellow?'

'Of course I know *of* him', Greg replied, 'and that, aside from being showbiz aristocracy, he's as big a petrol-head as you can find.'

'Well,' Peter said, 'he seems to be a really nice and genuine guy. He called me the other day and we had a great chat. He was very enthusiastic about Aurelias and keen on learning everything about them.' Then he added, 'Someone told me he does a talk show. What's it like?'

Paul Erdős was and Andreas Meyer and Peter Harding are crucial connectors within their own worlds. Within every intellectual discipline, every university, every school, every office, every church, every football or baseball league, every industry or commercial niche, every small town, and every social world imaginable, there are one or more superconnectors who seem to know everyone and connect everyone.

But there is another type of superconnector. Rather than connecting people within a given world, they build bridges between diverse worlds.

In 1999, Malcolm Gladwell wrote a piece in the *New Yorker* called 'Six Degrees of Lois Weisberg'. The article has since become justly celebrated. Lois, he said, was a 'connector'. She was then, and still is, Chicago's Commissioner of Cultural Affairs, but during her long career she has been part of many diverse groups and still has vibrant links to them. She has directed the Chicago Council of Lawyers, founded a pressure group called Friends of the Parks, opened a used jewellery store, run a drama troupe, been Director of Special Events for Mayor Harold Washington, started an underground weekly paper, worked in public relations and a law firm, saved an old railroad from closure, worked in a flea market, masterminded Chicago election campaigns, raised money to put on plays, and — perhaps most important of all — established the famous Gallery 37 project, which each year teaches thousands of unemployed youths how to make and sell art and jewellery. The kids also study painting, sculpture, drawing, poetry, textile and graphic design, acting and music. The project has since been replicated in many other cities.

One day, Cindy Mitchell was protesting in a freezing Chicago park, vainly trying to stop the Parks Department from lugging away a beautiful statue of Carl von Linné. Lois happened to drive by, saw the fuss, and started interrogating Cindy. What was going on? Why did Cindy care? Lois jumped back in her car, but later she persuaded two journalists from the *Chicago Tribune* to contact Cindy and turn her protest into a huge story. Cindy ended up as president of Friends of the Park for a decade and met hand-picked contacts of Lois, many of whom became her close friends. Gladwell quotes Cindy as saying, 'Almost everything that I do today and eighty to ninety percent of my friends came about because of her, because of that one little chance meeting . . . What if she had come by five minutes earlier?'[23]

Lois knows civic activists and politicians, lawyers and flea market peddlers, housewives and musicians, actors and journalists, nature-lovers and science-fiction writers, jazz players and intellectuals, artists and property developers, volunteers and antique-store proprietors, actors and railroad buffs. She has a huge range of acquaintances, and misses no opportunity to introduce them to each other.

If you ring Central Casting and ask for a typical Canadian grandmother, they might send you Eleanor MacMillan. At first glance, she ticks all the boxes: five-foot-one, bifocals, faded hair, Scottish descent, won't admit her age but her grandchildren will tell you she was born around the same time as the Queen. She's in good health but for a bad posture and a tricky heart valve. The widow of a noted orthopaedic surgeon, she spends most of her time between Ancaster, near Toronto, and the Muskoka Lakes, Ontario's cottage country where well-to-do Canadians and Americans have summered for more than a century.

Eleanor is of the inter-war generation, yet grows with the times. Conservative and frugal, she saves leftover food, no matter how small the portion, until it goes bad. She seems to be building a strategic stockpile of chairs. She's careful with people too, sizing them up before giving her confidence. Even so, she's a world traveller with thousands of snaps from bus trips through the likes of Iran, Mali and Burma. Not a knitter or doter, but a former biologist, she's happy to show her grandkids how to catch a snake. She's also swift on the freeway – and no one dares to tell her it's time to slow down.

She also hangs out with Rastafarians.

You see, Eleanor bridges the worlds of Ancaster and the time-less former smugglers' island of Carriacou in the West Indies. Each winter she flies to Barbados, then climbs aboard an eight-seat Britten-Norman Islander, which hops down the Grenadines to Carriacou's tiny airstrip, usually scattered with grazing livestock. A local minibus takes her cross-island in twenty minutes, through the main village of Hillsborough, where she greets old friends Cuthbert Snagg and Barnabus Quigley, while avoiding the local thief. Her destination is an isolated house up a deeply rutted track, where iguanas climb the trees, a donkey brays and the Caribbean shimmers beyond an overgrown yard. It's a three-mile walk back to Hillsborough, but only a few minutes to Bogles, a tiny village of one- and two-room shacks, some with electricity, several inhabited by dreadlocked, bleary-eyed Rastas. They grow vegetables, tend goats and chickens . . . and smoke ganja.

Everyone in Bogles knows of the old lady from the house in the bush. The children yell her name when she passes, and have been visiting her for years. One of them, then in his late teens, was Levi Thomas. Levi's middleweight prize-fighter physique and mound of dreadlocks might seem intimidating at first, but he is one of the gentlest souls you could ever meet. He used to sit on Eleanor's settee for hours in silence, flipping through old issues of *Canadian Living*, just looking at the pictures.

Perhaps these photographs made Levi want to visit Canada. He finally got there, stayed with relatives, and worked hard at two kitchen jobs. The money was good, and when his tourist visa expired, he borrowed his cousin's ID. One day the police came looking for the cousin, figured out Levi wasn't their man, but still charged him with overstaying. A thirty-day term in Toronto's violent Don Prison stretched to six months after the police lost his passport – they wouldn't deport him without one, yet wouldn't release him while he was awaiting deportation. No charges. No legal representation. Unaccountable functionaries did nothing to resolve the situation, even though they admitted they had misplaced the passport.

Eleanor got wind of Levi's predicament and went into battle. After getting nowhere with uninterested officials, she managed to reach the archdiocese in Grenada. A priest found Levi's birth certificate and faxed it to Canada. Levi was deported a few days later, but you wonder how long he might have languished in jail, because absolutely no one other than Eleanor took any interest in his plight.

Can you imagine an Aussie backpacker falling into a similar bureaucratic black hole for that offence? The world can be terribly unfair, marred by our differences and divisions. When alien worlds collide, more than likely random relationships made by superconnectors will cross the divide.

Lois and Eleanor both connect across different worlds – Lois across almost every sub-culture in Chicago, and Eleanor across countries and social groups. Of course, there are some differences between the two women. Lois knows or knew a lot of famous people from wildly different walks of life: Isaac Asimov, Arthur C. Clarke and Robert Heinlein – the Big Three science-fiction writers of their time; legendary jazz musicians Art Farmer, Thelonious Monk and Dizzy Gillespie; comedian Lenny Bruce, who once lived in her house; as did Nichelle Nichols, a singer and dancer who became famous as Lieutenant Uhura in *Star Trek*; novelist Ralph Ellison; and, of course, the Mayor of Chicago, whoever that may be at the time. Eleanor knows no celebrities, and doesn't particularly want to. Lois is quite renowned; Eleanor is obscure. Lois knows more people in far more diverse worlds than Eleanor, and has worked for a very long time in jobs that both require and enable a wide range of acquaintances.

Yet, the quality of Eleanor's individual connections and the

value of the bridges to the people she connects – such as Levi
Thomas – are absolutely of the same stature as the connections
made by celebrated figures such as Lois or Paul Erdös. Eleanor is
not a premier league superconnector but, as an octogenarian
grandma, she still participates in powerful and useful acts of linkage that bring some of the same benefits to individuals and
society. Without Eleanor, the worlds of Ontario and Bogles in
the West Indies would be much less connected. Without
Eleanor, Levi might still be incarcerated. In her own modest way,
she has reduced the degrees of separation in the world.

As we know, it was Stanley Milgram's experiment that led to
the idea of the 'sociometric star', which we have transmuted into
the superconnector. And who was Exhibit A for Milgram, the
star who slashed the degrees of separation between Nebraska and
Boston? Was it someone famous, like Lois? No, it was a clothes
merchant in Sharon, known by nobody outside the suburb but
by everyone inside it. Mr Jacobs is clearly more in Eleanor's
league than Lois's. Yet, the main difference between Jacobs and
Eleanor, on the one hand, and Lois, on the other, is simply the
scale of the canvas on which they operate. With a bit of poetic
licence, Jacobs is to Sharon, and Eleanor is to Bogles, what Lois
is to Chicago.

Lois and Paul Erdös represent such a high and virtually unat-
tainable degree of superconnection to most of us that they are
almost intimidating as models. When we think of superconnectors or superb networkers, we may visualise prominent people
with thousands of live contacts who have the inclination and
opportunity to spend their whole lives networking. However,
this is wrong. Certainly, Lois and Paul are superconnectors, but
the *typical* superconnector is someone much more like Eleanor
or Jacobs or Andreas Meyer or Peter Harding. These are relatively humble folk who can connect because they have placed
themselves at the centre of a social system, even a little-known or
newly concocted one, or because they intrude into two or three

systems that would otherwise be isolated from one another. The illustrations of ordinary superconnectors should give us pause and hope. Perhaps on some level this world is open to us as well; perhaps we are already very close to being a superconnector but have not realised the value of our role.

So what is a superconnector? And what does it take to be one? Clearly, it's essential to have a large number of friendly acquaintances, probably hundreds. The vast majority of these will be weak rather than strong links, which rations the amount of time available to cultivate and feed each contact. Paradoxically, though, the lack of time dictates a reasonably high level of trust and cordiality between the contacts: like a cactus that can live on limited and infrequent watering, the relationship has to survive on rare meetings, so it must be good from the outset. Contacts from past lives, where there might have been frequent contact and the ability to assess each other's character, may be fertile ground. Or you may just have met someone and instantly develop a mutual amity and trust. Some people, such as Lois, appear to be virtuosos at making friends on the hop. For the rest of us, it's helpful to realise that friendly acquaintanceship is a skill that improves with practice. Keeping contact details is a good start.

It's also necessary to know many people who are not well connected, at least in your circles. Some of this is intuitive and a matter of personality – curiosity, the willingness to meet disparate people, or building your life around a passion, like Peter or Andreas, which automatically requires connection or puts you in the middle of a spider's web. And it may be possible systematically to increase the number and diversity of one's contacts. Figure out how to find new characters to whom you are drawn, and talk for a few minutes. Be self-aware – appear open and approachable. A really good way is to change jobs or roles, or move house, every few years, especially if the jobs or residences are remote from each other.

A final superconnector characteristic is obvious but neglected – the willingness to act, to go ahead and connect people, when there is no ulterior motive or potential gain. The biggest network in the world is worthless if it is never used. The United States' Internal Revenue Service (IRS) is connected to more than a hundred million people. Information and hard-earned money pour into it all the time, and tax demands flow out relentlessly. Yet, the IRS is not a superconnector because it does not connect a single user with any other user. Traditional television is similar. As is a bestselling book. They are *connected* to millions, but they do not *connect*.

The same is true of some people. In theory, they have fantastic networks: they may have known hundreds or even thousands of people, and got on well with them, throughout their lives. But if they do not take the trouble to connect these contacts, they are no more use in this regard than television or the tax man. In researching this book, one veritable old saying keeps cropping up – *what goes around comes around*. People who connect one contact to another get contacted in return – albeit probably not immediately, and sometimes by a very convoluted and asymmetrical route. I may connect A and Z, who then connect their contacts AB and ZY, who then link up ABD and ZYW . . . and then, eventually, one of these derived and untraceable contacts comes back to me when I need it most. It works by reputation, too. Anyone who is known to connect people attracts other contacts; there is less fear of rejection or awkwardness. However it works, though, it works on a grand scale. As we've seen, the universe is one great connection machine, ramshackle and random, but highly effective. And the fuel that keeps connections racking up and ricocheting around is reciprocity.

Few of us use anywhere near our connecting potential, even with our existing networks. The value in our networks is latent; the value to us and our contacts increases enormously when we connect people. One of the great connectors we spoke to said that every time she meets a contact, she asks what kind of people they would like to meet. Then she finds one potentially relevant person and makes the introduction.

Interestingly, many of the superconnectors we interviewed for this book turned out to be rather diffident or self-effacing, far from the popular image of extrovert, dominant, magnetic net-workers. Malcolm Gladwell describes Lois at a reception in Chicago's Museum of Contemporary Art as looking 'a bit lost': 'She can be a little shy sometimes, and at first stayed on the fringes of the room, standing back, observing.' Nor, he says, is she charismatic in a conventional way. 'She doesn't fill a room,' he says, 'eyes don't swivel toward her as she makes her entrance.' This is reassuring and endearing for those of us who are also sometimes ill at ease in a big group. You don't have to be a party animal to connect successfully. Lots of us, deep down, hate par-ties, because the connections made at them are often forced and shallow, without the context and background of friendly acquaintanceship. Valued links come from natural connections, affinities that may surprise us but have some basis in common interests or the pull of personality, where we don't have to talk about trivial things or feel under any obligation to connect.

Superconnectors can even be prickly and difficult. For me, the best example of this is a man who was routinely avoided by his colleagues, yet was one of the most effective and significant super-connectors I have ever met.

Bruce Doolin Henderson was born on a Tennessee farm in 1915 and sold Bibles as a summer job. After studying engineer-ing and business, he worked for eighteen years at the Westinghouse Corporation, where he became the second-youngest vice-president in the company's history. In 1953, President Eisenhower chose Bruce as part of a five-member team to evaluate the Marshall Plan in Germany, which was odd, con-sidering that Bruce spoke no foreign languages and had no connections there. Despite his early promise, Bruce didn't make it to the very top of Westinghouse, and he quit in 1959 to join consulting firm Arthur D. Little. Four years later, he left that post too – rumour says he was fired. At the age of forty-eight, his career looked largely over.

Then fate gave Bruce his break. He was encouraged to start a consulting department within the Boston Safe Deposit and Trust Company. This department originally comprised just himself; he didn't even have a secretary. By 1967 Bruce had renamed his outfit the Boston Consulting Group (BCG), but it was still a very small operation. Then he sold a project to a timber company in Tacoma, and needed to recruit some temporary help to undertake the assignment. This came in the form of Alan Zakon, a teacher at Boston University, who recounted the call he received from Bruce:

> 'This is Bruce Henderson. I'd like you to do some consulting for me.'
> 'Wonderful.'
> 'What do you charge?'
> At the time I would have worked for fourteen dollars, but . . . I went for what I thought was a huge fee in those days: 'I charge one hundred and twenty-five dollars a day.'
> 'Wrong, too much,' he shouted. 'Take your annual income and divide it by three hundred and sixty-five, multiply by four and add twenty-two.'
> 'Mr Henderson,' I said, 'if I knew how to do that, I wouldn't need to do outside consulting.'
> There was dead silence . . .
> 'I'll pay you a hundred bucks. Come down tomorrow.'[24]

From this inauspicious beginning, Henderson's firm became one of the two most prestigious consulting firms in the world, with more than 60 offices all over the globe, 7000 staff, and revenues of around 2.5 billion dollars. Clearly, Bruce connected a lot of clients with a lot of consultants, some in exotic locations, which alone would make him a master superconnector. In 1992, when he died, the *Financial Times* said: 'Few people have had as much impact on international business in the second half of the twentieth century.' But, for me, Bruce is a stellar superconnector because he linked the world of business with academia, including thinkers in the business schools, and funnelled a large number of top graduates from liberal arts backgrounds into consulting and business. He hired some of the best professors in Boston and forced them to think about business in a way that nobody else had done before, resulting in such insights as the growth–share matrix and the huge value of being the leader in a high-growth market. He built a close alliance between Harvard Business School and BCG, recruiting some of the best professors and alumni. He started the practice whereby top consulting firms would take on not just MBAs but interns in their senior year of college and graduates, whether they were scientists, historians or English majors.

Yet, Bruce has to be the most contrary and difficult connector to feature in this book. When he came to visit the BCG office where I was working, one of the vice-presidents told me, 'Don't have anything to do with him. He can only do your career harm, never good.'

Later, I attended a client conference with Bruce at Chewton Glen, a delightful country house hotel set in Hampshire's New Forest. I thought the event went very well. But afterwards Bruce berated all of us for the staleness of the presentations. 'I was saying all this stuff *three years ago*,' he declaimed, as if an Ice Age had since intervened. 'Haven't we learned anything new since then?'

At his memorial service, the first speaker was Seymour ('Sy') Tilles, a BCG veteran and former Harvard Business School professor, who was my boss in the late 1970s. Sy quickly got to the point:

At BCG, 'founding father' is decidedly in the singular, for in the beginning there was Bruce Henderson. Of course, after the beginning there was also Bruce.

He was not always easy to deal with. My vivid recollection of those early days is that periodically some brilliant young person would come into my office and say, 'Do you know what he did to me?' It was never necessary to ask to whom they were referring.

The third speaker at the service was George Stalk, who joined BCG in 1978 and is still there today. 'He was physically and intellectually imposing,' George told the congregation, 'and I feared him greatly . . . I struggled to avoid him in the office.'

The final witness was John Clarkeson, BCG's chief executive officer at the time of the memorial service. He was hired, he said, during a period in BCG's history which 'Bruce often referred to . . . as "when we couldn't hire anybody". I expect many felt the need to resist the power of his influence, but everyone who came near him had the trajectory of their career changed. Some, I'm sure, in ways they could not have imagined.'

Bruce connected people whether they liked it or not. It was lonely work, but it made the world smaller and richer.

The heroic work of superconnectors who connect dissimilar worlds can be fully appreciated only if we reflect on what would happen if they did not exist. The natural tendency is to mix with people like us – we are more relaxed with people we know than with strangers, and less comfortable with folks from un-familiar cultures and backgrounds. There is a natural human instinct to favour our in-group and ignore or even stigmatise groups that are beyond our experience. The great economist Thomas Schelling showed in 1978 that the consequences of this can be highly divisive, even when the preference for our own kind is mild and people are tolerant.[25] Using a chessboard as an illustration, he showed how two different kinds of people in a city could initially be pretty mixed up and yet over time become segregated. Schelling's model works for any two groups of people, businesses or places that are not natural bedfellows: black and white people, Shias and Sunnis, young and old, beautiful people and the rest of us; or churches and brothels, motor supply stores and high-end boutiques, hospitals and night-clubs. Schelling did not assume that any of the people involved were prejudiced against the other group, but simply that anyone would feel isolated and uncomfortable if most of their neighbours were dissimilar.

Taking the case of black and white people, Schelling's model had the following rules: someone with one neighbour will try to move if that neighbour is a different colour; someone with two neighbours will want at least one of them to be the same colour; and someone with three to five neighbours will want at least two of them to be the same. Now, these preferences are not incompatible with an integrated town. Schelling used his chessboard to represent sixty people, half black and half white, leaving four spaces free at the edges of the board (a chessboard comprises eight by eight spaces). He set up the black and white chess pieces in such a way that, according to his rules, everyone was happy yet also integrated.

Then he upset the system's harmony. First he took twenty pieces off the board at random, then he filled five of the empty spaces, also at random, with white or black pieces. After this random scrambling, at least a few pieces tended to be isolated from their own kind, so the people they represented, according to Schelling's rules, became unhappy. These people would then move closer to their own kind, thereby often isolating others and forcing them to move, too.

You can try this with your own chessboard.[26] The result is fascinating. Remember that the residents were happy enough in a totally integrated town (the starting point), yet, when some people move randomly the end result is that the white pieces cluster together and so do the black. Eventually, more or less total segregation ensues.

Happily, in most places in the real world, people are more tolerant than Schelling's code suggests, and variety persists. Nevertheless, it is a compelling illustration of how we tend to mix with those of our own ilk, and how even mild preferences can result in clustering of similar people. Recall Stanley Milgram's small-world experiments – the question he was trying to answer was whether the world comprised largely unconnected, separate clumps of homogeneous social structure, or whether everyone in the world was connected to everyone else. It is reasonable to guess that Schelling would have placed his bet on the former, depressing theory.

If so, he would have lost his bet; but that in no way invalidates his model or the truth it approximates in real life. The tendency identified by Schelling exists. In fact, it is omnipresent – people *are* clannish and cliquey, often with unpleasant results. Only one thing overturns the Schelling tendency – the presence of superconnectors who link dissimilar groups. The superconnectors are a thin slice of humanity, yet they link us all together, making connections that otherwise would not exist. Without them, we would be plunged back into tribal enclaves, and life would be perilous, oppressive and poor.

Yet, life can be rich and free because superconnectors bridge the divisions in our world. But their influence doesn't end here. Personal opportunity often flows from a type of superconnector we have not yet described, one who is not particularly bothered about connecting people in the usual ways.

No plants, animals or insects live here, but in late August a naked lady with dragonfly wings might ride by on her bicycle.

We are in one of the largest completely flat places on earth: the empty, dimensionless Black Rock Desert in Nevada. Seared by the intense sun, temperatures rise above 110 degrees Fahrenheit, yet they can be near freezing at night. The cracked surface of the playa breaks easily into a fine powder, making a gluey, intractable mud when it rains and a choking fog when the dust storms sweep in.

Around fifty thousand people journey to this elemental Mecca at the end of August; they come in cars, campervans, trailers and buses. Construction begins immediately on shelters against the sun and wind, a temporary encampment that is Nevada's third-largest city for its fleeting existence. Art and apparition, on an apparently impossible scale, soar up from the desert floor, constructed of wood and scrap metal, but rendered eerie and ethereal by light and fire at night. There are bizarre costumes, spontaneous perform-ances, trippy raves. Multicoloured mutant vehicles – 'art cars' – prowl at walking pace; wacky games and pagan rituals play out; proportion is distorted, and convention challenged, at every turn. The week is a collective art party of deeply alternative reality, an altar of wild expression. The festival climaxes with the burning of a giant wooden man, a glittering beacon against the desert sky, the prehistoric image of humans huddling around a fire fused with contemporary confidence in unbounded possibility.

The roots of the Burning Man Festival, now the largest counter-culture event in North America, can be traced back to 1986 and a group of friends on Baker Beach, San Francisco. Larry Harvey and four pals – all with links to the city's under-ground art scene – held a bonfire featuring the burning of an eight-foot wooden effigy. As the event gained popularity and moved to the desert, Harvey and his friends created the set of magnetic ideas and practical organisation that has made Burning Man a cultural phenomenon.

A consistent thread of community, nature, fire, participation and freedom runs through the event. There's no profit motive, and no commerce except the sale of tickets, ice and coffee – the economy functions largely on gifting and volunteering. Everyone extends a helping hand. Dogs, guns, regular vehicles and mobile phones are banned. When it's over, the city vanishes without trace. Behind the scenes, there is a largely volunteer organisation that works for months in advance to pull it off. Many of the giant art pieces take a year or more to construct off-site.

Most people who attend are inspired by the event, sometimes permanently changed. They've been part of a huge experiment that temporarily rewrites the rules of society, and puts the way things are in a new light. Many feel it's the most free place they've ever been. And, undoubtedly, Burning Man is an extraordinary superconnecting structure, marking people with a shared, provocative, often spiritual experience carved out of a hostile environment. Harvey and his friends may struggle to maintain the purity of the Burning Man movement as it expands; but whatever happens next, they have already created an amazing new arena for deep human connection.

Superconnectors, then, may do more than link everyone within an existing world or bridge diverse worlds. The most creative of them may also bring people together in a completely new world. Burning Man is a perfect example of how the creation of weak links between strangers can lead to the formation of a wholly new hub. As an eight-day event once a year, run largely by volunteers, Burning Man is quite unlike conventional hubs, most obviously in structure, but also in results – while encouraging collaboration, the festival adds more to the freedom of participants than it takes away. Yet, Burning Man confronts us with the paradox that the most powerful and appealing acts of personal connection, however anarchic, need some form of group structure to maximise and perpetuate the individual connections. We'll find in the next chapter that hubs, though often in tension with weak links, are necessary complements to them; that progress has always come from our ability to work together in groups.

We've seen that there can be some pretty unlikely superconnectors out there; many are surprisingly normal, down-to-earth, fully paid-up members of the human race. But still, there are some mathematical laws we'll examine later which suggest that the great majority of human connection is the work of a small minority. We are all linked, not because we share the work of connecting in roughly equal proportions, but because a few people, like Mr Jacobs in Sharon, are so good at connecting that they do most of it for us.

But even if we are not superconnectors and never will be, we should not sit back and let the likes of Mr Jacobs do all the work. We can expand our repertoire of weak links and make them more useful by connecting other people more intelligently and more often. We can identify the superconnectors around us, and make more use of their networks – remember, superconnectors (with the odd exception such as Bruce Henderson) tend to be open and accessible. And we can choose the groups we join much more carefully, and consider leaving them when they hold us back.

Now we must turn to the hubs in our lives, and the peculiar hold they have on us.

CHAPTER FIVE

# HEAVEN, HELL AND HUBS

*What are hubs and how do we choose them?*

> The way to get ahead is to join powerful groups.
> The key to social life is not unfettered
> competition, nor universal cooperation, but a
> subtle mix of the two – competing fiercely to join
> up with the most attractive cooperators.
>
> *Paul Seabright*[27]

## Hell and heaven, a long time ago

The disciple asks, 'Buddha, what do heaven and hell look like?'

Buddha smiles, and escorts him to hell. People are seated around a long table laden with mouth-watering delicacies. However, with chopsticks a metre long tied to their hands, nobody can get the food close enough to their mouth to eat. Hungry and frustrated, they tangle and quarrel.

Buddha then takes the disciple to heaven. At first sight the picture is identical – a table groaning with tempting food. But here the people are smiling. They are using the chopsticks to feed each other. In small and large groups, they cooperate to achieve a common purpose.

Happily, by this measure, human life is more heavenly than hellish. From the earliest times our progress has been driven by success in groups – from the hunting party herding prey through a narrow pass where they can be easily taken, to the intricately choreographed team of scientists at CERN, the nuclear research institute near Geneva, smashing atoms to glimpse the fabric of the universe. Hubs are the places where people gather to socialise, collaborate, organise and achieve those works that are unthinkable for the individual. They are where we have our most intense and structured relationships – our strong links.

Hubs are the main places, the main means, for human cooperation. For sure, we can cooperate through weak links: I stop a stranger and ask the way; an acquaintance calls me to ask if I have information about a job she wants. But the deepest and most fruitful forms of cooperation, whether emotional, social or economic, take place in hubs with strong, structured relationships: in families, groups of friends and work groups. These human groups achieve new miracles of cooperation and production daily, extending our scientific and economic achievements well beyond our biological heritage. And this cooperative drive is so ingrained in us that it arises in the most unlikely conditions.

## The Western Front, France, 1914–18

In the most horrific fighting known in modern times, the armies of the French and British empires confronted their German counterparts. Both sides were dug into trenches stretching for 475 miles and competed to advance a few thousand feet either way into no man's land. The cheap and depreciating currency of competition was human life. More soldiers were involved in the war (seventy million), and more people died (twenty million, including civilians; with another twenty million serious casualties), than ever before. On one day alone, 1 July 1916, the British army saw 19,240 of its men killed and suffered more than 38,000 other casualties as the Battle of the Somme began. Most were slaughtered in the first hour of fighting.

Despite the carnage – which was completely unexpected before the war started, and out of all proportion to any war objectives – the generals and politicians on both sides remained resolute in seeking to exterminate the enemy and gain unconditional surrender. Yet, even in this hell, spontaneous cooperation arose between opposing front-line soldiers. Troops from one trench shelled the other with mortars in compliance with their orders, but at precisely predictable times and locations. Enemy soldiers reciprocated. As a result, casualties were sharply reduced. Somehow, without any formal communication, groups of troops on both sides managed to signal a cooperative strategy that brought at least temporary relief.[28]

Most of us instinctively understand the importance of hubs, particularly the cooperation that happens within them, to our lives. And, unlike weak links, hubs are familiar. Look at the group structures we participate in every day – family, workplace, clubs, and all the other nerve centres of our world. A school is a hub, as is a gang or a church. So, too, is our circle of friends, or, more likely, several largely distinct circles.

At the centre of hubs are the people who run them. Close to the centre, too, are the founders of the hub and, if it is a corporation, its main owners. Then there are the people who spend a substantial part of their life within the hub – employees, volunteers, other participants.

Outside the hub, yet essential for its success, are the people who connect to it – the users of the product or service, its suppliers, the local community. A flourishing hub usually has many more outsiders connected to it than there are people within it. All popular hubs generate an economic, social or psychological surplus. The proof of a hub's popularity is that more people connect to it than to similar – competing – hubs. Google is far more popular than any other search engine; the Roman Catholic Church has more followers and is much richer than the Church of Scientology.

Since we spend most of our waking hours in hubs it's not surprising that they are familiar to us. But like many intimate things viewed from a close vantage point, it's often hard for us to put hubs in perspective. Considering that our usefulness and happiness in life are substantially determined by these hubs – by their quality, how they fit with our aspirations, and our roles within them – this is a little curious. For reasons we'll explore, we often don't think consciously or carefully about our hubs. In which hubs do we participate? What do we give them and what do we get out of them? Are we in the right ones? What forces are keeping us there? Should we be in different ones? Apart from our families, we can select which groups we should belong to and our roles within them. Clearly, choice of hubs is crucial to what happens to us in life, but there are good reasons why we make bad choices about them. First, though, we need to probe a little deeper into why hubs are so important to humanity, and why there are so many more to choose from these days.

The key to human progress is that we specialise. Within hubs, individuals perform different tasks so that they concentrate on what they do better than anyone else; and each group specialises in what *it* does best. When you think about it, specialisation – what economists call the 'division of labour' – is the pinnacle of cooperation. It rules out individual self-sufficiency, and the more specialised the world becomes, the greater everyone's dependence on everyone else. We can't eat shoes, maths lessons, carefully riveted aeroplane wings, or legal opinions. So it follows that when we specialise, we must also trade goods and services. To do so, we must cooperate in a dense web of mutual reciprocation. Our differences bind us together; divisions of function do not divide, but rather unite us.

It seems that humans were the first intelligent beings to specialise and trade. *Homo sapiens* organised into the very first specialised hubs – the family, with different roles in which men exclusively hunted large animals, while women collected plants, looked after small children, and sometimes hunted small animals. Archaeologists say humans began trading very early, at least forty millennia ago, with some tribes making superior hunting weapons, and others bartering with seashell ornaments hundreds of miles from the sea. So humans specialised both within groups and between them.

Neanderthals, who were around before *Homo sapiens* and were also contemporaries, were apparently stronger, faster and at least as intelligent as our ancestors. But they did not divide tasks by gender – men, women and children all hunted large beasts. Nor did the Neanderthals have specialist tribes or trade between them. So specialisation was a human innovation, and it is probably the reason why humans survived when the Neanderthals did not.

Ever since, humans have specialised more and more.[29]

Stephen Pinker, a celebrated Harvard psychologist, says there are three intertwined attributes explaining humanity's pre-eminence among species – language, social cooperation and technological expertise. All three evolved together, making it possible for humans to work in groups to ever-greater effect.[30] Fellow psychologist Daniel Goleman adds an intriguing twist, highlighting the way that empathy has become a human characteristic, making it easier for us to work together in groups by thinking and feeling in similar ways.[31]

Goleman argues that humans have become subconsciously attuned to each other in a way that harmonises and resonates, resulting in our instincts for compassion, empathy and altruism. Over time we have developed neural responses that automatically mirror the feelings, experiences and actions of the people around us. In the transcription of a radio broadcast that you are about to read, look out for the speaker's instantaneous mirroring, and monitor your own responses as you imagine the scene.

### Lakehurst, New Jersey, 7 p.m., 6 May 1937

The *Hindenburg* was a German commercial passenger-carrying Zeppelin airship – a hydrogen-filled blimp – the largest and most luxurious flying machine ever built. During 1936 it made seventeen Atlantic crossings, including one round trip in less than six days, a record. It left Frankfurt on the evening of 3 May 1937 and crossed the ocean uneventfully. We pick up the radio commentary of its landing in New Jersey, three days later. The speaker is journalist Herbert Morrison.

> It's practically standing still now. They've dropped ropes out of the nose of the ship; and they've been taken hold of down on the field by a number of men. It's starting to rain again . . . the rain had slacked up a little bit.
>
> The back motors of the ship are just holding it just enough to keep it from—
>
> It's burst into flames! It burst into flames, and it's falling, it's crashing! Watch it! Watch it! Get out of the way! Get out of the way! Get this, Charlie; get this, Charlie! It's fire – and it's crashing! It's crashing terrible!
>
> Oh my! Get out of the way, please! It's burning and bursting into flames; and the . . . and it's falling on the mooring-mast . . .
>
> Crashing, oh! Four or five hundred feet into the sky and it . . . It's a terrific crash, ladies and gentlemen. It's smoke, and it's flames now; and the frame is crashing to the ground, not quite to the mooring-mast.

Oh, the humanity! And all the passengers screaming around here. I told you, it—

I can't even talk to people. Their friends are out there. Ah! It's . . . it . . . it's a . . . ah! I, I can't talk, ladies and gentlemen. Honest: it's just laying there – mass of smoking wreckage. Ah! And everybody can hardly breathe and talk and . . . Lady, I, I, I'm sorry. Honest: I, I can hardly breathe. I, I'm going to step inside, where I cannot see it.[32]

It took just thirty-seven seconds for the *Hindenburg* to be com-pletely engulfed in flames, so Morrison had no time to analyse what he was seeing. We get an unfiltered stream of consciousness where he tearfully implores those who can't see or hear him to get out of harm's way. Empathy dominates his reaction, to the point of rocking him physically.

Of course, Morrison's famous broadcast is an extreme example of empathy. But typically we use it every day, probably every hour or even every minute, across the spectrum of human interaction, from the mundane to the extraordinary. Here, Greg describes an empathetic moment in his office, a barely noteworthy event that occurred while we were writing this section, the sort of thing that happens all the time in a billion people's different realities:

'The name of your manager, please,' in an emphatic tone. '*I asked you for the name of your manager.*' The voice of a colleague broke into my thoughts.

*Curiosity*. As his insistent tone permeated the office I was compelled to listen to the dispute, half in English and half in French, with the Iberia Airlines customer service counter in Marseille. I pieced together that his fourteen-year-old daugh-ter was stranded in Malaga, Spain, because Iberia had bumped her off her flight. He now swore quietly, viciously, I think with the telephone on mute, and it was clear how upsetting this was for him.

*Alarm.* I have a daughter as well, younger, immeasurably precious. The thought of her being stranded in some foreign country by administrative incompetence – or, worse, some commercially calculated deceit – *was* upsetting. The language became more heated and rapid. He struggled with the service staff, in tersely enunciated French, powerless but for voice and word.

*Anger.* This was wrong! How could they do this? The atmosphere in the office was tense, and I shared some of his anger. I found my jaw set, as if I were about to get into some imaginary punch-up.

Then, ever so gradually, he started to make progress. The tension receded. She'd be on the flight home after all.

*Relief.*

We seem to be wired to connect to those around us. Our empathy is most powerful in face-to-face groups, among people we know intimately. Goleman says that groups generate 'a subtle, inexorable magnetism, a gravity-like pull toward thinking and feeling alike about things in general among people who are in close relationships of any kind – family members, workmates, and friends'.[33]

The number and variety of human hubs have steadily increased throughout history, but, until the last three hundred years, it was a slow process. In the Stone Age, people experienced just two or three hubs: the family, the tribe and – for men – the hunting party. Around 9000 BC our ancestors began to move from hunting wild animals and gathering fruit to 'agriculture' – domesticating animals, planting crops. But this made little difference to the number of hubs – for most people there were still only the family, the tribe, the farm and possibly a market. Typically, the hubs did not change over the course of a lifetime. Only explorers, traders and the upper echelons of society routinely experienced a life with more than three or four hubs. For thousands of years, human existence was incredibly predictable and local.

Then came the Industrial Revolution. Ordinary people began to move into the modern world – the cosmopolitan orbit of cities, schools and universities, multiple jobs in a career, travel and migration, clubs, leisure activities, voluntary groups, and friendship circles that could be freely adopted. People roamed; like me in my backpacking days, they came across individuals and groups they never knew existed.

These developments led to a momentous change in the human condition – a huge increase in both the number and choice of hubs in our lives. Think of all the hubs that you have experienced – the family into which you were born; the family you may have entered through marriage; the different groups of friends to which you have belonged; the schools and colleges you have attended; your jobs and perhaps different work groups within the same firm; the sports clubs, gyms, societies or hobby groups you have joined; social or volunteer groups; other affinity groups or collections of people with whom you have travelled or socialised. You have probably participated in dozens or even hundreds of hubs.

Moreover, the number of *potential* hubs, those in which we could participate, runs into millions and keeps rising. Frictionless communications and affordable travel have intensified the dense and wide-ranging web of human connection. We can form, maintain and renew links easily. We can even interact simultaneously with hundreds or thousands of people – in cities, in market places, in social groups, and all these again in cyberspace. New groups can form and change their shape at the drop of a hat, in ways that were previously unthinkable.

In the blink of an eye, in terms of human history, we have exchanged a life with very few hubs to one with a multitude of them. We have gone from interacting with a few highly predictable groups to interacting with many fast-shifting and unpredictable groups. The transformation from a society with few hubs per lifetime to one with many – from one where our hubs were largely preordained to one where we can select or create any number of hubs – is about as profound a social change as could be imagined.

What's good about this change? And what is not so good?

## Langres, eastern France, 1713

Denis Diderot was born into a prosperous French family. When he was twenty-one, he defied his father by refusing to become a priest or a lawyer, determined to pursue a career as a writer. His father cut him off, but Denis didn't care. He slowly established himself and was eventually approached by a leading publisher to provide a translation of Chambers' *Cyclopaedia* into French. Diderot read it and was disappointed: it was safe and unoriginal, confined to academically respectable subjects. So, instead of translating it, he had a vision of a totally different kind of project – one that would make every branch of knowledge, including that of every practical trade, readily available to anyone who could read. In 1750, a prospectus for Diderot's *Encyclopédie* created a flurry of interest, and a year later the first volume rolled off the press.

It started well. Diderot gathered a large number of contributors – both famous writers and obscure tradesmen – and attracted four thousand subscribers, a fantastic achievement at the time. But then the French authorities noted the encyclopedia's rather subversive tone. There was too much respect for the common people and reason; too little for tradition, the monarchy, the aristocracy and the Church. The establishment began to harass the writers, and Diderot's collaborators fell away.

He did not give up, however. He wrote several hundred articles himself, supervised the printing, and spent endless days and nights correcting the proofs, ruining his eyesight. After twenty-two years of constant drudgery, police interference and increasing isolation, the work was finally completed in 1772. Then Diderot discovered that his publisher had axed swathes of the manuscript at the very last minute, deleting anything deemed politically sensitive. It is little exaggeration to say that the project practically killed its originator.

Ultimately, then, the *Encyclopédie* was a great practical and intellectual achievement, but it was achieved at high cost and it never fulfilled its objective of letting ordinary people gain access to all available knowledge. The cost of subscription and the absence of public libraries confined the work largely to affluent readers.

### Saint Petersburg, Florida, 2001

Jimmy Donal Wales had the bright idea of a free, multilingual, online encyclopedia. Each entry would be written and edited, without reward, by anyone who wanted to contribute. Wales had enough faith in his idea to bankroll it himself, and soon he hired Larry Sanger, a philosopher with whom he had worked on an earlier encyclopedia project, as the chief organiser. It was Sanger who thought up the name Wikipedia and championed the use of wiki technology – a wiki is a web page or pages specifically designed to enable anyone to change its content easily.

To many people's astonishment, it worked. By the end of 2001, less than a year after its launch, Wikipedia featured 20,000 articles in 18 languages. As I write in 2009, it has 2,750,000 articles in English and – including articles in another 260 languages – 12 million in total. It is the seventh most visited site on the World Wide Web.

Wikipedia is an amazing resource – in a few seconds, you can get generally high-quality information on almost any subject.

But its most extraordinary facets are the dedication and expertise of its contributors, all of whom work for nothing. According to David Weinberger, fellow of Harvard's Berkman Center for Internet and Society, Wikipedia is 'epically important'. It has 'really proved something . . . we now know without a doubt that some immense and immensely complex works of humans can be created by removing most of the elements of control'.

Yet, it is worth asking what, precisely, is so different about Wikipedia, compared with Diderot's project a quarter of a millennium earlier?

The resemblances are striking. The objective was the same – Diderot's vision was the original. He was a philosopher; Wales hired a philosopher. Both projects were ground-breaking, collaborative exercises. Both achieved impressive, though inevitably controversial, products. Both reached a wide audience that had not previously had such easy access to the knowledge they provided.

There are, however, two telling contrasts. The first is the scale of the collaboration and the achievement. Diderot, at least initially, had more than a hundred collaborators. Wales has more than 150,000. Diderot had to find, cajole and pay his partners. Wales is able to use people he never knew existed, without paying them a penny. Diderot's product reached a few thousand users. Wikipedia reaches hundreds of millions.

The second difference is the ease with which the projects were achieved. Diderot toiled slavishly on his for over two decades. Wales worked part time on Wikipedia and it was hugely successful within twelve months. Diderot poured his life energy into the *Encyclopédie*, and it wore him out. Wales's life was immeasurably enhanced by Wikipedia. Diderot was persecuted by the establishment. Wales was welcomed into it. In 2006, *Time* magazine named him one of the hundred most influential people in the world.

What explains these disparities? It seems doubtful that Wales is more intelligent, or more dedicated, or a better networker than Diderot was. Rather, he is fortunate to live at a time when human collaboration on a grand scale is so much easier and can achieve so much more. Because of advances in technology, the cost of cooperation and communication is so much lower and its quality so much higher today. There is also much less political interference with knowledge. It is far easier for ordinary people to contribute what they know to any hub, and for others to connect easily to it.

As history has unfurled, there has been a cumulative increase in the number of humans, in the number and variety of collaborative hubs, in what they can achieve, and in the number of weak links binding together nearly everyone on the planet. The ease of making connections has increased exponentially, while the cost of making them has declined at a similar rate. The differences between the nature of human cooperation in the past and the present are relatively superficial; the continuity is profound and the results grow ever more impressive.

This all sounds very upbeat. Hubs, as we've said, are at the heart of human cooperation and advance. And in recent years, their number, diversity and achievements have soared off the scale. But listen to Martin Luther King: 'All human progress', he said, 'is precarious, and the solution to one problem brings us face to face with another.'

This is certainly true for hubs and their current abundance.


## Oxford, 2005

Psychology professor Barry Schwartz is lecturing a large group. Only he doesn't look professorial in his purple T-shirt, black shorts, white socks and black-and-white trainers. He paces the stage, sounding more polemicist than psychologist. He uses cartoons rather than research to make his points.

Society's dogma, Schwartz says, is that choice gives more freedom and welfare. When we have no choice, life is intolerable. More choice is better. But beyond a certain point, too much choice adds little value and might even become destructive. A high degree of choice has become embedded in our lives. The professor's local supermarket stocks 285 varieties of cookies, 75 iced teas, 230 soups, 40 toothpastes and 175 salad dressings. Using components on sale at the consumer electronics store, he says, you could construct 6.5 million different stereo systems. It used to be that there was one type of telephone and you rented it from the phone company. Now, there is almost unlimited choice and you can't buy a mobile phone that doesn't do many other things, too.

In healthcare, the doctor used to tell you what to do, but now she says, 'You could do A or B. A has these benefits and risks; B has these other benefits and risks. Now, what do you want to do?' This is more choice, but it is also shifting the burden of responsibility from someone who should know the right answer to someone who does not.

And what about work? We are now blessed, Barry says, with technology that enables us to work every minute of every day, anywhere on the planet – except, he adds to appreciative laughter, in the Randolph Hotel, which has almost no Internet connection. So (except in Oxford) we have freedom of choice regarding work – for every waking moment, whether to work or not.

But is all this choice good news or bad news? 'The answer is "yes",' says Barry. Everyone knows the benefits of choice already, so he is going to talk about two of its bad points. The first is that too much choice induces paralysis. Barry cites research into the choice of pensions. When people were offered more choice, fewer of them participated because it was too hard to decide between the various funds. 'So, not only will they have to eat dog food when they retire, but they are also giving up matching funding from their employers.'

The second bad point is that we are less satisfied when we have more choices than when we had fewer. More choice means more 'opportunity costs' – what we *could have* been doing if we hadn't decided to do what we *are* doing. Barry displays a cartoon of a couple on holiday in the Hamptons – they have a beautiful beach to themselves and the sun is beating down. The man says to the woman, 'I can't stop thinking about all those available parking spaces back on West Eighty-fifth Street.' Barry seems to take this joke literally, as an expression of genuine angst.

More choice also means that expectations escalate. Barry tells a long story about buying a pair of jeans, spending an hour trying on numerous different pairs. He walks out with the best-fitting pair of jeans he's ever had, but is dissatisfied because, although they're good, they're not perfect. 'I did better but felt worse,' he says, 'so I had to write a whole book to try to explain this to myself.' He shows another cartoon, with a man saying to his wife, 'Everything was better back when everything was worse.' Why? 'Because back then, pleasant surprises were possible.'

Who is responsible for everything not being as wonderful as we expect it to be? Well, you and I are. Given all the choices you had, if you had made the right decision at the right time, you could have done better. Clinical depression and suicide have exploded over recent decades. One reason for this, Barry says, is that too much choice makes people miserable.

'We have long since passed the point,' he concludes, 'where more choice is better.' In his aforementioned book, he says, 'After millions of years of survival based on simple distinctions, it may simply be that we are biologically unprepared for the number of choices we face in the modern world.'[34]

Some economists, in particular, have taken issue with Barry Schwartz. Certainly, some of his illustrations – particularly those related to shopping – seem a bit far-fetched. Choice in trivial matters is no big problem, and it is hard to believe that buying a decent pair of jeans caused him so much distress. But let's relate his views to the choice of hubs. He does not discuss this issue, but the problem of choice is greatest with regard to hubs – the families we start; the groups of friends we choose or create; the work groups, churches, clubs or gangs we join.

Why is the choice of hubs so hard today? Because the choice is almost infinite; because each choice we make will change our lives; because those choices may not easily be reversible; and because none is clear cut – the information regarding potential new hubs is ambiguous and we will never know what they are really like until we are living inside them.

It is vital to choose well, yet, as we will see, forces at work within hubs can lead us astray.

In the summer of 2008 the Japanese Ministry of Health ruled that a forty-five-year-old lead engineer working on Toyota's Camry hybrid project had died of *karoshi*, clearing the way for his widow and child to receive benefits from his former employer.[35] The official count of *karoshi* in Japan runs between one and two hundred each year, although some estimates put it at over ten thousand. The English translation is 'death from over-work'.

How alien to those of us in the West. Then again, maybe not. Do you know someone who sacrificed their marriage for work? Compromised their ethics? Lives somewhere they don't like? Endangers their health through stressful work? Or makes life miserable for themself and their loved ones by staying in a job or social group too long? There can be forces acting within hubs that are not in our best interests.

## The Bay of Pigs, Cuba, 17 April 1961

In January 1959, Fidel Castro's troops stormed into Havana to popular acclaim and overthrew the hated Batista dictatorship, proclaiming a new era of democracy. In April, Castro visited New York on a charm offensive. He ate hotdogs and hamburgers and told New Yorkers, 'I don't agree with communism. We are a democracy. We are against all kinds of dictators.'

But when he didn't secure the American support he wanted – President Eisenhower refused even to meet him – Castro started cosying up to the Soviet Union. Before long, Eisenhower instructed the CIA to start planning to topple Castro. When he became President at the start of 1961, John F. Kennedy took over the invasion plan. The CIA trained about fourteen hundred Cuban refugees who were to land at the Bay of Pigs, which would be the signal for a popular revolt against Castro. No American forces or air cover were to be provided, as the Cubans, it was confidently asserted, could do it all themselves. Almost to a man, the Cuban exiles in Miami were anti-Castro. Kennedy's advisers and generals were unanimous that the plan would work, just as Eisenhower's advisers had been – a rare example of Republican/Democratic bipartisanship. Everyone agreed that the invasion was essential, because Castro was known to be shipping in Soviet nuclear missiles, and their presence so close to the United States was totally unacceptable.

The intelligence about Soviet missiles was correct. But the Americans were wrong to assume that Castro lacked popular support. When the Cuban refugees landed at the Bay of Pigs they were easily defeated by Cuban forces, while in Havana Castro's victory was widely celebrated. Kennedy took responsibility for the debacle, and his reputation was so badly tarnished that he began to contemplate a dangerous gamble to force the Soviet leader, Nikita Khrushchev, to withdraw the missiles.

Curiously, before the invasion, the Institute of International Social Research at Princeton had conducted a survey of Cuban public opinion, and concluded that Cubans 'are unlikely to shift their present overwhelming allegiance to Fidel Castro'. The survey was published and copies provided for the US government. There were no contradictory opinion polls, either public or secret. The warning was very clear, yet the Princeton findings were completely ignored – at a high price.

## Washington, DC, 17 June 1972

Five employees of CREEP, the Committee to Re-Elect the President (Richard Nixon), were arrested trying to break into the Watergate Hotel. Their aim had been to plant bugs in the Democratic National Headquarters and steal campaign documents. Gordon Liddy and Howard Hunt, former White House aides also employed by CREEP, were arrested later. All seven men were indicted on 15 September 1972.

Nixon and his close advisers were not unduly alarmed. They were operating a massive slush fund out of Mexico to pay the burglars; now it could be used to buy their silence. The fund was financing campaign fraud, political espionage and sabotage, and illegal wire-tapping. But none of this would have come to light had Nixon not been recording his own conversations with close associates in the White House. Through a chain of accidents the existence of the tapes became public knowledge, and when transcriptions were published they revealed a massive illegal conspiracy and cover-up by Nixon and his key advisers – John Ehrlichman, H. R. Haldeman, John Dean and John Mitchell.

Under threat of certain impeachment, Nixon announced on 8 August 1974 that he would quit. The next day, he became the first US president to resign.

For more than two years the President and his top aides had been engaged in massive illegal operations; throughout that period, none of those involved dissented or showed any signs of conscience or regret. There was huge loyalty to the President and, among the conspirators, a universal view that their activities were right and proper. Even senior government figures not

involved in the affair were often blinded by their allegiance to
Nixon and the importance they attached to his administration's
work. For example, as evidence of Nixon's wrongdoing
mounted and became irrefutable, Henry Kissinger, the distinguished Secretary of State, predicted that history would view
Nixon as a great president and relegate Watergate to a minor
footnote.[36]

The Bay of Pigs and Watergate exemplify 'groupthink' – the
drive for unanimity, so that thinking alike becomes a virtue; the
division of the world into 'us' versus outsiders, who are often
stereotyped or stigmatised; the insulation of the group from
external information, opinions or data; and a belief that if the
group sticks together, it can safely ignore outside criticism.
Groupthink is an extreme form of empathy, the glue of cooperation in groups.

Without groupthink, Kennedy's inner circle could not have
merrily ignored the evidence of Castro's popularity inside Cuba;
nor could Nixon's gang have flouted the law and outraged even
Republican lawmakers so blithely. It is a paradox that the
strongest and most prestigious groups, comprising highly intelligent members, can sometimes make extremely stupid decisions.
Groupthink is often responsible for both the hub's ascent and its
ultimate fall.

Then, there's authority, which can make matters worse. Here
we return to our friend Stanley Milgram, this time in his
enlightenment-by-electrocution period, before his envelope
period. Recall, the subjects did what they were told by white-
coated authority figures, administering what they thought were
electric shocks to 'help' the hapless, helpless learners. Milgram
concluded that his experiments showed 'the capacity for man to
abandon his humanity, indeed, the inevitability that he does so,
as he merges his unique personality into larger institutional
structures'.[37]

You may feel that his conclusion is a little overwrought, but the direction is clear. In organisations, we tend to do what we are told, whereas in personal life many of us do the opposite. Authority occasionally leads us to do things that our conscience wants to reject – sell a mortgage that we know cannot be afforded, make the numbers say what the boss wants to hear, miss our child's Christmas play to attend a business meeting.

Another of these dark forces within hubs is conformity. Experiments by the psychologist Solomon Asch in the 1950s attempted to measure this. When subjects were asked to go along with a clearly incorrect statement – to say, for example, that a slightly shorter line was longer than a long one – only one in a hundred concurred when tests were administered individually. But once the subjects were put into groups, and the first people to speak up gave the wrong answer, up to *three-quarters* of respondents went along with it. They must have known it was wrong, but they wouldn't rock the boat.

Psychologist Jut Meininger suggests other reasons why we may be reluctant to leave a group, even when we know it's bad for us:

we all operate within systems of people [in which] very often people will distort themselves, absorbing great pressure or abandoning life-long principles just to accommodate a system [hub], just to remain in it or keep it intact. This holds true for family . . . as well as business systems.

Time and again, mature business people force themselves to stay in systems detrimental to their personal health . . . people trap themselves into staying in unhealthy systems out of fear (afraid to leave a job for fear they won't find another), inadequate planning (by keeping up with the Jones's, they can't afford to quit, or spend time looking for another job), or useless 'Parent' data (quitting is for cowards, job loyalty supersedes personal goals, no one likes a failure) . . . such people will usually have to choose between leaving the system or feeling bad within it.[38]


## Manhattan, 1995, and San Francisco, present day

Razorfish is an international online advertising agency, set up on a shoestring in 1995 by Jeff Dachis and Craig Kanarick. At first they couldn't afford an office, so they ran the firm from Jeff's Manhattan apartment. Razorfish now operates in eight countries, out of more than twenty offices, and has over two thousand professional employees. In 2007 Microsoft paid six billion dollars for aQuantive, the holding company for Razorfish and two other digital advertising agencies.[39] Razorfish is highly regarded; last year alone, it won more than seventy-five creative awards.

It is also marked by exceptional employee commitment and morale. Len Sellers, managing director of the San Francisco office, acknowledges, 'We've been accused of creating a cult-like atmosphere here.' Expecting a denial? Well, Len doesn't oblige. 'I used to be an avid sailor,' he says instead, 'but haven't been on a boat in a year. I used to have girlfriends, but they left out of boredom and frustration.' And the clincher: 'I used to have a cat, but it moved in with a neighbour.' His final verdict: 'It's one thing when a girlfriend leaves. But it's another when your cat moves out.'[40] Catastrophic.


## Redmond, Washington State, present day

Walk around Microsoft's beautifully manicured grounds any day, any time, and you'll run across plenty of employees. 'People are working here twenty-four hours a day,' an insider says. 'It's set up so you never have to go home.'

Lawyer Andrew Brenner recently went to Redmond for a job interview. Everyone he met, he says, 'seemed to think it was a foregone conclusion Microsoft would take over the world. It's a very strong culture.' Too strong for Andrew – he pulled out of the recruitment process.

What is the Microsoft culture? According to Michael Gartenberg, an analyst at information technology research group Gartner, it has 'four key parts – a tremendous work ethic; Bill Gates is always right; an us-versus-them mentality; and Bill Gates is always right'.[41]

Dave Arnott, Professor of Management at Dallas Baptist University, says that Microsoft, 3M, Enron and Southwest Airlines have this in common – they were or are all corporate cults. Cults, he says, whether corporate or religious, have three characteristics. They demand complete devotion and subordinate the individual to the organisation. They have a charismatic leader who is 'always right'. And by being such intense and time-consuming experiences, they separate their followers from the outside world. 'It starts with a refrigerator in the lunchroom,' Arnott writes, 'and ends in a full-blown corporate cult.'[42]

Have you ever been inside a cult? I certainly have. When I was at Bain & Company, the management consulting firm founded in Boston by Bill Bain, we were known as 'Bainies' – a reference to the Moonies, then a prominent cult. Bain & Company certainly ticked Arnott's three boxes. Curiously, though, I derived enormous benefit from my three years at Bain. And most of my colleagues, past and present, seem to agree. Bain regularly tops surveys of the best place to work. All excellent businesses have strong cultures, and most are cultish. For sure there are dangers, especially to family life, if outside links are neglected, if you don't share the firm's values, or if it fails. But intense experiences are sometimes hugely empowering, especially if you are aware of the dangers and don't stay too long.

So what do we make of hubs?

They are wonderful, and they are flawed.

They are wonderful because they are the main locus of human cooperation, the reason why we humans have freed ourselves from the tyranny of nature and been able to build a world richer in every way. Human cooperation has flourished through the division of labour – by building ever more varied and specialised hubs which do better things than our ancestors ever dreamed possible, and do them more competently and using fewer resources than in the past. Trading between hubs and nations has been at the heart of progress, creating a more interdependent world, where variety and individual differences soar alongside our number of personal connections and the links between all humans.

The upshot has been a huge increase in the number of hubs we join during our lives, and in the choice we have of hubs to join. The choice is great, but so is the opportunity to make the wrong choice, and the cost of doing so.

Choice and specialisation are marvellous, because they increase personal opportunity and diversity, allowing each of us to become a distinctive individual with unique talents and roles. We gain the freedom not only to benefit and learn from an infinite variety of hubs, but to start our own, whether this comprises a new venture or a new group of friends.

But choice can also overwhelm us. With so many options and so much time pressure, we often neglect to spend sufficient time on the few decisions that will make us happy or miserable – the groups we decide to join or leave. It is as well, therefore, to acknowledge the traps that hubs present. The psychological forces we've cited – groupthink, authority, conformity, fear and our tendency towards empathy with the people we see, which can make us stop thinking and acting independently – combine to produce what we call 'the gravity of hubs'. Powerful hubs – those to which we make commitments of time and emotion – exert a strange control over us, dragging us ever deeper into the purposes of the groups and powerful members within it, restricting outside influences or even cutting them off, and often causing us to stay within the group longer than is good for us.

The gravity of hubs, and their bias towards authority and groupthink, exhibits itself in all kinds of ways, from the false consensus leading to the launch of a faulty space shuttle, to protectionism, communism, apartheid, mindless violence in support of a football club, suicide cults and many other ills. How could so many big banks in the United States and the United Kingdom, with full complicity of regulators and almost no internal dissent, have built their businesses on sand? How can the most democratic and open societies bring themselves to lock up suspects for years without trial, or practise rendition and torture? These are grave phenomena indeed, and are not just due to the villainy of bankers or politicians, who, after all, are much like you and me.

More prosaically, the gravity of hubs may lead us to spend years working or living where we are not happy or most useful. In business, hubs often supplement their natural pull with financial manipulation, which itself has insidious routes into our minds – golden handcuffs and options or bonuses that 'vest' in the future a sum of money that is 'ours' but which we can't access yet. Of course, we don't want to 'lose' what is rightfully ours, so we stay. We may cut ourselves off from wonderful contacts and opportunities, and sacrifice our time, judgement, conscience and freedom to explore the outside world. Being wired to connect may mean we're just not wired to disconnect; and we probably should more often.

It pays to be discriminating and demanding of our hubs, just as they are of us – to experiment, to find hubs where we are truly part of the same network in body, mind and spirit, where we share the same values and aspirations, where our individuality is not curbed, but rather enhanced.

We said earlier that humans are constantly evolving new hubs and new types of hub. The Internet is further evidence that we are moving to a world of ever more hubs – cyberspace makes it easy for us to join increasing numbers of hubs, and many of us spend a lot of time in them. Pundits claim the Internet changes everything, that it's the biggest change in communication since the invention of language. Is that true? And is it good for us? The network perspective can show what the World Wide Web really means for our lives.

## CHAPTER SIX

# CYBERSPACE – BRAVE NEW WORLD?

*Does the Internet change everything?*

I was trying to describe an unthinkable present. Science fiction's best use is the exploration of contemporary reality . . . Earth is the alien planet now.

*William Gibson*[43]

## Vancouver, Canada, 1984

Having told the Vietnam draft board that his life's ambition was to try every mind-altering substance known to man, William Ford Gibson fled the United States for Canada. By 1984, he's a struggling science-fiction writer hunched over a typewriter, writing his first book. Perhaps inspired by the year – or the pursuit of his life's ambition – he imagines a future where consciousness, reality and technology blur. He coins a new word:

Cyberspace: A consensual hallucination experienced daily by billions . . . in every nation . . . a graphic representation of data abstracted from the banks of every computer in the human system. Unthinkable complexity. Lines of light ranged in the non-space of the mind, clusters and constellations of data. Like city lights, receding . . .[44]

It's striking that a computer illiterate using an ancient typewriter created the idea of cyberspace – and of *netsurfing* and *the matrix* – a decade before the Internet took off. Gibson's book, *Neuromancer*, went on to sell 6.5 million copies. *Time* magazine named it one of the top hundred modern English novels.

The Internet does seem to maintain a futurist aura. Perhaps it's the lingering ghost of Gibson's writing – inspired sci-fi can be amazingly predictive, and his vision was pretty strange. Or is it the overworked prophecies by 'experts' that the Web changes everything? Perhaps it's just our fear of the new and fast-changing Internet. Huge hubs like Facebook seem to spring up from nowhere, often displaying behaviour that seems, to the uninitiated, hard to understand or even weird. Is cyberspace really so distinctive and important?

Have you ever asked, 'What has the Internet done to my life? Has it changed me at all?' In 1964, as television began to dominate our media diet, Canadian communications theorist Marshall McLuhan famously claimed that 'the medium is the message'. He meant that the dominant medium affects our thought processes in a fundamental way, so that when the dominant medium changes, so too, in profound ways, do society and even human nature. Is this true, and has the Internet generated such fundamental changes?

McLuhan claimed that society had previously been dominated by print media – books, magazines and newspapers – but television became the controlling medium and changed us all.[45] Towards the end of the television era, the average American household had the set on for seven hours a day, with actual viewing estimated at four and a half hours per adult. Japan had even higher figures – average household television time in 1992 was eight hours, seventeen minutes. These numbers constitute a huge share of our leisure hours. Moreover, the ascendancy of television coincided with a burgeoning of the consumer society and proliferation of branded consumer goods, whose growth was stimulated by new, sophisticated marketing, centred on television advertising.

Television is an inflexible mass broadcast system, simultaneously spreading the same experience to everyone in the audience. With only a single message sent at peak viewing times, the broadcasters – dominated in most Western countries by commercial networks – naturally sought messages that appealed to the largest audience, and hence to advertisers with the biggest budgets. Witness the success of *The Brady Bunch* or *Starsky and Hutch* – a clear bias towards trivial and escapist content, the pursuit of the sensational, and to soap operas which could engage the viewer and in many cases provide a more gripping narrative than was enjoyed in 'real' life.

McLuhan noted that television's one-way broadcast created an immediately gratifying, uniform, passive and unexamined experience. He claimed that TV was taking us backwards, beyond the civilised life of reason and individuality created by European print culture, to the time when our ancestors lived in tribes and were afraid of mysterious outside forces. The new village might be superficially modern and 'global' rather than local, but essentially, he said, it was the same – everyone heard the same news at the same time, communal terror was easily stimulated by the graphic depiction of disasters, and the immediacy and inescapability of human suffering shown on television led us to emotional rather than rational responses. Instead of witch doctors, we were in thrall to the broadcasters and the spin they put on events. Furthermore, since McLuhan first published his theories, psychologists have discovered that people who habitually watch several hours of television a day typically experience mild depression.

But now it appears we have a new dominant medium. If you

are connected online, you are probably spending more time on the Web than watching television. A comprehensive US study shows that the average Internet user now spends nearly thirty-three hours online each week, double what they spend watching television. The researchers conclude, 'the time spent using the Internet will continue to increase at the expense of television, and to a lesser extent, print media'.[46]

Of course, the Internet is different from television and earlier media in substantive ways. Consider, for instance, the ubiquity of Internet connection. For television, there was typically only one connection point, in the home. We might also have listened to the radio in the car on the way to work, and read a newspaper at breakfast, on the bus, train or at our desk. For sure, we used to spend many hours a day 'consuming' various media; but if we are connected, the Internet is much more prevalent in our daily lives. We can be, and increasingly are, online at home, in the office and anywhere and everywhere else with an increasing array of powerful desktop and mobile devices. As more participants are drawn into online networks, their value and importance in our lives are likely to rise and rise.

Another difference is the vast increase in information that resides in cyberspace, far surpassing television's informational power. Storage technology (memory), display technology (xml, html), search technology (Google), publishing technology (wikis, blogging and Twitter) and organising technology (social networks such as Facebook) have multiplied the amount of knowledge available and the ease of accessing it – and we are only in the early stages of this astonishing and bewildering cornucopia.

Earlier media – whether sermons from preachers or lectures from professors, print, radio, the movies or television – transmitted information in a single direction, from the few to the many. But the Internet is two-way. When we're online, we not only receive information but transmit it; we can all be publishers as well as readers. Earlier media were inherently hierarchical and could bolster the central power of elites; in theory, at least, cyberspace is more democratic.

A final difference is the overwhelming choice the Internet offers and the possibility of tailoring its output to the needs of small groups or even individuals. The Web can 'narrow-cast' on demand.

So has cyberspace changed us? Researcher and author Don Tapscott claims it has and that the purest indications come from the young generation that has grown up with the Internet. Tapscott has conducted more than ten thousand interviews with this 'Net generation' and he paints a glowing picture. They use sites such as MySpace and Facebook to manage several hundred contacts – Tapscott says 700 is not unusual, far beyond the 150 contacts that anthropologists consider the typical limit of people we can know properly. Young Internet users, he says, do not accept information on the Web at face value; they are consummate sceptics, researchers, authenticators, referrers and critical customers. Given that cyberspace presents information disconnected from real-world clues to quality or reliability – you can't squeeze the merchandise – this is a vital skill. The Net generation has figured out which sources to trust, when to get second opinions, and how to navigate the ocean of unverified information.

Perhaps Tapscott's most revolutionary argument is that this generation is conditioned to thinking and acting in an interactive world. It is natural to be connected, to 'talk', to provide feedback and to collaborate; it is unnatural to be a silent recipient. The new generation will carry these critical and collaborative attitudes into every realm that they encounter. Tapscott implies that the new expectations will collide with existing practices in education, business and government, all of which still basically assume that knowledge and instructions travel in one direction, from top to bottom.

Not everyone, however, shares this rosy view of the Internet. The opposite case is that the new generation's reading and writing have suffered; that they can't focus or concentrate for long periods; that they plagiarise without guilt; and that they blithely create a permanent public record of their personal lives that they may later regret. The distinguished novelist Salman Rushdie has critiqued today's 'blurt culture' – where people push spontaneous reams of private information into the electronic ether in a ceaseless stream of low-quality self-expression. 'Blognate' Arianna Huffington has celebrated 'first thoughts' as 'best thoughts'. Rushdie does not agree – he fears we are moving to a future where people will not think and communicate in a considered and structured way. As the world grows more complicated, not less, he sees a looming problem.

Yet, there are some problems even with McLuhan's judgement on the impact of television, let alone the 'all-change' view regarding the Internet. One immediate difficulty with the idea that television changed society or human nature is that one might have expected such a powerful, centrally controlled, top-down medium to have led to a docile, conformist and mindless generation, gullible, easily manipulated, willing to do what they were told. But where are these people? Despite the forebodings of George Orwell in *1984*,[47] William Hollingsworth Whyte in *The Organisation Man*,[48] and Pete Seeger in his 1963 hit song 'Little Boxes',[49] the heyday of television coincided not only with a dose of bourgeois conformity but with the opposite – an explosion of individuality, diversity and soul-searching, an increased tolerance or encouragement of minority norms or eccentric behaviour, together with an unprecedented rejection of central authority and distrust of society's leaders.

Of course, if these social trends had coincided with the birth of the Internet, theorists would be claiming that the change of dominant medium had clearly changed society. But history is messier and more ambiguous than that. The idea that the

Internet is making young people more critical and less deferential seems a little odd, when, as we saw in Chapter One, these trends were already there in the 1950s, with James Dean, the Beats and the birth of pop music. The biggest youth and student revolts of all time – which took place in 1968 – came smack-bang in the middle of the TV era, not the Net era. And is the collaborative attitude highlighted by Tapscott really new? We've seen how the instinct to cooperate was one of the fundamental advantages of early humans, and that this characteristic has probably been honed by evolution. For sure, the Net hugely facilitates collaboration, but the instinct has been there for thousands of years. Of course, the Internet might be having numerous effects on young people; but if so, at the moment it's unclear precisely what they are.

Moreover, many other forces, besides new means of communication, are also at work, moulding society. If we were forced to pick one single technological change that has transformed society since the eighteenth century, it would be the invention of the steam engine, which facilitated the Industrial Revolution and led to massive increases in both the number of people in the world and their living standards. Given the same task for the nineteenth century, it would probably be a toss-up between the invention of railways and the automobile – both of which essentially derived from the steam engine – and the practical exploitation of electricity. None of these developments was in communications media. For the twentieth century, the invention of the transistor – which led to the silicon chip – might top the poll.

Beyond inventions and new technologies, society is most profoundly changed by radical ideas, such as the dignity of all human life, liberalism, nationalism, democracy and socialism, or more practical concepts, such as Keynesian economics and the importance of maintaining purchasing power to avoid depressions and mass unemployment. Despite the regressive tendencies of some recent world leaders – some now mercifully dead or retired – most people in Europe and the Americas are now free from the fear of being tortured, something that was not true three hundred years ago. Ideas and social norms are at least as important as the means of communication that propagate them – to some extent at least, the message really is the message.

So, if you grew up with television or the Internet, ask yourself whether either of them has fundamentally changed your attitudes, your behaviour, or the way your mind works. It seems a dubious claim.

What would a big change in attitude and thought look like anyway? Let's compare the impact of electronic media with two earlier shifts in the prevailing means of communication. (Incidentally, with these, we think McLuhan was right about their profound effect on humankind.)

In the previous chapter, we saw how the invention of language – the most fundamental and important change in communications technology ever – not only affected human nature, but helped create it in the first place. Language really did change everything. You've probably observed the ease and speed with which a child acquires language, or even two languages simultaneously. The software certainly downloads easily. Over millennia, our brains have become, in part, wonderful language machines, purpose-built for this function. The medium of language has become so important to humans that the species appears to have become specifically designed for it.

But we don't have to go that far back in history to notice another epoch-making change.

Contrast television and the Internet with the effects that gradually flowed from the advent of typographic print around 1450. This separated speech from the speaker, made ideas portable across physical and social distance, and moved us from communal to private thought. Before printed books, only a minuscule elite of people could read books, all of which had to be copied by hand. Everyone else – 999 people out of 1000 – relied on their leaders for new information: kings, tribal chiefs, lords, priests, landowners and occasionally merchants. Ordinary people had little opportunity to think, read or reflect internally. They were too busy listening, obeying and just scrambling to survive.

Johannes Gutenberg and his co-inventors changed all that. The demand for, and supply of, knowledge increased faster than ever before – the Renaissance transformed ideas, art, medicine and science. There was a tremendous outpouring of new writing and knowledge: as the Scottish anthropologist James Frazer (1854–1941) noted in *The Golden Bough*, the pace of innovation speeds up enormously with written books: 'For literature accelerates the advance of thought at a rate which leaves the slow progress of opinion by word of mouth at an immeasurable distance behind. Two or three generations of literature may do more to change thought than two or three thousand years of traditional life.'[50]

The authority of priests and the Church of Rome became fatally compromised. Everyone could now read the Bible and many other books and make decisions about the meaning of life, the universe and everything. New forms of Christianity proliferated; scepticism and atheism were born. Nationalism became possible, because for the first time since ancient Greece and Rome there was such a thing as public opinion within each country. Europe entered an age of reason that led eventually to the American and French revolutions and modern democracy. Attitudes towards commerce and industry changed. The so-called Protestant work ethic emerged and spread to all civilised countries, whatever their religion, transforming the self-confidence and power of ordinary people. They began to think and reflect; the individual could find inner direction towards remote objectives. Inventions proliferated. While the printing press with movable type did not directly cause all these phenomena, they would have been inconceivable without it.

At a personal level, printed books, popular journals and

private reading really did transform life, but it was not an easy process. Readers had to embed a complicated symbolic technology in their minds – to learn the alphabet and each letter's phonetic representation, how they combined to form words, how to read those words, how to write them, how to think them. Given the oral society that had preceded it, typographic society imposed dramatic changes on personal lives.

Once mastered, though, a whole new world of thought, structured and linear organisation of ideas, private reflection allowed by non-synchronous correspondence, and ultimately individual interpretation and individualism began to prevail beyond the intellectual elites of monastery and court. Movable type touched millions of people in lower echelons of society – merchants and traders; craftsmen and guild members; parish priests and teachers; artists and scientists. The alphabetic mindset changed and extended our thought processes in a highly significant way. Together with the emergence of language, it is the clearest and most profound example of how a new medium altered human life forever.

Frankly, any changes to human nature or conduct that have been wrought by electronic media, so far at least, pale by comparison.

Rather than being an unprecedented development, the Internet simply combines and repackages a range of older media in a very flexible and convenient way. It uses established modes of communication – we read, write, speak, listen, watch and project ourselves, in much the same manner as we did before, but without having to leave our chair so often. It doesn't impose any radically new mode of communication or novel way to use our minds. It does advance the creation and circulation of knowledge, but not to the same relative degree as when printing catalysed the Renaissance and the Scientific Revolution.

We may even question whether the Internet is really a new medium, rather than a fantastic transformation and heightening of all our earlier communications media – language and writing, letters, public assemblies and lectures, libraries, market places, newspapers, the telegraph and telephone, radio and the movies, network television, computing, videoconferencing and interactive TV. In making these earlier media much cheaper, more powerful and accessible, and presenting them in more combinations, on demand at any time to many millions of people, the Internet may be less a new medium and more a media supermarket whose aisles contain every means of communication, only in new and improved versions.

A summary of these competing views might be that the Net changes everything, and nothing. It pervades our daily lives – changing, for instance, how we communicate, our work routines, the way we access and process information, and how we consume media. No doubt, to some degree, the changes Tapscott foresees in education, government and business will come. And yet, against the benchmark of how speech and text fundamentally altered the way we think – the way our minds actually work – thus far, at least, the Internet has changed nothing.

So, conventional views of the Internet's impact on humans might be wide of the mark. Therefore, to try to understand the significance of cyberspace, let's adopt a different approach, the particular perspective we're exploring. What light can the simple network model of human relationships – hubs and links – cast on the subject? How far does the Internet change the opportunities presented to us by our choice of hubs and weak links? Will it mutate the network structures that rule our lives?

Consider weak links first. Mark Granovetter wrote the first draft of his paper on weak ties back in 1969. From then to the rise of the Web in the 1990s, breakthroughs in communications technology made it much easier to develop and maintain a mass of weak links – cheaper national and international phone calls, the mobile phone, the PC and digital information, and increasingly affordable air travel allowed the average person living in a rich country to manage a hundred times more weak links than would have been possible a generation earlier. Think of the richness of links you or your parents had in the 1970s compared to those of your grandparents or great-grandparents. The small world and the proliferation of wonderful weak links are not just Internet-era phenomena.

The impact on hubs was similar. When weak links proliferate, we might expect hubs to do the same. And the 1970s and 1980s did indeed see an explosion of new hubs, especially in communications and technology, such as the founding of Microsoft (1975), Apple (1976) and CNN (1980), and the launch of the World Wide Web (1989).

What happens when the Internet and related technologies allow easy, almost costless creation of links and hubs? Well, we exploit them in much the same fashion as before, following our social and cooperative instincts, only more vigorously, because there is less holding us back. Facebook was founded in 2004 and has just passed a quarter of a billion registered users – it's currently the third most visited website in America. Social networks, email, instant messaging, blogging, texting and every new little twist in our online communication options make it much easier for people to connect to each other. There has been an explosion of communication. All of this is undeniably impressive and important, but isn't it just a more efficient way of doing what people have always done – talking to friends and acquaintances, consuming, and collaborating for work or pleasure? With a few exceptions, it is unlikely that anyone is doing anything online that they didn't do – or at least want to do – before. Now they've just found a way to do it that is easier, faster, often more fun – and less inhibited.

The hub–link structures that emerge in the virtual world are already familiar components of the real world. Both worlds exhibit such phenomena as stores, market places, schools, clubs, cliques, charities, and pulpits for preachers, protesters, bullies, ranters and ravers.

Think of any website you know. Most resemble real-world structures, or hybrids of real-world structures. For instance, eBay is an auction room or flea market. Amazon is a record and book shop, and increasingly a shopping mall of smaller vendors. Wikipedia is an encyclopedia. Google has elements of a library and an archive, plus targeted advertising. Facebook comprises a club of clubs, a database organising the social map, a directory of people's profiles, and a software store. These are not novel inventions, but translations and combinations of old ones.

It also works the other way round. Most communications media have online equivalents, or soon will. For instance, the telephone became Skype; television became YouTube. Even cities, which are one of the oldest and most important means of multiplying human connections and making the world smaller, have parallels in cyberspace – for example, in Second Life, online property is bought and sold for real money. Arguably, too, the great new hubs of the Internet are 'cities in the air', places where everyone congregates simultaneously for social and business reasons. The value of the 'real estate' is expressed in the rent it can command, not from tenants but from advertisers. The online rent reflects the number and purchasing power of the people attracted to the site, just as places in 'real' cities command rents according to the number and spending power of the humans passing through them.

When thinking of websites as new cities, it's telling that many people spend more time in cyberspace's cities than they do in real-world ones. Take World of Warcraft, the world's favourite massive multi-player online game, with over ten million monthly users. Players inhabit the world of Azeroth, where they explore, defeat hostile creatures, and complete quests, often through teamwork. Knowledge and expertise grow; property, status and friends are gained.

A hardcore gamer will spend an impressive amount of time at it. So much so that China forced gaming companies to incorporate anti-addiction software to discourage minors who play for more than three consecutive hours each day. In Korea, the most wired nation on earth, a few per cent of the population, with another 10 per cent borderline, are thought to suffer from game addiction. There are even reports of game-related deaths, typically from continuous play without enough sustenance or sleep. Online hubs, apparently, can even exhibit the insidious gravity of their real-world counterparts – a cause for concern, maybe, but more vindication for the argument that there is little essential difference between offline and online hubs.

The similarity between online and offline structures supports the view that the Internet is not another communications medium, but *another dimension of existing forms of communication*. It is like suddenly being able to live under the sea or in the clouds, to create valuable new places where people may congregate, socialise and do business. It is truly magical in that new places can be created almost overnight with a good enough idea, with relatively little investment; and these new places can be reached in seconds from anywhere on the globe. If the pioneering science-fiction writer H. G. Wells (1866–1946) could join us in the time machine he conceived, he might enquire about cyberspace, 'Where is it? How do I get there?' Cyberspace would seem just as fantastic and miraculous to him as his time machine – more so, as it now exists. (In a manner of speaking. We would have a hard job explaining to Wells precisely where cyberspace is located. And he would suspect it was a capitalist trap, a mirage to make the masses spend more of their money to conjure up new billionaires. He would have a case!)

In this respect, we may look backwards and claim that television is just a primitive form of electronic communication, a step towards the Internet, with the television stations also creating virtual cities – assemblies of people at precise times for one common purpose, to watch a programme. And from the con-sumer's viewpoint they are entirely compatible media. In fact, 31 per cent of Internet use occurs when we are also sitting in front of a television; and cyberspace increasingly features television programming – Hulu and other sites like it now provide many television shows online. Owned by NBC and Fox, Hulu increased its viewers by 57 per cent in the second half of 2008.

Many aspects of television and the Internet are more alike than different – especially in their economic impact. Advertising is the commercial lifeblood of both – Google's advertising rev-enue in Q3 2009 was $5.94 billion, up 7 per cent from Q3 2008 despite a recession.[51] The owners of television sites also enjoy the advertising rents that flow from creating cities in the air. In social terms, too, television and the Web both reinforce the consumer society, making it ubiquitous and inescapable at any time of day, every day; incubating ever more sophisticated forms of market-ing, and ever more valuable brands; and concentrating markets, with the leaders taking more of the spoils.

And what are we doing with the Internet? We are colonising it in much the same way as we did with previous connecting technologies. We've rushed to build the same hub–link struc-tures as we've done before in order to support the same types of activities and desires as before – the desire to be social, to trans-act, to be heard, the gain information, to belong, to be entertained – yet with more flexibility and freedom than before.

From this perspective, the Internet is important not because it is a new world, but because it is an *old* world. It has brought a terrific *intensification* of the communication and network trends seen in the decades and even centuries before its invention. So, far from being a discontinuity, the Internet is a *profound continu-ity*. It has not created fundamentally different ways of communicating, but there has been a dramatic change in tempo and volume. We do similar things, but we do them more often and faster, while expending less energy, time and money: almost effortlessly. The world is getting smaller while our opportunities and choices are becoming staggeringly greater.

Imagine the universe of relationships, hubs and links available to someone living in a small town in rural England a hundred years ago. Only a couple of hundred people in the town would have been the same age, and far fewer of those would have been suitable marriage material. The town might contain twenty shops, a single factory, one or two institutions, perhaps a library sparsely populated with dusty books. If you were lucky, one of a few small businesses might have provided you with something resembling a trade, profession or career. Imagine how few interesting new conversations most people would have each day, and how hard it was to escape from that existence.

Compare what is available to an equivalent person today. She can research any book or idea on the Internet. She can meet people with similar interests online. She can escape her town by visiting other places or tapping into other people's experiences on innumerable websites. Within her budget, she can find and buy anything she fancies. She can hold simultaneous conversations with dozens of people across the globe. She can participate in a business enterprise located anywhere in the world from her home computer.

From a network perspective, our degrees of separation from others have decreased. More profoundly, our degrees of separation from people's thoughts and ideas, their words and images, have plummeted practically to one – we can find all these 'proxies' for people on the Web. For instance, in writing this chapter, we needed to find statistics for media consumption and so they were Googled. Much of what we don't know is only a Google search away.

Choice – of hubs and links, information and communication – and diversity are the two aspects of our society that have been increased most by the Internet. For the first time ever, we can have *too much information* and a *surfeit of choice*. More networks bring more variety, more information, more chances to succeed, but also more chances to feel that we are failing. We're as dependent on the half-hidden structure of hubs and links as ever before, but the choice of hubs and links is vastly more complicated and visible than it used to be, stretching before us in confusing complexity. And the more mobile and successful we are, the more choices we have – hugely multiplying the number of wrong moves we might make.

How do we deal with this? The simple answer is to realise that life can be better than it used to be and to embrace the opportunities, while avoiding the pitfalls of the new environment. These opportunities can be charming and simple. Avoid being dispossessed – a grandmother can easily learn how to video-call her grandchildren for free on Skype. But to use the new tools effectively in a world of excessive choice, we must build and hone our screening capabilities, our personal online and offline spam filters. We should remain open to high-quality new ideas and contacts, but screen out the dross that will steal our time and drive out original thought and creative contact. Ideally, we will be open to random new weak links, especially from different worlds, but selective when turning a weak link, new or old, into a friendly acquaintance. We should examine many potential hubs where we could spend our time, but ensure that *we* choose *them*, rather than the other way round. There is huge cost to not selecting or not selecting well, simply because there is so much choice. As we'll see later, there are many small payoffs in life but only a few really big ones.

Happily, there's a lot of help online. Runaway choice has spawned technologies and services that let us search, list, sort, compare, review and sift through the flood of information. Sites compete to become *the* trusted adviser or market place – Amazon for books and CDs, Rottentomatoes.com for movie reviews, Etsy.com for handmade goods, and thousands of others. For instance, most of us have looked with interest at Amazon's recommendations based on what other customers like us have bought.

Even without such filters, there's a network phenomenon that lets everyone else help us pick our sites. Within any particular category, from the huge number of websites that are available, users tend to gravitate by unspoken agreement to just a handful, and usually only one or two. How convenient! Strikingly, concentration – the share of the market taken by the leaders – is usually greater on the Internet than it is offline.

Take any offline manufacturing or commercial category – cars, publishing, salad dressings, insurance, advertising agencies – and you'll typically find that the top three suppliers account for between a third and two-thirds of the market. For instance, the top three US car-makers command 53 per cent of their market; globally, for mobile-phone handsets, the top three manufacturers take 64 per cent; and the top three ice-cream-makers have 39 per cent of their trade. Considering the total number of suppliers in any of these fields, the picture is pretty concentrated.

On the Web, however, concentration is even greater. In the American online search market, Google and Yahoo command 84 per cent. Globally, Betfair has 95 per cent of online betting-exchange transactions; Wikipedia more than 95 percent of online encyclopedia enquiries. Amazon controls a stunning 34 per cent of the *total* American e-commerce market, with almost complete dominance in books. All this is more than a little weird, considering that the Internet allows free and easy access for anyone – the barriers to entering a market are far lower online than they are offline, yet online concentration is so much greater.

Choice is so overwhelming, and the difficulty of deciding so great, that most people opt for the easiest solution – which is to trust the judgement of everyone else. We gravitate to the largest online hub in any particular category, and once there is a clear leader it tends to become even more dominant. Like contestants on *Who Wants to Be a Millionaire?* we 'ask the audience'. So does the 'wisdom of crowds' work on the Internet simply because it's too difficult to decide on our own? Or do the search engines determine where the crowd goes? Google's recursive algorithm ranks search results by a site's links to other popular sites. It's rather like the powerful and famous voting on who should remain powerful and famous.

We have argued that the most important decisions in our lives are our choices of links and hubs. How does cyberspace affect these decisions?

Clearly, the Internet makes it possible to cultivate many more weak links and participate in many more hubs. Social networks and tools to mine our relationships have proliferated, helping us record, organise and manage our online connections, acquaintances and memberships. The social networks can give us a glimpse of our social graph – our links through immediate and intermediate contacts – which is very useful for seeking introductions, recommendations and references. They allow us to map our links to friends and the links between them. We can see whether our network is open and bridges unconnected worlds, or whether it is incestuous and densely interconnected. The Web really does allow us to forge and manage hundreds or thousands of weak (and strong) links. You don't have to spend hours a day on Facebook or LinkedIn – just put up your profile and start rediscovering and tracking long-forgotten friends and contacts with very little effort. We can use these networks like a living phonebook, without spending our life on them. If this results in more real-life reunions and exchanges, the potential benefits are considerable.

Yet, even the most dazzling improvements in technology may struggle to change the basic social, economic and even physical rules governing human interaction – the structures that our genes and cultures have evolved over myriad millennia. Language and communication can be compressed into movable type and even more into cyberspace, but we have evolved to understand more, be happiest and feel most alive when communicating face to face. Anthropologists say that technology does not multiply our biological capacity to manage meaningful relationships, those in which some degree of trust and reciprocity are taken for granted.

They are probably right. Can you imagine falling in love over the Internet without ever meeting your beloved? We hope not. By contrast, love at first sight often endures in real life. Have you ever experienced 'email cross-purposes', when an innocent and uncritical line of text unintentionally makes the recipient really angry? Although such misunderstandings can also occur face to face, they are surely much less frequent and more easily corrected. The virtual world has tremendous range, but far less depth and emotional power. It cannot convey subtle and personally rich information, especially between people who do not know each other well, and it is most effective when allied to traditional face-to-face communication. We need personal connections. The addict needs a frequent fix, and nearly all of us need frequent face-to-face connections – the warm, complex, unpredictable and response-inducing banter of human interaction, even with people we barely know. It keeps us going. We need to collaborate, even if only for a moment. So it seems unlikely that many serious human purposes can be fulfilled solely through virtual means. Wikipedia may be an exception, but even there its heavy-duty volunteers often seem grumpy and at each other's (unseen) throats. Consensus, empathy and harmony are much easier to achieve when we see each other almost every day, and see the hurt dissent may create.

We hope you agree that the online world requires balancing with a large dose of offline reality. The aspects of our lives that really matter – who we're with, what we do for a living, our health, where we make our home – must take place primarily in the real world. Perhaps our children will evolve into cyberspace versions of *Star Trek*'s Mr Spock, where knowledge is perfect and everything is rational and calculated. We shudder at the prospect, but we also doubt it. The emergence of language and the spread of printed books greatly enriched and facilitated exchanges between humans, and especially the spread of ideas and inventions. But language and books did not diminish human emotions or our desire to meet people and richly connect with them. The new media add to our powers without diminishing our humanity, neither improving nor worsening human nature.

Just as we should strive not to be dispossessed, we should be equally careful not to be possessed. We know that we are wired to connect naturally, and this may mean we aren't very good at disconnecting. We saw earlier that real-world hubs exert gravity, making us take them too seriously, luring us into spending too much of our lives in them. Virtual hubs can exert a similar baleful gravity. They attract; then they can addict, trap and distract. Time spent online necessarily diminishes time in the real world.

If cyberspace enables us to encounter dissimilar people we would not otherwise have met, or re-establish old links, it may play a part in improving our lives. But it will not be the main means. The Internet is a very convenient, powerful and enjoyable way of gaining information and communicating, but it is no substitute for something that helps us choose wisely and is as old as humanity itself – face-to-face communication that can jolt and redirect our lives.

## CHAPTER SEVEN

# ROLODEX ROULETTE

*How to tap the power of weak links*

I have met so many people . . . who have proved
unexpectedly useful . . . I don't see them very
often . . . [but] it is like spinning a roulette
wheel – you never know what will come up.

*Antony Ball, doyen of South African
private equity industry*

## Mayfair, England, 1996

Here's how accidental weak links helped me, without my knowledge, as a result of Robin Field's network. After Robin had turned around Filofax, he was looking for businesses Filofax could acquire. One of these was Topps of England, a stationery company, and Robin began negotiations with a corporate financier who was working for its owner.

The deal went quiet for a couple of years, but the corporate financier stayed in touch with Robin and invited him to lunch at his Mayfair office. Another guest at the meal was Luke Johnson, a serial entrepreneur and now chairman of Channel 4 Television. Luke told Robin about the circumstances surrounding his departure from Pizza Express, a restaurant chain he had co-founded. After a glass or three of red wine, Robin, who is noted for his random ebullience, extravagantly told Luke that he should buy Belgo, a restaurant chain where the waiters dressed as monks and served mussels and chips. Robin added that he knew the main owner – me. Then the conversation moved on to politics and Robin thought no more about it. A year later, Luke – who had never met Robin before, nor saw him again – called him out of the blue and asked for my phone number. After some negotiation, we sold Belgo to Luke for a price beyond our expectations. He really wanted the company.

Curiously, Robin did not mention this introduction to me until I told him recently that I was writing this book. I am now wondering how many of my 'strokes of good luck' were really due to tenuous weak links – a chain of contacts where something happens at one or two removes, without our involvement, courtesy of our acquaintances and their networks.

This is really 'passive networking', because the network itself does nearly all the work – it rolls on regardless of our efforts. Having good networks is more important than active networking. Maybe people in their twenties and thirties should think carefully about getting into a small number of networks that may be life-long blessings, even when the network links appear to be rusty or in abeyance.

Or does it start even earlier, for some people anyway: in the nurseries and prep schools of the privileged, leading to the benefits of the Old School Tie. Or in the networks cemented in Ivy League varsities, or at Oxbridge, or in their equivalents around the world? Certainly, upper-class solidarity continues to thrive, especially in Britain, and is gently satirised by the narrator in the novel *Snobs* by Julian Fellowes (it might as well be Fellowes himself speaking):

I have always been uncomfortable with the *jejune* pseudo-informality implicit in the upper-class passion for nicknames.

Everyone is 'Toffee' or 'Bobo' or 'Snook'. They themselves think the names imply a kind of playfulness, an eternal childhood, fragrant with memories of Nanny and pyjamas warming by the nursery fire, but they are really a simple reaffirmation of insularity, a reminder of shared history that excludes more recent arrivals, yet another way of publicly displaying their intimacy with each other. Certainly the nicknames form an effective fence. A newcomer is often in the position of knowing someone too well to continue to call them Lady So-and-So but not nearly well enough to call them 'Sausage', while to use their actual Christian name is a sure sign within their circle that one doesn't really know them at all. And so the new arrival is forced back from the normal development of friendly intimacy that is customary among acquaintances in other classes.[52]

But it cuts both ways. The privileged may network very well among their own kind and exclude others, but in doing so they may isolate themselves from a larger body of variegated contacts. And, if the argument in this book is correct, that is an increasingly perilous stratagem. In worlds where the numerically small upper class no longer dominates the action, relying on the old magic circle might not work; and if it doesn't, the closed world of the establishment and the wealthy is not much more use than the equally isolated enclaves of the poor. Certainly, there was scant evidence from our interviews that contacts from school or university – be they exclusive or not – helped in the rise of remarkable people. Most of them flourished from playing an increasingly central role in good job networks early in their careers, then moved on to another good network, with the range and variation in their contacts building cumulatively.

Yet networks can be built at any time in our lives: it is never too late.

## Boston, Massachusetts, and London, England, 1990s

Geoff Cullinan had made the biggest mistake of his life. After co-founding and building up a successful consulting practice, and taking eighteen months out to work on personal investments, he'd been headhunted to become chief executive of Hamleys, a leading toy store. But after six months Geoff fell out with the chairman and co-owner of the firm, and abruptly resigned. Everything had gone smoothly in his career to that point. Now it looked a mess.

But Geoff had a precious fallback. The previous eighteen months without a paid job had been spent enjoyably and, though Geoff did not yet know it, very constructively. 'I had no office,' he told me.

> It was just me and my Rolodex, working from my study at home. I talked to lots of people and groups of people about many things. It was this access to a great variety of contacts that allowed me to be entrepreneurial, which I'm probably not naturally. The time when my network was most dispersed, it was most valuable. It did a lot for me and subsequently for my reputation. This period was golden, putting roots and connections down without having to commit myself.
>
> I had many offers of jobs but turned them all down. I wanted to start another business. I knew the top people in Bain & Company in Boston and London and they seemed to like my track record. Equally, I had always admired the Bain culture; it fitted my own view of the world. They were also impressively persistent in trying to persuade me to join them, but I didn't want to go back to 'plain vanilla' consulting. But in conversation with them we saw an opportunity to build a new business within Bain, advising private equity firms on deals, and investing alongside them. I wouldn't have recognised

this opportunity but for spending so much time looking around, and getting to know the private equity world and many of the key players. The turning point for me was meeting a Bain partner from California who had spent some years trying to develop a business model so he could advise and co-invest with private equity investors. It was a real light-bulb moment – I saw the connection at once and the potential to do this on a big scale globally.

So I agreed to join Bain to build a new line of business that hadn't really been invented in Europe. Now, twelve years later, the private equity consulting business we started comprises more than a quarter of Bain's global revenue and we are far and away the leaders worldwide, dominant in big deals. It worked brilliantly for them and for me.

Geoff's relaxed approach in his eighteen-month pre-Bain odyssey was crucial. Of course, as he freely admits, he was in a privileged position, having savings to fall back on – most people would not have that cushion. Still, his story shows the advantage of being able to focus more on contacts, information gathering and ideas than on finding a job immediately – something that perhaps we should all do if we are lucky enough to be employed, before we really *need* to find another job. Geoff's method brought many opportunities, so he could act by choice rather than out of necessity. He waited until he could see the best fit and chance to make a big splash. His range of contacts and information made this much more likely, and his reputation as a well-connected individual with many alternatives made it easy to close the deal on favourable terms.

Geoff is one of dozens of people whom we interviewed for this book. We selected contacts that we knew were accomplished, happy and fulfilled in their work; and, if they wanted to, had made plenty of money. We asked them about their weak links and hubs, and their responses are sprinkled throughout these pages. The interviewees were a mixed bunch – seven nationalities, sixteen professions and a wide range of personalities and attitudes towards life and work. But they all had one thing in common, which made a deep impression on us. Without exception, they had an unusually large and varied assortment of friendly acquaintances with whom they maintained infrequent but fairly regular contact – at least once a year.

We hope you'll agree that the strength of weak ties stands the common view of strong and weak relationships on its head. We all tend to think that friendship is the ideal relationship, while anything else is shallow and futile, or at least less worthy of our attention.

But what if friendly acquaintanceship is a great thing – not the same as close friendship, but something distinct and valuable – a whole raft of highly efficient, loose and flexible relationships, absorbing little social energy but potentially providing significant benefits to both sides?

When we understand the rules of acquaintanceship – that it is not a poor substitute for friendship, but something totally different – it can begin to play a vital part in our lives. Having wide-ranging contact with mutually respected acquaintances enhances our humanity and enlarges our opportunities, and all without the commitment of time, concern and emotion that is an essential component of deep friendships.

Adrian Beecroft reckons he owes his success to two tenuous weak links. He is one of the most successful investment professionals in Europe, having built up Apax Partners from three people to become a hugely profitable giant and take over Apax's US arm, which had not been quite so successful.

However, after earning an MBA from Harvard, the early part of Adrian's career was not so smooth. 'I was clear that I wanted to get a job in industry and become a chief executive eventually,' he confided over breakfast in Luxembourg.

When I left Harvard I tried to find a job in high tech in England, which in those days meant principally Plessey and GEC. But they were staggeringly uninterested in MBAs, even those like me with a technical background. I never wanted to become a consultant – I like to do things, not advise – but I had to join a consulting firm as a fallback. I told myself that I would stick at the Boston Consulting Group (BCG) for three years maximum and then move into industry.

But that plan failed. Adrian spent eight years of his life at BCG, and though he did well and became a vice-president, he wasn't happy. 'The last two years were particularly hard. I had no ladder left to climb, I didn't feel I was contributing much; it was a thoroughly miserable period.' Eventually, though, Adrian was approached by venture capitalist Ronald Cohen, who ran a very small fund, Apax, in London. Ronald got in touch after talking to a former acquaintance of Adrian, John Baker, who had been one of eighty people in the same section of Harvard Business School, but not one of his closer friends.

Joining Apax was not obvious at the time. They only managed ten million pounds, and they would pay me only a third of what I made at BCG. Would I enjoy working in a three-person start-up? They courted me for ages and eventually, with many misgivings, I said 'yes', because I wanted out of BCG.

Well, I realised that I would have to find my own deals. I had no idea how to do that. But that is where two weak links came from left field. I belonged to a cricket club in Cropedy, north of Oxford. A chap there I didn't know well introduced me to a friend of his who owned and ran a chain of small record shops. This became my first deal. Six months later we sold the chain on to W. H. Smith, a big UK chain, for three and a half times what we'd paid.

That helped to establish my confidence and reputation in
my new job. My second deal was Computacenter, a chain of
stores selling computers, which was run by Phil Hulme. [Phil
had been one of the bosses at BCG.] But I didn't get the deal
from Phil. Instead, I bumped into John Burgess, whom I knew
had left BCG before you and I joined. John mentioned the
deal to me, so I called up Phil and we did the deal. We put in
£10 million over a period of time and got out £270 million.

Of course, weak links operate well beyond the business world,
and in personal lives as well as careers. Whenever we talk to
anyone, however casually, about networks and weak links, we
find almost everyone has a story to tell of how the course of their
life pivoted on an accidental contact.

## Hampstead, England, 1990s

Alice Wallace was an artist holding a private view in a
Hampstead gallery. She invited Petra, someone she'd met only in
passing,

> very much on the off-chance she'd buy one of my water-
> colours of the area. Anyway, she brought along Ann, a friend
> of hers but a complete stranger to me. Both of them were very
> much the type to drop into a private view every weekend.
>
> Neither of them bought a painting, but I got talking to Ann
> and she told me it was her fortieth that day and invited me to
> her bash that night. Ann, looking stunning at her party, had
> invited Dave, a jazz pianist, a brilliant accompanist who made
> every girl sound like Ella Fitzgerald. There was no shortage of
> women who wanted to sing with him, at the very least.
>
> Meanwhile, I'd always wanted to sing jazz and blues, but
> never had in public. Since childhood I'd played piano for my

mother, who had a beautiful voice and had sung jazz standards on Karachi Radio for many years. Somehow, twenty years of frustration at being in her shadow reached fever pitch, and I did something completely out of character. Fighting off the other women who were squeezing up to Dave, I grabbed the microphone. I chose 'Organ Grinder', a raunchy blues song from the 1920s which was not too well known but with which any pianist could shine. It finishes rather provocatively, and I milked it:

> Your sweet music seems to ease my mind,
> Well, it's not just your organ – it's the way that you grind!

A few notes were all it took to seal a completely unexpected musical and romantic partnership. For the next five years, Dave played and I sang in basement jazz clubs and chichi restaurants all over London, and we had a ball. I discovered a great new career as a singer and later as a song composer. None of that would have happened if I hadn't spoken to someone I didn't know earlier that day, who was a friend of another person I barely knew.

## Cape Town, South Africa, 1995–2007

At the end of a recent tennis lesson my coach, Stan Hasa, originally from the Czech Republic, asked me what I was doing at the moment. I said I was writing a book, and quickly explained about weak links. He got the idea right away and told me about two important events in his life:

When my wife and I arrived in Cape Town from Germany in 1995, we stayed in a guest house owned by a gay couple and we remained in brief contact after we moved out. I was not sure what work to do in South Africa and was looking around. Four months later, I hadn't found anything that interested me, money was running out, and I was a bit down about it. Then, out of the blue, one of the guest-house owners called to say that the Health and Racquet Club in Green Point, where he did his gym, was looking for a tennis coach. I had been a semi-professional tennis player but never a coach, and I hadn't even thought of that. So it was actually that gentleman who figured it out for me and made the connection.

After an interview I got the position, and remained coach there for twelve wonderful years. I gained a number of great friends while I was there, and was able to bring together quite a few other people who hadn't known each other before, who became close friends of each other. You might say it was all pure luck, but I think at some level I was really looking for that kind of job, not just to teach tennis, but to connect people I met on the court. Certainly I was very happy doing it.

There is a flea market in Hout Bay, where we used to buy honey from a beekeeper. One day in 2007, he told me about an international yogi master giving a blessing in Cape Town. I had become interested in spiritual issues and decided to go along and it really clicked with me. I didn't think too much about it, though, and not long after we decided to return to Germany, mainly because of the girls' education. But then I discovered that the yogi has a spiritual centre less than two hours from where we are living. I now make regular visits to the centre and am learning from him.

I do not believe in accidents or coincidences. I think that we will receive in life what we are looking for, even though we may not know exactly what that is. The world is a giant radar machine and what we are radiating will not go unanswered. Our needs vibrate in a universe where everything is interconnected and related. Most of this help comes from people we don't know well, as long as we are open to receiving help from them, and as long as we give other people the help they really need. That may sound a bit far-fetched, but it's what's happened in my life so far.

## Cambridge, England, 1970s

Colin Smith is a highly respected artist. One great accolade in his career was when London's Tate Gallery decided to purchase two of his large works for its permanent collection. (It is highly unusual for the Tate to buy more than one work from a living artist.) Colin's leap forward came about through a couple of weak links, one of whom he had never met but who had known of Colin more than thirty years previously:

> About ten years ago, I ran into an ex-tutor of mine, someone I hadn't seen for ages. He said he'd just found out, quite by chance, that twenty years ago [as it was then] I had nearly been given a prestigious art residency at a Cambridge college. I had been considered for this award without knowing anything about it. Anyway, the director making the decision had eventually decided that, though he thought highly of my work, I was too young. At first I was just bemused, but then I thought, Why not get in touch with the director now, wherever he was? I asked around and through another acquaintance I found out that the former director now worked at the Tate Gallery. I was filling in an application for a grant at the time and it required two referees, so I sent it to the man at the Tate and asked if he would mind vouching for me. He agreed, but then asked if he could visit me at my studio in Hackney. He and another curator turned up and that led to the Tate buying my work.

More recently, I had another stroke of luck through a couple of people I see from time to time, though less than once a year. Manuel and Alison, a security consultant at a Spanish bank and his wife, came up to me after a talk I gave at the Whitechapel Gallery on another artist. We got chatting and met again, and I was really touched because they decided to delay the fitting of a new bathroom in their flat and buy a picture from me instead. We stay in touch and I sometimes see them at my London exhibition openings.

Two years ago, Manuel sent me a text message – he'd just read my name in the weekend *Financial Times*. I would have missed it completely – the financial world is not mine – but a successful entrepreneur was being interviewed and said that he had two of my paintings. I used Google to find an email address for him. Contact was established and eventually he came to my studio, bought several more works, and sponsored a research project. And we are becoming quite close friends as well – my studio in Spain, which is in a remote place, is not far from a home he has there.

## London, England, 2003–5

Sir Stephen Sherbourne is not a household name, but to the cognoscenti of British politics he is known for two important roles. The first was as Margaret Thatcher's Downing Street secretary between 1983 and 1987, the key years when she broke the power of the British miners, led by Arthur Scargill. (Stephen and Margaret had hit it off during the 1983 election campaign, when he'd briefed her every morning before her press conference.) The second was as chief of staff to Michael Howard, Leader of the Opposition between 2003 and 2005, during which time the Conservatives began their long climb back to electability. When I met him in the Wolseley, a smart café in Piccadilly that he uses as an office, Stephen explained how weak links had been crucial throughout his career:

> On the one hand, there are your dear friends, people you lavish with love; like plants, you water and fertilize them. And in politics there are always close friendships, because of the intensity of the experience and the fact that it's not a nine-to-five job. On the other hand, there are people you barely know, but to whom you have some faint, friendly connection. In my career, my close friends − people from whom, in so many ways, I've learned so much − have not produced leads (perhaps because the friendship was so personal). Whereas quite casual acquaintances have come out of the blue to give me some very interesting jobs.
>
> For example, my time as chief of staff to Michael Howard came this way. I knew him very slightly − he had been a junior minister when I was at Number Ten. But there was no direct connection. I knew a young guy called Steve Hilton, who worked for Maurice Saatchi in public relations. Steve's girlfriend happened to be a close adviser to Michael Howard. She told him he needed a chief of staff and said, 'Why not Stephen Sherbourne?' I loved my time in that job, getting back to the centre of politics, and it would never have happened without those two weak ties.
>
> Today, when I make my living as a consultant to companies, my best client is a property company. I got a phone call two years ago from a woman who said she had worked with me − I didn't recognise her name, but she had changed it when she married. It turned out that fifteen years ago she had been way down the line at the Milk Marketing Board, then a client of mine. Anyway, she was now head of corporate affairs at this property company, told the CEO he needed strategic advice, and recommended me.
>
> I think I have been lucky to have done so many different

things and have so many connections that I have forgotten about, so that these thousand-to-one jackpots come up more often than anyone could expect.

There is something fascinating in the way that our personal relationship machines occasionally produce a bonanza. We might not know why we talk to someone or keep in touch with them – we might forget all about them for 99.9 per cent of our lives – yet if *they* have a good network of weak links, *we* might suddenly benefit. So is there something we can do to make such serendipitous events more likely or frequent? Can we rig the odds in our favour by investing in a larger number of appropriate casual contacts, like sprinkling a large number of small bets on all the roulette tables we can find?

Antony Ball, probably the most accomplished venture capitalist in South Africa, thinks we can. He suffers the occupational disease of most serious business folk – he is unbelievably busy. Yet he always makes space in his agenda, once a week, for a lunch with a new contact or acquaintance from the past whom he has not seen for a while, with no specific plan or purpose in mind.

I asked how he could justify this. He grinned – or was it a grimace?

Well, there are people in my organisation who criticise me for spending time with outsiders for no particular reason; they say I tend to go towards people I find fascinating. And it's true!

Randomness so often works. Think about investment bankers – their whole professional lives depend on working the field. They don't know ahead of time who's going to be useful, or for what; but they get results by putting together chance connections. Everyone in business could do the same.

Substance comes back to relationships with people, always back to that and nothing else. If people are inclined to hang out with you, they will bring things to the table for you in preference to anyone else. Friendly acquaintances work for me and they work for most people who deliberately cultivate and maintain them. You can test ideas easily with people and select the few ideas that may work.

Some people have been so helpful, people that I really don't know all that well. Mark Paterson, for instance. We went to the same school, not at the same time, but I had a tenuous contact from that. He is a superconnector in New York, and when I'm there I take the time to look him up. He runs a distressed-debt fund and is very successful. He has been exceptionally helpful on many things. He tells me how to price an offer or a sale, he told me ten things about one of our American investments, and so on.

I have met so many people like that who have proved unexpectedly useful in business. I don't see them very often, maybe four or five times a year. It is like spinning a roulette wheel – you never know what will come up.

All you need to do is contact people you think might be able to help and ask for that help. I would do the same for any contact who asked me. If you have this attitude, it's natural to ask for help. There are always things you can do which are easy for you and hard for them, because it's outside their experience.

I believe in giving and am strongly into that – there may not be an immediate payout, maybe not one at all in any particular case, but there is a lovely big cycle to all these things. There is a chain of reciprocity stretching around all your contacts, and their contacts, what you call the invisible links, and what goes around comes around. If you give, you will receive.

Geoff Cullinan agrees, but says that diversity of contacts is crucial:

I buy the idea that avenues of opportunity come from people we don't spend much time with, because they are outside our world. Whenever I see people I ask, 'What's happened to X?' – someone we both remember. Ms X is usually walking on a different planet. In a fixed network people become inbred, which is why it's essential to have a jumbled and assorted network. If you wait until you have a reason to see someone before you contact them, you may never meet and you miss so much.

Does this seed-planting sound rather aimless, at odds with the advice we are constantly given to 'focus' our lives? It needn't be.

Focused ends; random means.

Here's my own story. As soon as I became a management consultant in my mid-twenties, I wanted to start my own firm, with one or two colleagues. It struck me that to shape and direct my own firm would be so much more fun, that it was the only way to stop being a wage slave and start gaining control. But I didn't want to do it on my own (too lonely, too risky) and there were certain things, such as the day-to-day business of running a firm, at which I knew I'd be hopeless.

So I'd always wanted to do this, but never saw an opening.

Then it came, but in such an oblique, sideways manner that if I had not *always* been on the lookout, the chance would have slipped by.

After four years at BCG I jumped ship and joined what was then quite a small offshoot, Bain & Company. I moved to London and two of my colleagues there were Jim Lawrence – initially my boss – and Iain Evans, who was promoted to partner at the same time as me. I liked and admired Jim and Iain, but they were acquaintances rather than friends.

Then, in my third year at Bain, something strange happened. It was a Saturday morning and I was calling another Bain colleague, Ian Fisher. We chatted about a case we were working on and then he suddenly blurted out, 'Something bad is happening.'

I asked what he meant, but he was cagey – he'd witnessed something in Boston, but had been sworn to secrecy. However, he did admit, 'It's really bad, Richard.' Putting two and two together and making fifteen, I asked, 'Is it to do with Jim and Iain?' He wouldn't say, but he didn't need to.

As soon as the conversation finished, I tried to call Iain and Jim. Both phones were engaged for ages. Were they off the hook? Were they in cahoots? Had they resigned to start their own firm? If so, could I get in on the action?

I cycled from my house in Bayswater to Iain's riverside pad at Kew. I found them together, shocked and bedraggled. They'd flown from London to Boston to offer their resignations in person to Bill Bain, expecting him to appreciate the gesture. He'd responded by calling in a federal marshal to slap an injunction on them, stopping them setting up in competition or taking clients.

I said I'd like to join them – if they ever got started. They were impressed that anyone would want to throw in their lot with them in their darkest hour. Within a few months, we had co-founded Lawrence, Evans & Koch, which became LEK.

Opportunity's knock is often muffled. It may come, as it did for me, from weak links and faint signals when you least expect them.

Your skill at cultivating and using weak links will be reflected in how open and varied your networks are. A simple way to assess this is to count the total number of social or business meetings – even quick cups of coffee or drinks – you have had over the last few months with friendly acquaintances you don't see very often, or new ones. And can you think of the people with whom you last discussed something significant in your life – a big decision, a favour needed or given, a plan or project not directly related to your work? Are these people very different from you and from each other by age, sex, ethnicity, religion, social, educational and occupational group, political views, workplace and hobbies? Tellingly, if they are a diverse crowd who don't know each other, the chances are your network is open and assorted. If they all know each other and are similar, or if you discuss important things only with your close friends, your network is closed and introverted, so it might be hard for fresh information to seep in.

Failing this test can be a good thing. The more we fall short of a big, open, varied network of weak links, the greater the opportunity.

In listing our weak links, we shouldn't forget people from our past. The past, it is said, is a foreign country. Maybe, but it's also eerily familiar and easy to revisit. Most of us have huge latent networks that can be reactivated easily.

I met Paul Judge through the Wharton alumni network. He's one of the most superconnected people I know, and has achieved a tremendous amount in business, financial circles, politics and education. An Englishman, in 1973 he left Wharton and returned to the UK. Later, he was knighted for his creation of the Judge Business School, which is housed in a fabulous new building in Cambridge. Paul has more weak links than anyone else I know – he is always getting on or off a plane to some remote part of the world for a meeting, and he never seems to be visiting the same people.

For Paul, connecting is driven by social urges, by his fascination with meeting people, and sometimes by reliving good times from the past:

For instance, recently when I was moving I found my work phone directory from 1976. And I thought, Gosh, I remember all these people! I got two of the secretaries to contact all the other people and we had a big party. Everyone was thrilled. It was twenty-five years on, yet everyone knew everyone else instantly, just like with school friends. I think that is why old contacts are such great weak links. You can resume your old relationships with no cost, it's easy to do. You *know* them and can immediately have a deep conversation if you want. But I think it's important to be spontaneous and not to look for any benefit over and above the pleasure of seeing people. Serendipity happens, but it happens when you're not expecting it, and you certainly can't bend it to your will.

The main way we can build and maintain a large repertoire of excellent weak links is to keep a broad circle of friendly acquaintances and to be open to new people or worlds while continually thinking – at a patient, submerged level – how they might be relevant to our aspirations. Some people – Richard Branson, for example – always carry a 'day book', an A4 bound notebook, to jot down conversations, ideas and the contact details of anyone they meet who could prove useful in the future.[53]

Besides openness and serendipity, we see three other tactics – much less important, but worth a quick mention. One is to target a new world deliberately and immerse ourselves in it. We add a new social *context* to our life – by taking up golf, joining a cycling club, doing yoga, getting a new job or doing volunteer work. Clearly we can't do this all the time, so one new activity a year might be a sensible target.

We can also position ourselves in a variety of places where there is plenty of opportunity for random contact with strangers or acquaintances – read or just watch the world go by on a park bench; walk the dog in a popular locale; patronise a specific coffee shop, with or without a laptop; become a regular at a club, bar, restaurant, bookstore, market or other spot where people congregate. People have been socialising in particular places for millennia, but it was only in 1999 that Ray Oldenburg coined the phrase 'the third place' (after home and work) to describe locations where we habitually relax.[54] Regular visits to familiar third places, and irregular forays to new ones, are good ways to renew or forge weak links.

The third way is ad hoc, in response to a pressing need. If you desperately want to change jobs, for instance, you would use all your existing contacts, revive the old ones, and create new ones, such as friends of friends who may have some connection to your target position. (Online social networks can come in handy here. They can reveal chains of contacts and a path to the desired introduction that you'd never discover otherwise.)

Finally, cutting across everything, let's not neglect to connect people we know who don't know each other yet but might be better off if they did. That is the first step towards doing a little superconnecting ourselves.

Weak links are so interesting and useful because they are predictably full of surprises. They're our outreach to distant planets. They supplement our world and put it into context. They enlarge our empathy and humanity, and our ability to enjoy the infinite variety of people and the stories they have to tell. Yet weak links are not the only reason why people enjoy remarkable lives.

The other half of the story concerns hubs – the groups we join. They are wonderful and dangerous things.

## CHAPTER EIGHT

# HUB TO HUB

*How to choose hubs, and when to
move from hub to hub*

It's not a corporate ladder; it's a corporate trapeze.
You jump from one swinging trapeze to another.
If you're lucky, you catch the new trapeze as it's
about to go up, and then swing to an even higher
one.

*Jim Lawrence, chief financial officer, Unilever*

### London, England, 1983

My life was transformed by the six years I spent in LEK,
after resigning as a partner of Bain & Company. In that
time, LEK went from three professional consultants to a team of
350, opened new offices around the world, and doubled its size
every year.

Anyone who has started a new venture will be familiar with
the buzz it provides, particularly when the firm grows very fast
and things mainly go your way. I was able to pick some incredibly talented young people and watch them develop in the new
company. I learned a lot about myself, too – what I did well and
what I did badly. I used LEK to test some theories about business,

particularly the idea that most firms do far too much and can multiply profits by halving sales. By bringing in extraordinarily gifted raw talent, then honing it, I felt that I was helping to build a great firm. When I left in 1989, I was able to look back with pride at something unique and self-sustaining.

That, I thought, was that – a compelling chapter of my life closed. To my great surprise, though, LEK has proved most beneficial to me *since I left*. This first manifested itself in my social life, as four people from LEK became very close friends. But the business benefits kept on rolling, too. Over the years, people in the LEK network have brought me four great new business deals. Two of these have already been mentioned: the rescue of Filofax and the launch of Belgo. The third was to buy Plymouth Gin, a great name if you went back far enough, but at the time a defunct brand. The last was the online betting exchange Betfair. These four ventures have made my fortune; and two decades after I left LEK, the links made there are still working brilliantly for me.

In my experience, then, if you've been a key part of a fine hub, it will automatically help you later. You get two lives for the price of one: the one you're living now; and the one you lived before, which continues to deliver significant emotional, social and economic dividends.

This sheds new light on effective networking. It's not a frantic fight to connect superficially with anyone you happen to meet. The lesson I learned accidentally is to select a new hub and work creatively inside it, every few years, to make life even more fulfilling. Work networks in particular build cumulatively – each move creating a new network that we can use for our next upward leap. This inspires me. A career is a chain of events; each step can be the springboard for the next, whether business or social, because we know more people and are known by them.

My instinct seems to be supported by research. Mark Granovetter, the sociologist we met in Chapter Three, says,

'Mobility appears to be self-generating: the more different social and work settings one moves through, the larger the reservoir of personal contacts . . . who may mediate further mobility.'[55]

All the accomplished people we interviewed recognise the value of previous hubs and have stories about how former hubs helped them. Jim Lawrence – my former partner, the 'L' in LEK – is well aware of how important LEK was for him after he left: 'LEK gave me money, stature and reputation,' he says, 'as well as a network of great people that just keeps getting more and more valuable.' Many interviewees refer to former hubs that they have used increasingly over time. But there is no universal pattern – some former hubs prove very useful, usually for social *and* business reasons, while others are no use at all. 'It's a funny thing,' says Jim, 'the hubs I've got most out of after leaving are also the hubs where I've been able to help a lot too. PepsiCo is a great example of that. I stay in touch with many former colleagues there, and try to put them in touch with other people in my network whenever I can. And the contacts from PepsiCo have proved enormously useful to me.' This was echoed throughout our interviews – a hub will be most useful if you feel affinity with the people, make small efforts to stay in touch, and try to give something back, such as a deal, job or contact that might be interesting to a former colleague.

Our interviewees give many examples of how they had benefited from former hubs. One says that, in a general commercial career, hubs are even more valuable after we leave because we now have distance and perspective, which help us work out how to use our contacts more constructively. To do this, we have to keep moving in our career: 'Infuse it with kinetic energy,' he says.

Another notion is that success in a hub gives kudos and confidence in using that network later. For example, everyone I hired directly from university for LEK has benefited from their experience with the firm, and I have no hesitation in approaching any of them. Some are now in top jobs and very busy, but they always respond quickly.

There is also general agreement that the most successful hubs are the most useful for subsequent networking.

But not everyone concurs. A few point out that *failure* in a hub can contribute to future success through the productive use of the former network. 'I think the most important thing in determining success', says Chris Outram, the co-founder of OC & C Strategy Consultants, 'is the willingness to take risks, to leave a hub even if it is well paid and go somewhere else.' Chris and another interviewee both cite the Boston Consulting Group as one of their most valuable hubs after they left, although neither thrived there. 'I learned a tremendous amount from my time at BCG,' says Chris. 'I met some amazing people and participated in some great work, but there were just some things that I was less strong at than other people. I learned that my strong points were conceptual strategic thinking, relationship building and connecting with people. There are four or five friends from BCG I've kept in touch with who have been terrific in terms of social and business contacts.'

Refreshingly, one interviewee says that we should not view leaving firms where we did not thrive as failure: 'You keep going, you keep moving, until you find the place that fits you entirely.' Another confides,

I worked for Virgin for a couple of years and I absolutely loathed it. My boss had poached me from another firm by offering me much more responsibility and a big salary hike. But my relationship with him was difficult and I felt miserable. I realised my mistake almost at once but I thought I'd better stick with it, to prove myself. I learned many things from the job – especially how *not* to treat people – but I wish I'd had the confidence to leave earlier. It's interesting that I only see

two people from my days there, which is much less than anywhere else I worked.

So how long should you stay in a firm? Clearly, there is no universal answer, but here are a few cautionary tales. Back in the
early 1970s, Mark Granovetter was the first to notice an intriguing tendency. He talked to several people 'who seemed
personable and intelligent, who had stayed in one job for fifteen
or more years, and had then had remarkable difficulty in job
search'. He cites the case of 'Victor O', a chemical engineer.
When Victor left the army he worked in one firm for two years,
before going to work for a small company near Buffalo:

> He held this job for eighteen and a half years; many of his
> workmates stayed there the whole time. The company was
> then bought out in a conglomerate acquisition, and Mr O's
> position was eliminated. He began searching by contacting
> friends and acquaintances and by answering ads. He wrote to
> 115 companies; as time passed and his frustration mounted, he
> began keeping a scrapbook of the ads and his letters along
> with the responses.

None of these approaches resulted in a job, and Mr O became
angry and unhappy. From this and many other cases, Granovetter
concludes that 'long job tenure cuts off the accumulation of personal contacts and thus reduces the chances for mobility'.[56]
    Recently, I met an old colleague from Shell International.
Let's call him 'Adam'. He stayed longer than I did – eight years
in total. 'I should have left earlier,' he says, comparing himself to
his best friends in the firm. 'James went into headhunting, Steve
and Rick into venture capital – they all stayed less than half the
time I did. They ended up with more interesting jobs and they
made far more money.' Adam then joined a small firm, where he
still works, fifteen years later. 'In the last recession, I felt that I

should leave, but it was a tough time for the firm and I felt some obligation to stay and help put the business back on track again . . . To be brutally frank, moving here was a mistake, and staying here was a worse one.'

Now, Adam has not done at all badly. But by staying in two firms for a total of twenty-three years, he has gradually moved from the fast to the slow lane. He has not renewed his contacts in the same way as former colleagues have done; nor has he created a dispersed network of contacts by moving from hub to hub. He is as intelligent and personable as any of them, but he's stayed in the same gene pools for too long.

As he walked me back to reception, I said it was great to see him again. 'Yes,' he replied ruefully, 'but I have to admit that you've depressed me. I never realised the full consequences of staying put too long.'

I can relate to this, because I've been there myself. When I left business school, I thought I had landed the perfect job. Snazzy offices, first-class travel, bright and personable colleagues, interesting work, and the opportunity to learn about a whole new area, business strategy. I was confident and got on well with clients. But I didn't impress most of my bosses. They felt I was weak at heavy-duty analysis. And they were right. So I redoubled my efforts. I put in eighty or ninety hours a week. I was always there on Saturdays and Sundays. I became tired. I started staying in the office at night and ordering in pizza, or popping out for a quick burger and fries. I had no time for exercise, so I put on weight and got chubby in the face. My personal relationships suffered. Most of all, work was my life, and I wasn't even winning at that.

I stayed for four years and resigned just in time to avoid being fired. Looking back, I can't believe I was so stupid to continue for as long as I did: two years was enough to learn almost everything, and then it stopped being fun. So I pretty much wasted two years; in fact, I went backwards in everything that mattered.

But I know why I stayed: I didn't want to admit defeat. I wanted to prove that I could win. Eventually I did the sensible thing and joined another firm where brilliant analysis was not the only measure of success. But by then my ego had doomed me to two years of misery.

'Don't underestimate the power of inertia,' one of our respondents says. 'I knew I should move, I knew I wasn't happy, but I was too busy and thought I was too locked in financially to make the break.'

'I reckon the ideal time is four to five years,' says another. 'Two years means you come and go. Any longer than five years and you're stuck.'

On the other hand, it's not necessary to move hubs very often. The fewest work hubs experienced by any of our interviewees was four; the most, nine. The typical time between moving hubs was four to six years, but this increased as the interviewees got older, perhaps because stability and pensions seem more important later in life. 'You had better move quite a bit when you are young,' one person says, 'or you won't move at all in later years.'

Regardless of how long we've spent in a hub, the most pressing reason to move is unhappiness. Yet, as we saw earlier, 'the gravity of hubs' tends to make us stay too long; and, paradoxically, we might cling most tenaciously to the hubs that make us most depressed.

When I co-owned a consulting business, a very intelligent consultant called John came into my office one day and said something that took me aback: 'You're ruining people's lives by making them work too hard.'

'What?' was the best response I could muster.

'You're making people unhappy. They never see their wives, husbands or children,' he said.

'Who are these unhappy people?'

'Well, me, for a start.'

'I don't want to lose you,' I said, 'but if you don't like the job, why don't you leave?'

'I don't want all the effort I've put into the job to be wasted,' he replied, 'and anyway, I still have to prove myself, to show that I can cope with the pressure.'

John stayed for another two years, but then he had to leave because he had a nervous breakdown. This troubled my conscience for a long time.

A friend who was a mayoral adviser in a large Portuguese city relates that she stayed in the job because it was well paid, near her home, introduced her to interesting people, and allowed her to bask in the status of representing the mayor. 'But every time I wanted to do things, they didn't agree with my proposals. It took me a long time to realise that they never would. There was a generation gap between employees and bosses.'

An American acquaintance, Anna, admits that she stayed too long in her job as an accountant. 'The sad truth was that I didn't like accounting. I could do the job, it was convenient, and I had a good relationship with my boss. But I hated being an accountant. Now I design websites and I love it. I work when I want, I work fewer hours, but I make more money. I wish I'd moved years earlier.'

The writer and broadcaster Charles Handy reckons he always used to stay in organisations for far too long. He finally became a freelance writer in his mid-forties, and only after his wife gave him an ultimatum: 'I'm not prepared to continue living with a stressed-out zombie.' He became much happier when independent of formal hubs. He found it a relief to be his own boss and not to have to pretend to be someone he wasn't. Why did he stay so long in organisations where he was unhappy? Money, he says, and an unwillingness to take risks.[57]

We've seen many reasons why people end up trapped in unsuitable hubs. Many explanations revolve around personal insecurity – the need for money or status, the urge to demonstrate

competence, fear of the unknown, wishing to live up to somebody else's expectations, lack of time or contacts to find a new
job, and risk aversion. How can we know when it's time to move
on, when a hub is good or bad for us? Our interviews suggest
some easy diagnostics for bad hubs: those where we don't feel at
home or where we have divergent values; where we are frustrated
or unfulfilled; where we feel underpaid or overworked; or simply
where we are despondent.

If in doubt, leave.

When someone moves from one hub to another, they automatically create the possibility of new weak links – probably many –
between their old hub and their new one. So job mobility – like
social or geographical mobility – helps create more weak links of
the most valuable kind: those that bridge previously unconnected groups. It is characteristic of an open and dynamic
society – one inevitably thinks of the United States – that there
is frequent mobility from hub to hub. Every time we move from
one to another, we help sew together society.

Links from the past, where we've been deeply engaged, toiled
side-by-side, shared formative experiences, endured hardship,
suffered failure or enjoyed success, are bound to have a deeper
quality than recently formed contacts. Whether it's a hard season
on an oil rig, an Internet start-up, the McKinsey analyst programme, or the crucible of the Special Air Services, intense
shared experiences forge trust and bonds of personal loyalty.
When you reach colleagues from the past – even after decades
without any contact – the old collaborative responses snap back
into action. There is automatic rapport; communication is rich
and fluid. As many of our interviewees have attested, there is real
joy in meeting a colleague from the distant past who now lives
in another world, and experiencing again the trust and ease of a
different time and place – with the added bonus of tapping into
decades of their insights and ideas, one of which may provide the

missing link in your life here and now. We saw in Chapter Seven how Paul Judge arranged a party for colleagues he'd known a quarter-century earlier, and how there was instant rapport. Three interviewees, all in their fifties, mentioned that they had recently started attending college reunions, having never gone before. 'It's a strange sensation,' one said, 'seeing someone you knew at eighteen. Apart from the fact that they look so much older, it's just the same as back in 1968. You can talk about your life with absolute frankness.'

When we asked our interviewees to describe their history of hubs, and the moves they made in their careers, few sounded very logical. None marked smooth, linear, upward progress. Perhaps that's not surprising. Imagine choosing your first set of university courses, or your first job. At that stage we don't know what we don't know; we can't even say what we *should* know. Yet, our image of people who make it to the top – an image that is often reinforced by what they claim in interviews – is that they planned their careers perfectly from the get-go.

By contrast, the people who talked to us frankly acknowledged the role of trial and error – especially the latter – in their careers. They told us that the only way really to understand the world and one's place in it is to sample different experiences; and this involved some casting about. Errors were unavoidable. We asked all the interviewees: 'If you could have your time in hubs over again, would you do anything differently?' No one invoked Edith Piaf. Everyone said they would change at least one thing.

Jim Lawrence says:

You jump from one swinging trapeze to another. If you're lucky, you catch the new trapeze as it's about to go up, and then swing to an even higher one. But then again, you might catch it on the way down or fall off altogether. What can you do? You can't plan all that. You just have to experiment until you end up where you want to be. You remember when I went to work for that airline? It didn't work out how I wanted, but the experience enabled me to become an outside director of another airline, which I greatly enjoy. And by becoming chief financial officer of the airline, it meant that I could be considered for any CFO job in the world, whereas that would never have happened otherwise. I thought at the time it was a disaster for me, but I moved on, and things have worked out just fine. Even when you make a mistake, you can turn it to your advantage.

Chris Outram advocates what he calls end-gaming:

The idea is to be specific about the type of hub you want to work in, say in ten years' time, and what your role is in that hub. Then you can test your activities and hubs to see whether they are taking you from here to there. You may need two or three hub changes en route. If you keep the end-game in mind, you'll know if it's time to move on.

But Stephen Sherbourne doesn't think planning is necessary:

I'd worked for Mrs Thatcher for four and a half years, and as you know I think five years is enough in any job, even one as fascinating as that. So I gave myself a target to leave by Easter 1988. I had no idea, no clue what to do. The first person I approached for advice was advertising guru Tim Bell – he wasn't a friend, but had advised us during the 1987 election. 'You know a lot of people,' I said to him, 'so tell me whom I should talk to, so I can decide what to do next.' He told me he was setting up a new kind of agency, with people from different backgrounds – public relations, advertising, management, politics and media. To my great surprise, he offered me a job. I took it and it was fantastic. I have never, ever, thought about the next move. Yet as one thing has come

to an end, something else has always opened up. So am I
lucky? Yes. But on the other hand, if an acquaintance says,
'Come and have a drink,' I always say 'yes'.

I was at university with Mary Saxe-Falstein – a glamorous mathematician, a combination I'd thought impossible before meeting
her. She belongs in these pages because she has struck out on a
remarkable series of different careers, creating new hubs as she
goes:

Up to the age of thirty-six, I had a conventional career, mainly
in marketing and advertising. I enjoyed my work and did well,
but then I thought, It's time for a new adventure. Somebody
else could have done everything I'd done up to then. What
could I do that nobody else could do in quite the same way? I
decided to take a holiday with my boyfriend, who was a well-
known artist, and hoped inspiration would strike.

One evening, relieved that Mike and I hadn't argued all
day, I told him that I'd always wanted to try sculpture. This
wasn't entirely true, but I had been toying with the idea. 'I've
never even seen you playing with stones on the beach,' he said
cynically, 'so don't bother, you won't be any good at it.' Back
in London, his friends reinforced the message: 'Let Mike be
the artist, and you stick to marketing.' Now, this was all the
encouragement I needed to become a sculptress of bronze
portrait busts. It was terribly thrilling and I loved doing it and
my clients were delighted.

After five years, I wanted to try something new again, so I
moved into portrait painting. I loved that too, and it led on to
teaching art to the wives of some of my subjects. Then, in
2000, someone I'd known twenty years before started a pet-
food company, and asked me to do all the market research and
advertising ideas. There I was, right at the centre of a new
venture that took off. Sometimes I worked nineteen-hour

days but it was great – I did all the writing, I designed the packaging, and wrote the advertising scripts.

In 2005, he sold it to a French company and I wanted a new adventure, so I set up the Extraordinary Mind Company, working one-to-one with clients and applying techniques – hypnosis, coaching, relaxation – to develop the mind. Now I'm working on rejuvenation, turning back the clock on people's faces and bodies. I present myself as a kind of cosmetic sculptor – I have a vision of how clients could look, how they could change the lines and muscles on their face, and how to re-program the mind to lock in the changes. I know it sounds outrageous, but it does actually work; the clients can't believe how much younger they look and feel. For me, the most exciting thing is the zone of ideas, adapting and improving other people's techniques and inventing my own. It is early days, but I believe we'll create a new approach to rejuvenation.

Since 1987, my time has been totally my own. In your terms, I've created a new hub for each new venture – I suppose I'm at the middle of the hub, then there are a few people I work or cooperate with, then the clients. I've just done what I've wanted to do, but if I hadn't been able to get happy clients, then I would have stopped. I've had a huge party, but the guests have enjoyed it too!

So should we all just 'trust the universe', like Stephen and Mary? Not entirely. Our interviewees were not hot on career planning, but they did offer some guidelines. They agreed that the most important steps up in life generally come with a move to a new work hub. Unless the first hub we happen to join fits us perfectly and allows for personal growth, this must be so. There's almost certainly a hub out there somewhere that we could join in which we would have a better experience than we are having now. But how do we find it?

People talk about the value and ambience of organisations. So, if you are thinking of joining a new company, ask yourself if its values are similar to your own. Will you feel at home there?

Our interviewees strike a note of caution about dog-eat-dog organisations or very large ones. 'I decided not to join Shell,' says Paul Judge, 'when the secretary taking me between interviews got lost in the corridor.' Jim Lawrence contrasts the friendly atmosphere of branded consumer goods companies with the 'brutal' culture he encountered in another industry, where margins were thin, demand was unpredictable, and losses were a constant danger: 'The consumer products culture is much more friendly, partly perhaps because it's more stable and profitable, and partly because consumer product leaders take a long-term view and treat employees and customers well. If you can't decide between two jobs in the private sector, go for the one with nicer people.'

The accomplished people we asked suggested two main criteria for joining a hub – how much you think you can learn there, and how much you can contribute. Securities services professional Alex Johnstone says:

> Early in your career, I'd say you should select hubs on the basis of learning; but later on, by how much you can contribute *and* how much you learn. In my early career, I learned much more than I contributed. Now I am contributing a lot but learning very little. I'm not talking about technical skills. I think it's personal. You can learn only from the people around you. If you don't respect their superior knowledge or techniques then you can't learn. If you're not learning, it's time to move to another hub. So that's what I'm going to do.

Another important realisation our interviewees made was that their careers had not taken off until they'd first experienced a hub that had profoundly changed their outlook and capabilities.

They came out different from how they'd gone in. Typically when they were in their twenties, they experienced two or three hubs that transformed them.

For Chris Outram, the first life-changing hub was an extraordinary sixth-form college, and the second was INSEAD, the top business school near Paris, which he attended from the age of twenty-seven:

> I met people I didn't know existed – polyglot people who were ambitious, intellectually curious, and also attractive personalities. It provided a mirror for me, allowing me to hone many of my skills, and it also led to very firm relationships. There are sixteen people who were in my year and we now meet every year for a long weekend. It has a 90 per cent turnout. It's a very diverse group comprising a dozen different nationalities.

For another of our interviewees, the intense experience came when he joined EY Consulting Group (formerly Ernst and Young):

> My career took off there. I was only twenty-eight, but they gave me a lot of freedom. I was able to do my own thing and also meet and learn from the senior people. I worked in the corporate finance unit and thrived. I learned to link together people and ideas and create totally new business opportunities. The people were fantastic and it all came together. Really it was the time of my life. It changed me for ever.

Alex Johnstone accelerated his career when, at twenty-two, he joined Goldman Sachs:

> It was a huge springboard for me . . . a fantastic learning experience. Suddenly the idea of global, international business

dawned on me. What transformed me was not so much specific knowledge as the people. I learned how important
attitude was and I worked with the brightest people I have
ever met – not just bright but totally driven, almost to the
detriment of everything else in life. I never knew people like
that existed. It really changed me – before I was a provincial
lad, now I felt keyed into the whole world.

I eventually realised, however, that I didn't want to let my
life be taken over by any organisation, even if it would make
me rich. There are more important things in life. But seeing
how people in a top investment bank thought – seeing the big
picture – has been invaluable to me ever since. Now I only
work forty hours a week but I am able to do everything that
I think is important, and stay relaxed.

For many of our flourishing interviewees, the transformation
came by dipping their toes into entrepreneurial waters. Two of
them had 'dummy runs' by opening a new business within the
protection of their existing employer. Jim Lawrence flexed his
entrepreneurial muscles by starting Bain's London and Munich
offices, while Antony Ball started a new strategic consulting
business within Deloittes. The real transformation came when
Jim and Antony set up their own operations from scratch.

'LEK was different,' says Jim, 'because we operated successfully without the backing of a parent, with our own money, and
initially outside my home country.' Nevertheless, Jim reckons his
first transformations came at Yale – 'a complete educational
transformation, a gain in social status, and I acquired a world
view' – and at Harvard Business School – 'a knowledge transformation'.

Antony's big break came when he set up a new private equity
business, Capital Partners, in South Africa: 'I had had a practice
run in setting up the Strategy Group, but that was within a big
firm. Capital Partners was totally our own thing and it was an

unusual thing to do at the time in South Africa. We felt we were pioneers. It changed my life in every way.'

Typically, these people's careers have not been marathons. Rather, success has come as the result of a series of infrequent sprints – sudden staccato leaps from one hub to the next. After thirteen years working for Cadbury Schweppes, including a stint as chief executive of its food division, in 1985 Paul Judge was a successful career manager, but no more so than most of his business school peers. Then Cadbury decided that the food division was no longer a 'core' business. Paul surprised his boss by asking permission to try to put together a buyout. He arranged the finance using almost exclusively other people's money, but, unusually, without any venture capitalists to share the potential upside. Soon, Paul was back as chief executive of the division, separate from Cadbury and renamed Premier Brands. Within four years, Premier had been sold to Hillsdown Holdings and Paul had many million pounds in the bank.

Yet, he says that a much earlier job, as managing director of Cadbury's subsidiary in Kenya, was more of a step-up than running Premier Brands:

> Kenya was my first line-management job. I was four thousand miles from head office, and in those days there were no emails or faxes, and a phone call was an unusual event. It was a baptism of fire, because the local sales tax was 50 per cent and some of the local companies cheated by under-recording their sales, but Cadbury reported accurately. Kenya really made me tough and decisive. Contrast that with Premier Brands. By the time of the buyout, I had already been managing director of that unit and it was the same people and the same company. For sure, we were now on our own and we focused on cash and new products, but the really challenging part of Premier Brands was the months arranging the deal before we started.
>
> Premier Brands altered my life completely. Afterwards I

could choose how to spend my time. I got enormous satisfaction out of revisiting one of my earlier hubs, Cambridge
University, and funding what became the Judge Business
School there. But did Premier Brands transform *me*? That had
already happened earlier, with Cambridge and in Kenya.

This suggests that new hubs can provide two different types of
transformation.

First we may encounter an intense emotional experience – a
group of people and a set of activities that leave us feeling different, in some sense *better* and with more potential than before.
In recounting their experiences in transformational hubs, many
respondents talked in quasi-evangelistic language. They experienced something quite novel. They hadn't even known that such
an experience was possible. They realised what they wanted to
do. They *knew* that they could do it. All they needed was the
opportunity to open up somewhere down the line. 'I was transformed when doing my MBA at INSEAD,' says Chris Outram.
'It may sound a bit arrogant, but it's true – I knew then that one
day I might do something more ambitious – though I didn't
know then that it would involve setting up my own firm.'

The second type of transformation – the actual experience of
breaking through to unusual accomplishment – is the realisation
of something made possible earlier, when we were transformed.
We use the skills we acquired earlier to create something unique
and personal; we realise our vision. 'It was nine years after
INSEAD that I co-founded OC & C,' says Chris, 'but when it
happened I was more confident and less risk averse than I would
have been if I hadn't met the people at INSEAD.'

My own experience bears this out. My initial transformational
hubs – those that changed me – were the University of Oxford
and the Boston Consulting Group. Oxford gave me the tools to
analyse events and work out the few elements that were important in achieving results, whatever the arena. BCG showed me

the power of ideas in business, and convinced me that if you had new ideas and could communicate them to clients, then running a profitable consulting firm was not hard. Even though I was not successful in my time at BCG, I had total confidence afterwards that, as part of a two- or three-person group, I could start a new consulting firm. I knew that was what I wanted to do when the right time came along.

If you think about it, hubs either *are* or *are not* intense experiences. Have you been 'transformed' already? Is your present hub transforming you? Might it? If not, should you move on?

It is not always necessary to move organisations in order to move hubs. A single firm or university may comprise many hubs. Quite often, prominent individuals and their protégés comprise a pulsating, potent hub, though you won't find it on any organisation chart. When he was Warden of Wadham College, Oxford, Maurice Bowra, a rotund and witty don, made a habit of inviting half a dozen of the sharpest undergraduates round to his lodgings for uproarious intellectual sessions. I never made the cut, but the privileged few were well aware of their special status, and I am told that the friendships formed by being in Bowra's clique often last a lifetime.

But you don't need to be an eminent professor to form ad hoc hubs of this type. When he was quite junior at management consultants Booz Allen, Chris Outram created the grand-sounding Stafford Club:

> I invited anyone I'd met at my level whom I thought was interesting and might be going anywhere. We got in a speaker and met two or three times a year. Typically I invited thirty-five people and twenty would turn up. It ran for five years and it sort of 'came with me' when we started OC & C. Over the years it has been a tremendous source of social and commercial contacts for me, even though I never intended that.

Personalisation makes the hub more intimate and more like a club – you choose the people to work with inside and outside the firm. Alex Johnstone says:

> I've found that you always have much more freedom than is generally recognised, as long as you're performing. Your set of work contacts is *your* hub and nobody else's; you choose a particular mix of people and how you interact with them. It becomes your unique hub. Everyone can have a unique hub within the same firm. You can then add useful outsiders to your work network.

Older interviewees had typically made the transition from working in one hub at a time to working in many. None regretted it. 'After Premier Brands was sold,' says Paul Judge, 'my career changed. Before that I had just one hub. Now, with one exception, my career at any point in time has been exclusively many-hub. It is more interesting. You can achieve more.'

We asked everyone when they felt that their career really took off. 'Not until OC & C,' says Chris Outram. We also asked the first time they felt they had become central to the hub. 'OC & C again,' says Chris. 'It was the first time I felt I was contributing as much as I could.' Nearly all our respondents gave similar answers – they became really successful only when they became central to a hub. It seems that being at the heart of a small organisation is more rewarding than being on the periphery of a much bigger one.

About half of our interviewees say their aim was to make serious money. Most achieved this, and in the same way – through starting a hub and owning a chunk of it. 'If you are in business, you might as well be an owner,' says one. 'It's more interesting than working in someone else's firm and the upside is tens or hundreds of times greater.'

'I have started three businesses from scratch and I've made all my money from them,' says another. 'But this really isn't the most important thing. I'm most fulfilled when getting something going with a small team and no politics. You have to make it up as you go along. It's challenging and it brings out the best in people – it forces you to be resourceful. When a firm gets too successful, it gets political . . . and boring.'

It's telling that the typical route to material success for our entrepreneurs was through doing something they enjoyed or wanted to achieve, with colleagues they liked and chose. 'Put together the people and ideas you most like,' one advises. 'The easiest way is to start a spin-off from an existing hub, doing something you know how to do but adding your own special magic.'

'People should think laterally about hubs,' says Robin Field.

> You can experience more than one hub at a time, even if you only have one job. My boat is a great hub. Through sailing, I have established or re-established contact with several people who are now my close and valued friends. They wouldn't be, but for sailing. It's been useful for business and it's an enormously important social hub, as well as being what I love doing. Strangely, I've had more opportunities come to me when on my boat than anywhere else. If you don't like sailing, find another reason to invite friends – a reading party or weekend away perhaps?

Ray Hiscox, an old school chum of mine, makes a habit of assembling about a dozen friends for a day-long walk in the country, punctuated by lunch in a pub. 'This is ideal for talking at length in a relaxed way,' he says. 'You just walk alongside the person or people you most want to speak to.'

Robin has one final idea: 'My wife is French and she brings a whole new world of people into my life. Dominique has been hugely influential – nearly all my friends in France and many Chinese friends came from her. Extending your overseas network is a great way of breaking the circle that limits your contacts and information.'

Antony Ball, who wrote a South African version of *In Search of Excellence*, points out that a book can be a great hub: 'I met people I would never have met but for the book. All kinds of people wrote to me. It brought a lot of business.'

Our respondents typically juggle about half a dozen hubs, which often mix business, socialising and hobbies.

Alex Johnstone tells of a dinner party where one of the guests proposed doing an 'audit' of the social groups in which they all participated:

> It was a classic consultant two-by-two matrix in which you compare the time and energy put into each hub with the enjoyment or other reward derived from the hub. Hubs with high effort and high return were working well. Hubs where there was low effort and low reward might be due for more effort – or the chop. Hubs with low effort and high reward might deserve more time. Finally the problem area – high effort, low reward.
>
> At first, I thought this was a rather cold-blooded way to think about social interaction, but it made me talk to my partner about our circles of friends. We decided to stop making an effort for one group that never invited us anywhere, and to spend more time with the friends we enjoyed most. It made a big difference to our social life.

It's easy to see life as a series of jobs or family and social obligations. But a more inspiring perspective is to think of it in terms of the groups that have been, are, or will be important to us, the people with whom we want to do something serious or enjoyable in our lives.

Most people in the affluent world now have an extraordinary degree of choice of hubs to join, a privilege that was denied to most previous generations. We can sample several hubs and appreciate why they do or don't work for us. We can gain more contacts and discover which individuals and groups we enjoy. We can learn what type of contribution we enjoy making. We can understand what complementary skills we require from other people. We can become central to an existing hub and change its course: making it better, more useful to other people, stronger and richer. We can become a magnet for attractive, energetic, talented and unfulfilled co-conspirators, old or young. We can start our own hub, with partners who have different strengths and cover for weaknesses. We can gain money and time; and money *is* time, our own or that of other people we pay to work with us.

It's inspiring to think of life like this, where we have the luxury of choosing collaborators, and on what we collaborate. How marvellous to be alive, improbably, at a time when all this is possible. We can achieve and enjoy far more in groups than we ever could on our own. This is the destiny stumbled across by humans – not just to unite in groups, but to create new groups with unique and hitherto unimagined characters and purposes. Society grows richer, more variegated and intriguing as we form new hubs to boldly go where no group has gone before.

## CHAPTER NINE

# THE NETWORK STRUCTURE OF IDEAS

*Are weak links and hubs the key to
realising great ideas?*

> People like to think that businesses are built of
> numbers – 'the bottom line' – or forces – 'market
> forces' – or even flesh and blood – 'our people'.
> But this is wrong. Businesses are made of ideas –
> ideas expressed as words.
>
> *Business guru James Champy*[58]

## Roman Empire, province of Judaea, first century AD

Once upon a time, there was a Jewish preacher and faith-healer who, for a couple of years, exerted enormous appeal. His message was a brilliant synthesis of the teachings of the best Jewish prophets – such as Isaiah and Hosea – who called for social justice and self-improvement. The preacher said that God was intervening in history, using the Jews in general and himself in particular to bring history to a wonderful climax, establishing a special Jewish kingdom on earth. He talked of God's love, compassion and concern for social outcasts, the poor, the sinners, the impure, the untouchables. It was easy, he said, to love our friends and family, but the real challenge was to love people whom we would normally shun – such as foreigners, prostitutes, the diseased and criminals. The preacher had an idiosyncratic view of God – as a loving father who was more interested in sinners than the righteous and who reached out to all of his people. The preacher himself rescued an adulteress from being stoned to death, he restored the sick and deformed to full health, and he gave dignity and purpose to swindlers and the most hated group in Judaea, the men who collected harsh taxes on behalf of the Roman occupiers. God, he said, cared little for formal religion and meticulous observation of Jewish rites, being impressed only by human kindness, mercy, and care for the unfortunate and the oppressed. God could speak directly to the individual, however lowly, to women as well as men, to the disreputable as well as the respectable; and the individual, sensing God's unconditional love, could respond, using his or her conscience to interpret and follow God's will.

Although the preacher's message was just about within the best (albeit most radical) Jewish prophetic tradition, the priests of the Jerusalem Temple felt he was straying into dangerous territory. They were jealous of the crowds who followed him and nervous that he was going to lead a rebellion against their Roman rulers – who would be merciless in crushing the Jews, and might even destroy the Temple in retribution. So the high priest and his Temple police shopped the preacher to the Roman governor, a notorious thug. The preacher was tortured and executed. In physical and mental agony, he wondered, just before he died, why God had deserted him. The preacher had promised a new kingdom of God; but God had not delivered it.

The crowds melted away, but a tiny band of the preacher's family and die-hard supporters, led by his brother James, did not give up. The preacher had made a deep impression on them, and they could not imagine life without him. They insisted that he was not really dead. Jesus, they said, had been God's latest and greatest messenger, fulfilling the words of earlier prophets, the 'Messiah', God's chosen one. As a sign of approval, God had raised him from the dead and lifted him up to heaven. Soon Jesus would return in triumph on the clouds as the 'Son of Man' prophesied by Daniel, the Jews would unite, and God's new kingdom on earth would be inaugurated. The Roman Empire, and the whole earth as currently constituted, would end abruptly.

Apart from their beliefs about Jesus, the 'followers of the Way', as they called themselves, were conventional religious Jews, to be found worshipping in the Temple at Jerusalem, observing the ancient rites as meticulously as the Pharisees did, living austerely and engaging in good works. Some followers of the Way left Jerusalem and became part of the Jewish groups in Asia Minor, North Africa, Rome and elsewhere. The Greek-speaking Jews of the 'Diaspora' (dispersion beyond Judaea) settled in many ports, and a small minority of these – known as 'Hellenists' – also followed the Way. They popped up ten or twenty years after the death of Jesus in the cities of Caesarea Maritima in Samaria, Alexandria and Rome, all largely non-Jewish settlements.

The largest group of Jesus' followers outside Jerusalem congregated in the Syrian city of Antioch, where, around AD 46, they were first called 'Christians' (followers of the Messiah). Although they were exposed to Greek culture, and may have sought converts among the 'god-fearers' – non-Jews who were attracted to Judaism by its austerity and/or monotheism – the Way did not attract many non-Jewish followers. As with any other Jewish group, a Gentile (Greek or Roman) man who wished to join first had to become a Jew, submitting to the fearsome operation of circumcision and observing all Jewish laws and rites, including a ban on most meat. Like all Jews, the followers of the Way arrogantly refused to pay respect to the Roman gods, or observe Roman civil and religious rituals. And this form of Judaism, if any non-Jew heard about it, was the most extreme and unacceptable. To the average Roman in the Forum, there was something particularly offensive in claiming that a renegade who had been crucified – a loser's fate if ever there was one – had been raised from the dead by God, and would return to inaugurate God's kingdom and free the Jews from Roman rule. All of this may have been treated as nonsense, but it was also an affront to everything the Romans held dear.

The Jesus movement remained geographically and mentally within Jewish confines. In Rome, for example, the Way followers lived in the Jewish slums and, through anti-Roman riots, appear to have caused the expulsion of several Jews from the city in AD 49. As the years passed and the preacher failed to return in glory, his followers remained few in number – at most several hundred throughout the Empire – and still almost exclusively Jewish.

The Way looked set to remain at most a minor faction within Judaism, or more likely to die out completely. Then something very strange and unexpected happened. In the mid-to-late 40s AD, a new preacher and a new message erupted on the scene, probably in Antioch. The new man started life as Saul, born into a wealthy Jewish family in the cosmopolitan city of Tarsus in Cilicia, part of what is now Turkey. His family owned a business supplying large marquees and tents to the Roman army, and Saul became a Roman citizen. Tarsus, like Antioch, was home to a large community of Hellenised Jews, who would have been familiar with the views of thinkers such as Philo of Alexandria, who sought to fuse Jewish theology with Greek philosophy. Saul appears to have been a deeply religious man, initially a conventional Pharisee, and perhaps participated in a crusade to hunt down followers of the Way.[59] But at some stage, possibly around AD 33 or a little later, he had a mystical experience in which he saw a vision of Jesus, who commanded him to 'proclaim him among the Gentiles'.[60] Thereafter, Saul renamed himself Paul, and he began preaching his new faith around AD 45.

Unlike James and the other Apostles, Paul almost certainly never knew Jesus the man. Nor did he seem to care much about what Jesus had said or done in his lifetime. Paul was the first person to write anything about Jesus, in his long and influential letters to the Jesus house-cult groups in various towns, the first of which were written around AD 50–1, ten or twenty years before the first Gospel was penned. Yet, in all his surviving letters, there are only half a dozen references to the life or words of Jesus. Instead, Paul claimed a direct line to the risen Christ for himself, transforming the Way into a completely different faith. He turned a minor Jewish sect into the first universal, non-tribal religious movement. In complete contrast to Jesus and those who had known him in the flesh, Paul marketed the religion primarily to Greeks and Romans.

Furthermore, his message was stunningly original. He blatantly repositioned the Jesus movement in Greek terms. For Greek philosophers, the cosmos resembled a super-mind – nature made sense, and as men understood more about the world, so they came closer to God. As Xenophanes said, 'The gods did not reveal, from the beginning, all things to us, but in the course of time, through seeking, men find that which is better.' Paul took the incredibly daring step of elevating Christ to near equality with God, a move that compromised the monotheism of Judaism and the Way, and took two or three centuries to become generally accepted among Christians. Paul was not interested in the historical Jesus, but in Christ as a mythological symbol, Christ as the way for individuals to connect with God and receive God's love, grace and power. The living Christ, Paul said, made all the difference – now men and women could use Christ's divine power to improve their lives. They could live in God, and God could live in them.

This was an exciting new world-view, blending the appeals of Jesus and the Jewish prophets to become better people with the Greek view that men could share in divine nature. And as a further incentive to adopt the faith, Paul added the immensely beguiling idea that Christians – even those who died before Jesus returned in glory – would live for ever in heaven with God.[61] This promise of eternal life, and the avoidance of eternal damnation, became increasingly appealing as time went on and the kingdom of heaven did not appear on earth.

Paul also invented the extraordinary concept that the death of Christ on the cross was necessary for God to forgive man's sins, turning a terrible accident into God's most sublime plan, an epoch-making demonstration of the Almighty's love for mankind. It was not necessary for people to become good in order to be saved; on the contrary, only the grace of God could save anyone, and that grace could be made available only through the crucifixion of Christ. This bizarre thesis, the 'Crosstianity' wholly original to Paul, was at odds with the traditional Jewish view, which Jesus himself clearly held, that Yahweh was a God of mercy who was willing and able to forgive sins long before Jesus had lived and died.[62]

The grandeur of Paul's poetic vision, however, was that Jesus had instituted a new form of humanity, and reconciled everyone if they believed in Christ, giving unity to the world and freedom to all believers. 'There is no longer Jew or Greek,' Paul wrote, 'there is no longer slave or free, there is no longer male and female; for all of you are one in Christ Jesus.'[63] Paul was the first person to propose a universal faith that could unite different nationalities, connecting people through a common currency of belief and behaviour. It would be wrong to credit him with any intention to create a better civilisation, since he shared the Apostles' belief that Christ was about to return in glory at any minute, wrapping up human empires and indeed all life on earth. Nevertheless, Paul unintentionally created a network effect, which became ever stronger over time as Christ's return was 'delayed', the number of Christians grew, and their influence in Roman and later Western society became progressively greater. Eventually, with the religion becoming almost universal throughout Europe as nearly everyone joined the Christian network, its moral code spread and society improved, on the whole. For sure, by modern standards, medieval Christianity had some glaring ethical flaws. But when one compares it with Roman civilisation – in which the citizens were an exclusive minority, subject peoples and slaves were harshly treated, and crucifixions were routine – some progress had certainly been made.

Jesus' followers had adhered to all the traditional Jewish rites and rituals – circumcision, the cultic food requirements, the synagogue, and so on. In line with the new non-tribal faith, however, Paul insisted that they must all be unceremoniously dumped. He also used Rome's transport and communications network to spread the religion, and started new Christian hubs – groups of people in each town who met in one another's homes, and became what Paul called the 'church of Christ' there. The Romans ruled through a network of road and sea connections around the Mediterranean, with each large town linked to the others and to Rome. Paul travelled incessantly between them – like someone spinning plates in sequence, he lectured, corrected and condemned (he found much to dislike about many of the new Christians), established new churches and restructured others – all in a whirlwind of activity that involved multiple shipwrecks and imprisonments. This frenzied preaching only ended, as far as we can tell, with his execution in Rome in the early sixties AD.

Through sheer force of personality, a startlingly original message, inspirational speaking and writing, and full exploitation of the existing Roman network, Paul eclipsed the people who had worked directly with Jesus. His brand of Rome- and Athens-friendly Christianity grew rapidly and prevailed. Before him, there were only a few hundred followers of Jesus. By the time of his death, there were many thousand. By AD 200, there were perhaps two hundred thousand Christians; and a hundred years later six million, a tenth of the Roman population.[64] In AD 312, the Emperor Constantine converted to Christianity and made it Rome's official religion. Today, there are nearly two billion Christians world-wide, more people than follow any other religion.

Paul took a terrific Jewish idea, combined it with the best Greek philosophy, added his own twist about the earth-shattering importance of Christ's death, changed and hugely enlarged the target market, founded many groups of Christians throughout the Mediterranean, and used Rome's networks to spread the religion like wildfire. Perhaps unintentionally – since he expected Jesus to return soon, so presumably felt little need to set up an institution – he was responsible for the emergence of a non-Jewish Christian church and provided the message that made it take off.

All this must make him one of the most influential superconnectors of all time.

## Prussia and France, 1818–48, and England, 1849–83

Karl Marx was born in Trier, now part of Germany, in 1818. In the first thirty years of his life, he was, among other things, a philosophy student writing a doctoral dissertation on 'The Difference between the Democritean and Epicurean Philosophy of Nature', president of a drinking club at the University of Bonn, a radical journalist, and a would-be fomenter of revolution. In 1848, together with his friend and financial backer Friedrich Engels, he wrote and published *The Communist Manifesto*, perhaps the most innovative and well-written political manifesto of all time. In the same year, he hurried from Belgium to Paris at the invitation of French revolutionaries who had seized power.

Sadly for Marx, the revolution soon collapsed. After a brief sojourn in Cologne – where he started and wrote for a short-lived radical newspaper – and another expulsion from Paris, he and his family finally settled in three shabby rooms in central London's Dean Street. Apart from punctuating a hand-to-mouth existence by drinking rather extravagantly, and some gestures towards organising revolution throughout Europe, Marx spent much of the rest of his life reading and writing in the British Museum. His work became increasingly scholarly, complex, unreadable and unread; his quarrels with collaborators and fellow-revolutionaries ever more rancorous; and his health ever worse. Towards the end of his career, the redoubtable Jenny Marx, Karl's wife and the daughter of a Prussian baron, is said to have lamented, 'If only Karl had made some capital, instead of writing so much about it.' In 1867, when the first volume of *Das Kapital* was published in German to a resounding silence, she said:

> There can be few books that have been written in more dif-ficult circumstances . . . I could write a secret history of it which would tell of many . . . unspoken troubles and anxieties and torments. If the workers had an inkling of the sacrifices that were necessary for this work . . . they would perhaps show a little more interest.[65]

When Karl died in 1883, stateless and intestate, only the faithful Engels and ten other people attended his funeral. Few believed that Marx was a major thinker; he died in obscurity, deeply unfulfilled. Like Jesus of Nazareth, he could have had no inkling of his posthumous fame.

Marx believed that his lifetime had seen a shift from feudal-ism – rule by landowners over peasants – to an equally class-based but much more dynamic system – rule by the owners of capital, middle-class industrialists and financiers, over the new exploited class, factory workers. The phrase he coined to describe this system was 'capitalism'. Although this was in many ways a huge improvement on feudalism, increasing wealth and civilisation stupendously, it was a deeply flawed system. Marx said that it unfairly divided the world into a few rich people and a mass of poor ones, and was thereby digging its own grave: 'the bourgeoisie forged the weapons that bring death to itself; it has also called into existence the men who are to wield those weapons – the modern working class'.[66]

Capitalism could not last, Marx thought, because it brought ever more workers together in factories and cities, and increasingly capital would be concentrated into ever-larger organisations, which needed to squeeze workers' living standards in order to survive. The workers would not stand for this and would rise up in bloody revolution, probably first in Britain, the world's leading industrial economy. A communist government would follow, initially imposing 'the dictatorship of the proletariat' and abolishing capital. But this communist state would then 'wither away' in a world of free individuals, able for the first time in history to exploit their full talents for the benefit of themselves and society.

With the benefit of hindsight, we can see that Marx's diagnosis of the transition from feudalism to capitalism was wholly original, brilliant and broadly correct. A large working class, concentrated in ever-larger cities, did emerge and eventually grow more powerful.[67] But just when Marx predicted revolution throughout Europe, in the second half of the nineteenth century, revolutions became increasingly rare and unsuccessful. There were two main reasons for this: the failure of the revolutionaries to build a large network of committed followers; and, more fundamentally, in direct contradiction of Marx's thesis, capitalism delivered ever-higher living standards for the workers, who overwhelmingly supported socialist or social-democratic parliamentary reform rather than communist revolution on the streets.

But, as we all know, that was not the end of the story. Just as the Jesus movement would probably have disappeared without the efforts of St Paul, so 'Marxism' would not have triumphed without a similar transformation, again largely the work of one man.

Vladimir Ilyich Ulyanov (1870–1924) was born in the Russian Empire near the Volga River, the son of a prosperous schoolmaster. When he was seventeen, Vladimir's elder brother Alexander was arrested and hanged for plotting the overthrow of Tsar Alexander III. Ulyanov was a first-rate student and later a successful lawyer, but he became increasingly interested in the work of Karl Marx. When he was twenty-five, he was arrested for revolutionary activity and imprisoned for fourteen months.

Ulyanov, who renamed himself Lenin, had two great virtues as a revolutionary. First, he repositioned the geographical focus of Marxism and the whole revolutionary movement. He concurred with Marx's analysis of the inevitability of revolution and the moral and practical weakness of capitalism, but he changed the locus of intended revolution from Western Europe to Russia. Just as Paul made Greeks and Romans, rather than Jews, his main target group, so Lenin worked indefatigably to identify the cause of revolution with peasants as well as factory workers. The workers were not going to do the job alone, so the peasants had to be roped in – Russia was a backward, agricultural country with only limited industry. Through tortured logic, Lenin formulated his 'law of uneven development', which said that capitalism would break down 'at its weakest link', which happened to be in underdeveloped Russia. A Russian revolution would then become the signal for the workers' revolution throughout Europe.

Lenin's second great attribute was his organising skill. In 1903, he formed the Bolshevik revolutionary party, consisting solely of professional revolutionaries, not mere sympathisers, and organised into a network of local cells, much like Paul's house-cells of early Christians. In 1905, when revolution broke out in Russia,

Lenin and his fellow-Bolsheviks took the lead. But the revolution failed, and Lenin fled to Switzerland.

Early in 1917, however, the Russian Empire of Tsar Nicholas II was exhausted by three years of terrible war against Germany. Revolution flared again, and this time the regime was overthrown. Lenin, still in Switzerland, rushed to get home, and he arrived by train at the Finland Station in Petrograd, the major industrial city of Russia. There he received a tumultuous reception, and immediately set about undermining the new social-democratic government. He coined the slogan 'Peace, Land, Bread' – note the appeal of 'land' to the peasants, the great majority of the population. On the night of 7–8 November 1917, Lenin and the Bolsheviks staged a *coup d'état*: their forces stormed the Winter Palace and deposed the government. Lenin then seized the reins of power and jailed opposition leaders. Within a month, he had set up the Cheka secret police, which imposed his will through terror.

The dictatorship of the proletariat had arrived, as predicted by Karl Marx. But then reality started to diverge from theory. Far from withering away, the Soviet state grew into the largest and most powerful hub the world has ever seen. Over the course of the next seventy years, it took control of all but the smallest businesses, as well as all educational institutions, newspapers, radio, television, police, the army and civil institutions across half of Europe. It also murdered tens of millions of its own citizens. The Soviet state inspired both Hitler and Mao Zedong, who, regardless of apparent ideology, modelled their monstrously vast and hate-creating hubs on identical lines, and similarly succeeded in their programmes of economic and military growth, and barbaric slavery.

We have talked of the 'gravity of hubs'. In many senses, the Soviet, Nazi and Red Chinese hubs were the gravest of all.

These stories reveal that even astonishingly fresh and magnetic ideas – loving your enemies, the inevitable triumph of industrial workers over capitalism – do not live or die on their own merits. Without Paul, Christianity is unlikely to have reshaped the world. Without Lenin, statues of Marx would surely never have been erected across Russia, Eastern Europe, China and parts of South America. Nor, in all likelihood, would there ever have been a Russian communist state or civil war; or famines; or Stalinist tyranny, with its show trials, purges, mass murders and gulags; or the debilitating rivalry of the Cold War.[68]

Paul and Lenin breathed new life into the failed ideas of their forerunners. But they also did something even more vital, something which Jesus and Marx never effectively managed – they formed hubs. Paul organised his converts into house-groups in every port, churches that set out to convert more and more local people. Lenin formed revolutionary cells and built up the Bolshevik Party to the stage where it could seize power and then deny it to any other group. Simply because they formed incredibly powerful and important hubs, Paul and Lenin superconnected to an extraordinary and long-lasting degree, far more than Jesus or Marx had. All the world's most influential superconnectors have left behind hubs that long outlived them; and the founders of the world's greatest hubs, through that very fact, have all been great superconnectors.

Any idea needs a hub – an organisation of supporters – to become influential. A business idea needs a firm, just as the firm needs the idea. A religion needs a church. A political idea needs a party. A revolutionary idea needs terrorist cells. The supply of ideas always exceeds the demand for them, which is why some wonderful ideas die while others become widespread and even begin superconnecting themselves. The idea is not enough. It requires a coordinated group of zealous supporters to spread it far and wide, to find 'customers' who will support the idea against its rivals.

That is also why some terrible ideas – such as hell, the duty of religious persecution, communism and fascism – can become hideously pervasive: they are similarly supported by powerful hubs, and by protagonists intoxicated with power and dogma.

Ideas need networks to spread them – their own 'broadcast media'. These can be books, radio, television, rallies, church meetings, rock concerts, the Web, advertising or a sales force. In spreading the word, ideas need to fight for attention – against all the other information and noise that might drown them out. Ideas succeed if the network can persuade people that the benefit derived from using the idea exceeds the cost of understanding it.

Consider a new movie or a brand extension like Diet Coke. If the movie is entertaining or the soft drink has virtually no calories, the benefit is small but measurable. Consequently, it will spread only if the effort to understand the benefit is even smaller. It's easy to get the point of Diet Coke or the latest blockbuster movie. The purpose of brands is to make it easy to understand the product and the benefit it brings.

At the other end of the spectrum, think about a new technology, such as railways, cars, personal computers or the Internet. We now know that these can bring enormous gains, that they have rewired our daily routines of work and communication. But like all new technologies, they took a great deal of time and energy to invent, design, produce and distribute; and new users needed to devote a great deal of energy into understanding how to use them. However great the benefits, new technology spreads slowly at first – for instance, it took more than a decade for the Internet to become mainstream.

To spread an idea, operate on both sides of the equation – the benefits of the new idea, and the effort to understand it. Increase the benefits and make them obvious. Cut the energy required to grasp the new idea. Simplify it. Compress it into a soundbite.

The Sermon on the Mount was not a soundbite. 'Faith, hope and love, these three abide; but the greatest of these is love' was.

*Das Kapital* was no soundbite either. 'Peace, land, bread' was.

★

St Paul and Lenin did something else, too – they linked an original idea, from Jesus and Marx respectively, to another excellent but unrelated idea. In Paul's case, it was linking the personal, loving God of Jesus to the Greek concept of the universe as a super-mind in which humans could share, so that people could become part of God. Lenin linked Marx's idea of the inevitable triumph of revolution and the whole 'scientific' edifice of Marxism to the conditions in backward Russia.

Business people can similarly link two good ideas – or apply a good idea in a new context – and this can be a relatively easy way to remarkable achievement.

Venture capitalist Adrian Beecroft attributes his success to copying a simple idea:

I took the idea on which my career has been based from the Boston Consulting Group. BCG's philosophy was to take the top two or three people out of the best business schools. It meant that the consultants were smarter than their clients, which is the only reason BCG survived. BCG and McKinsey swept the world by having the best people and putting them together in networks. The best people learned from each other and became even better at what they did. Now, everyone thinks they hire good people but almost no firms in the world hire *only* the best. It makes recruiting difficult, time consuming and expensive. But that was BCG's idea and I experienced how well it worked.

And that is what we did in Apax Europe. I was totally uncompromising; I stuck to the idea completely. That was why my firm in Europe became bigger than Apax US. We eventually took over the US side and employed our idea there to great effect. When people ask me why we became so successful, they always expect me to talk about our investment philosophy or something directly related to our industry, and they are always surprised when I mention this simple idea and its overwhelming importance. But it is true.

## Cape Town, South Africa, 1950s–present

In South Africa, one of the most famous people from the business world is my friend Raymond Ackerman. He's known and loved by a huge number of ordinary people, because they shop in his Pick 'n Pay stores, because he is always willing to talk to anyone – his secretary June has strict instructions to put any customer straight through to him – and because he and his wife and business partner, Wendy, are generous and practical philanthropists.

But how did they make their fortune? In the early 1950s, they observed the large number of big supermarkets and hypermarkets being built in America. The idea behind big supermarkets is breathtakingly simple. If you can become the biggest supermarket chain in a region or country, you can buy goods to stock the shelves at lower prices than is possible for any rival; and if you then pass on the savings to customers, they will make a bee-line for your stores. The same principle applies in any retail category – DIY, computers, carpets, shoes, fashion, you name it. The art is to become the biggest before anyone else.

Raymond, then an executive at Greatermans, a South African retailer, persuaded them to start the Checkers chain of supermarkets and, at the age of twenty-four, put him in charge. By 1966, he controlled eighty-five stores. Then he was fired. He used his severance pay (and a large bank loan) to buy four supermarkets in Cape Town called Pick 'n Pay. Then he took all the cash this business generated and opened new supermarkets faster than anyone else, creating the largest chain in South Africa. In the 1970s, Raymond also became famous – to the country's rulers, notorious – for refusing to implement the colour bar and promoting and paying black people on the same terms as whites. He got away with it because he was so popular with the public.

## Bangkok, Thailand, 1962

One steamy day in Bangkok, Dietrich Mateschitz, an Austrian executive who was in Thailand to market toothpaste, took a tuk-tuk (bicycle taxi). He noticed that his driver and others he saw were all drinking a particular brew to keep up their energy levels, and he asked the name. Initially none the wiser for being told it was Krating Daeng, his hotel later informed him it meant Red Bull in English. Mateschitz patented the brand in Western markets and started selling something similar, though not as sweet. Recalling Bangkok's labouring cyclists, he dubbed it an 'energy drink' and sold it to bars and nightclubs. Today, Red Bull sells more than three billion cans a year and Mateschitz is the richest Austrian on the planet – *Forbes* magazine says he's worth four billion dollars.

## San Francisco, California, 1970

I arrived in San Francisco in 1969, a little late for the 'summer of love', but still a teenager. I was amazed at the concentration of stoned hippies driving Volkswagen camper vans, saying, 'Peace, man!' at every opportunity – and little else. It was a different world from the England I had left. Maybe a young British couple who arrived in California the following year had a similar experience. But a store on Berkeley's Telegraph Avenue called the Body Shop made the biggest impression on Anita and Gordon Roddick. It didn't sell bodies, but trendy creams, lotions and shampoos.

Back home in Brighton, Anita and Gordon tried their hand at running a restaurant and then a hotel, but neither was a success. Gordon returned to America while Anita remained in Britain, but she never forgot the sensual cosmetics store in Berkeley. In

1976, she opened a similar cosmetics and lotions store in Brighton. Unconcerned with originality, she called it the Body Shop. For a laugh, she wedged it between two funeral parlours.[69] Eventually, Anita would run a global empire of 2400 stores, which she sold in 2006 for £652 million.

There are countless other examples of a good idea spawning another, bigger and better one. They tell us something important about ideas and networks. Anita Roddick did not just copy the Berkeley shop's idea and name. She also positioned it six thousand miles away, where nobody would say, 'Ah, yes, that's just a rip-off of that store on Telegraph Avenue.' Instead, 'her' idea seemed fresh and exciting. When Dietrich Mateschitz launched Red Bull in Europe and America, it was hailed as the world's *first* energy drink, not as an adaptation of the tuk-tuk drivers' favourite tipple.

Distance gives respectability; it makes copying resemble innovation. When I backed two unemployed young men to open Belgo, the *moules-et-frites* emporium serving Belgian beers, it was seen as London's coolest new restaurant concept. Never mind that there was a long-established chain of such restaurants called Leon prospering in Paris and Brussels, not to mention a similar place in New York's Greenwich Village.

This is the essence of a 'weak link' – someone far away who has useful information. By talking to that person, or just observing what they do, we grasp that they have had a good idea – it's attractive; and if it's a business, it's growing and profitable. The next step is to ask if that idea could be applied in a different place, or in a different type of market, or in a different way. Forming a weak link between a distant source of insight and a new idea becomes the germ of our new initiative.

Earlier in this book, we explored the potential value of a weak link to a person, a remote acquaintance. In this chapter, we are examining another way of enriching our lives, by linking to a distant *idea* and then reinventing it in another place or another context.

For example, Anita Roddick did not hire the proprietor of the Body Shop on Telegraph Avenue, Berkeley; nor did she spend much time with her. Anita took the idea and ran with it. Before my business partners and I started Belgo, we studied the Leon restaurants carefully. First, we wanted to know whether the chain made a lot of money. It did. What seemed to make Leon special was its menu and the way the food and beer were presented. But my partners added a lot of new ideas to the mix – the restaurant itself was made to look like a monastery eating hall, with long communal tables, and the waiters were dressed as monks. We didn't spend much time chatting to the folks at Leon; nor did we offer them a share of our new venture. We took the concept and ran, reinventing their idea for our market. By linking into a far-flung idea, then adapting it closer to home, it is possible to create a new venture – a Body Shop in Brighton, not Berkeley; a *moules-frites*–Belgian beer hall in London's Chalk Farm.

You can greatly reduce the probability of a new venture failing by forming a weak link to an idea that has already proved itself in another place or context. Ideas have heritage; they have track records. If you like, we can think about them genetically. A good idea has good genes, the elements that work together to give it integrity and appeal. Good genes are valuable. They make a venture work. A child is not a replica of its parents, but there is usually a strong resemblance. So strong parents tend to have strong offspring. Similarly, good ideas are the best sources of new good, or great, ideas.

In business, a profitable idea usually spawns another profitable firm. Most start-ups fail, but I believe that a start-up carefully modelled on a weak link to a distant good idea has a much greater chance of success. Unfortunately, there are no statistics to back up this claim – nobody has yet divided ventures according to the previous success of the ideas behind them and then looked at the success rate for ventures based on proven ideas compared with those founded in other ways. But from my own experience, I have helped to start five new ventures that were reinventions of previous profitable ideas and they all succeeded, making several times the cash that was invested. I have also helped to start four ventures not based on successful ideas; three of them failed, and one was only moderately successful.

In this chapter, we've seen several examples of super-successful ventures that were less original than they seemed to their target markets. As Albert Einstein modestly said, 'The secret to originality is knowing how to conceal your sources.' Sam Walton, the legendary founder of Wal–Mart, said something similar: 'Most everything I've done I've copied from someone else.'

But if starting a new organisation based on a distant, thriving model tends to succeed, starting a venture based on *two* successful ideas might be even better. The approach would be to form a weak link between two distant ideas that have both proved their worth in worlds isolated from each other. Then a new venture can be created, combining the two original concepts. Anita Roddick did precisely that. She took the Body Shop concept from the store in Berkeley, but she also combined it with one of the best ideas in the venture firmament – franchising.

In retail businesses, franchisees are given the founder's brand and business formula, and sold the products sourced by the parent, in return for putting up the capital for new outlets and paying a royalty on their sales to the parent. If Anita had been forced to rely on her own cash flow to open new outlets, her business would never have grown so fast – initially at more than 50 per cent a year. Nor would it have reached sixty-one countries. An added advantage of using franchisees is that they know the business practices and traps in their own countries.

Of course, the owner of the original Body Shop could have

done the same as Anita, but sometimes distance is necessary to recognise the value of something. It is often easier to appreciate a good idea when you come across it in a different world than to realise the universal value of something you created in your own back yard. Dick and Mac McDonald, for example, created a very successful business between 1948 and 1954 – they opened eight restaurants in California that sold only hamburgers, cheeseburgers, fries and beverages. Unlike traditional coffee shops, theirs had no waiters or waitresses – customers had to line up, give their orders, pay and take away their food. By restricting the menu and using self-service, the McDonalds were able to shift enormous volumes of hamburgers and sell them at rock-bottom prices. The result was an extremely profitable business, but the brothers did not see the potential of their innovation. When Ray Kroc, a former travelling salesman, offered them $2.7 million for the business in 1961, they bit his hand off. McDonald's is now worth around $48 billion, nearly 18,000 times what the brothers accepted. Kroc, incidentally, combined the idea of the hamburger restaurant with franchising.

It may also be easier to make fundamental improvements to something that is somebody else's idea. Is extending a proven idea or combining it with another idea any less creative than having it in the first place? Perhaps, but it is also likely to be more valuable. Entrepreneurs do not need to invent anything. They just need to recognise an under-exploited idea when they see it – and then set up the organisation to realise its full potential.

## Boston, Massachusetts, 1963

'Strategy consulting' – advising big companies how they could make more money by concentrating on the areas where they are better than their rivals – did not exist prior to 1963. It was dreamed up in that year by Bruce Henderson, whom we met in

Chapter Four. Bruce changed the behaviour of firms all over the world and created a totally new type of consulting firm, based on intellect rather than experience. Yet, Bruce and his colleagues found it quite easy to conceive strategy consulting. All they did was bring together two previously separate but powerful disciplines – marketing and finance – and let off all kinds of cerebral fireworks from this combustible mix.

There are myriad examples of entrepreneurs blending two good ideas. Betfair combined betting between individuals with the electronic market. The motorbike linked the bicycle and the internal combustion engine. The school of 'positive psychology' took off by combining clinical psychology – previously reserved for treating people in poor mental health – with the mainstream self-help movement. The Sony Walkman merged the tape recorder with the portable radio; and, in turn, the iPod has linked the Walkman with Internet downloads.

Other combinations could be equally successful. All they need is someone to spot them and merge them together.

But as we have seen, the best ideas, like most opportunities, derive from weak links. Moreover, ideas can spread only through their own dedicated hubs. To succeed, the group needs to be well organised, and it must broadcast the benefits of the idea as simply as possible.

Ideas, then, are effective when they follow network rules; and are organised through hubs and bridging weak links. Like these structures, creative ideas help make the world smaller and richer. The numbers of weak links and hubs proliferate. By linking two or more ideas, or by applying them in a new milieu, the world is brought closer together. Good ideas unite us, yet they also increase our differences. They encourage further ideas, advances and replacements. They are *an* answer. They are never *the* answer. Voltaire said that the best is the enemy of the good. Jim Collins, the author of *Good to Great*[70], inverted that aphorism to say that the good is the enemy of the great. But when it comes to developing fresh ideas, there are no enemies. Good ideas point the way to better ones, and better ones to great ones. The only thing that will elude us is the perfect idea, because all ideas, happily, can be improved.

There is a structure to the way information is found in nature, in a library or on the Web. The structure is embedded, universal and follows mathematical rules. There is also a structure – a network structure – for the way excellent ideas are discovered and disseminated. Once this has been grasped, anyone can innovate with confidence.

## CHAPTER TEN

# NETWORK STARS

*Discovering the best type of business*

The future is already here – it's just not equally distributed.

*Science-fiction writer William Gibson*

### London, England, 2001

Greg and I first met in a brutal fight to the death. Each of us had invested and joined the board of a 'betting exchange'. Greg had supported Flutter, a UK company run by Americans; I had put money into Betfair, a British venture. In providing person-to-person betting websites, both companies were attempting to do something that had never been done before, and both had chosen the same means to achieving it. They started within a few months of each other. Betfair was bigger, growing fast, and had a crucial hold on betting for horse racing. But Flutter was threatening to catch up, having captured a third of the market through more stable software and deeper pockets. Everyone in both companies sensed that there could be only one winner, and that the loser would be left with almost nothing.

The traditional view of markets is that they can sustain several profitable competitors. But our situation was unfolding differently for one very specific reason. A betting exchange's product – the facility to place a bet against someone who takes the opposite view – improves every time the exchange adds a new customer. The key competitive advantage – the appeal to customers – is having more customers to bet against than can be offered by any other exchange. This is an inherently unstable system, and inevitably one firm will eventually command nearly the whole market, causing the other to collapse. Coexistence simply cannot work. We were in a game of Russian roulette and one of us would die. The odds were about fifty–fifty. Not appealing for any gambler.

So the board members of each company, after heated debate and some soul searching, eventually came to the same solution – merge the two exchanges. That would make one bigger and more liquid market, which would please our customers and dramatically expand the business – more people would bet, in bigger amounts, if the market were deeper. We'd each have a share in a much larger hub that would grow faster than before; the product would be even stronger with scale; and the new firm would dwarf its rivals.

And that's exactly what happened. Instead of each company growing at 5 per cent a month, the new, merged firm (which retained the name Betfair) grew at 15 per cent a month for eighteen straight months. The betting-exchange market took off. It changed the face of gambling, first in Britain, then in all other countries that allowed such exchanges to operate. By April 2006, just six years after its launch, Betfair was worth over £1.5 billion. The firm recently announced its two-millionth customer. We reckon it has 95 per cent of the betting-exchange market worldwide.

As we shall see, Betfair typifies the best kind of business anyone could hope to start or work in – one where the network itself enlarges the market, and also awards one firm an overwhelming share of that market. We think this is a new trend in business and a new way of thinking about it, although it is comparable to another conceptual breakthrough, made in the 1970s.

One of the 'Aha!' moments of my life came when I was twenty-five. I was finishing my MBA at the Wharton School of Business in Philadelphia and was looking around for a job. At that time, the hot field was strategy consulting – helping big firms decide where and how to beat competitors and build valuable businesses. Strategy consulting had been invented a few years earlier, in the mid-to-late 1960s, by the Boston Consulting Group. BCG seemed a great place to start a career – it paid well and provided fascinating work with top corporations willing to part with huge fees even for wet-behind-the-ears consultants.

At my interview with BCG, I rather naively asked the recruiting vice-president why big firms with plenty of bright people on their own staffs paid young consultants so much. 'Basically, we've got a model,' he said.

> We categorise business units into one of four types. By far the best businesses are what we call 'stars'. These are businesses that are number one [in market share] in a high-growth market. Nearly all the value in the stock market and the economy comes from stars. But stars are rare. A large company is doing well if it has a few star lines of business, or even one. Many have none. And they often don't realise how valuable these businesses are. We get our clients to focus on these stars and make them as big and dominant as possible. And we get clients to create other star businesses when they can. It's simple but powerful. It's why our clients thrive and why we can pay you ridiculous money. Your job is to analyse the companies' businesses in accordance with our model and see which category each business falls into, and therefore what to do with it. That requires no industrial experience, just raw intelligence.

This was my introduction to BCG's famous growth–share matrix, with its cash cows, question-marks and dogs, as well as stars. The cash cows are where a company is the leader, but market growth is low – such as Heinz in baked beans or soup. Cash cows are very solid, good businesses. They should be profitable, but don't normally require a lot of cash to be reinvested – they generate cash, but not much growth. Dogs are not good news – they have weak market shares in low-growth markets, and are typically not very profitable (their margins are thinner than those of cash cows in the same market, because they don't enjoy the same economies of scale). Dogs don't generate much cash. Question-mark businesses are not leaders in their markets either, but those markets are high growth. For example, in the 1990s firms flocked to become Internet service providers, but only one company in each country could become the leader. Question-marks will become valuable only if they seize leadership from the star business in their market. This usually demands an awful lot of cash, and it might not work even then. If question-marks don't become stars, and the market stops growing, they end up as dogs – having sucked in a lot of cash, they'll never pay it back. That's why they're called question-marks: either the firm should invest like hell to replace the leader, if that will work; or it should sell the question-mark, since buyers will often pay for potential growth even when there are no profits.

Well, I became a true believer in star businesses, a kind of business fundamentalist, simplifying everything down to one great truth: *stars are much more valuable than people realise.* Before long, BCG was moving on to newer, more sophisticated models. But I stuck with the star formula, eventually starting my own star ventures and encouraging everyone else to do the same.

So why are stars so great? BCG's explanation started with costs – with economies of scale and the benefits of greater experience. The biggest firm in any particular product or service would have greater volume over which to spread its fixed costs, so its unit costs would be lower than those of smaller rivals. Then the 'experience curve' kicked in – a business with greater experience than its rivals would find smarter and cheaper ways to operate.

The cost advantage came from being the market leader and it applies to 'cash cows', too – leaders in low-growth markets. (For example, Heinz can make baked beans more cheaply than any other firm; it is bigger than any other producer and has been baking beans since 1869.) So what was special about being the leader *and* being in a high-growth market? BCG said that a high-growth market enables a leader to add revenue faster than all its rivals, to gobble up experience at a faster rate, and thereby to drive down unit costs at a faster rate. Increasing revenue and falling unit costs would make profits soar in a way that a firm in another, less vibrant market could only dream about. Ultimately, a star business would have *much* lower costs and *much* higher profits than any competing firm. The gap between the capabilities and costs of the leader and followers would keep widening, increasing the value and security of the star business. For example, when mobile phones were growing very fast in the 1980s, the Nokia Corporation of Finland abandoned all its other businesses to focus exclusively on becoming the leader in that product. By investing heavily, growing faster than any other mobile-phone maker, and achieving much lower unit costs, Nokia eventually made 80 per cent of the world's mobiles. The company is now valued at eighty billion dollars.

Yet, in the early 1980s, it was far from clear that Nokia would win. When markets are immature and growing very fast, market share can be volatile – there is a lot to play for. Whoever gains clear leadership and successfully defends it ends up with a great star business. But an early leader might lose its star position – and most of its value – if a rival overtakes it in the early days of very high market growth. For instance, in the early, high-growth days of mainframe computers in the 1950s, the market leader was

Remington Rand. But it ultimately lost out to IBM. Similarly, in 1959, Xerox invented the plain paper copier and by the mid-1960s it had a great star business. But by the early 1980s, Canon had replaced Xerox as the global leader in copiers. And the early leader in search engines was AltaVista, launched in 1995 and an instant star. But it was comprehensively thrashed by Google, founded three years later, and now perhaps the most valuable star business in the world.

Stars are exciting and expanding places to work and learn, and they can afford to pay you well. What's more, stock options held by employees, or shares held by investors, can become life-changingly valuable. Yet, although everything BCG said about stars is true, that's not the whole story. Not all stars are equal. There's a constellation of stars that shine brighter than the rest, a distinctive type in their own right. In a critical extension of BCG's thinking, I've come to realise that the ideal business is a *network star* – a star venture that has strong network characteristics.

In 1999, Albert-László Barabási, a physicist at the University of Notre Dame, and one of his students, Réka Albert, published a landmark paper in the journal *Science*. Arising from work on the structure of the Internet, they saw a pattern in the world of networks that astonished them.[71]

The two physicists started to construct maps of the Internet, where each website was a point, with lines depicting the links to other hubs and to users. A popular hub, such as Yahoo, would have a huge number of lines converging on it, whereas your website or mine would have very few. The picture, then, was one of dense concentration in a few places, and wide open spaces or just a few lines in others. It looked a bit like a map of population concentration in the United States: a few hubs had a tremendous number of links to the other hubs or to individuals in the network; on the other hand, the great majority of hubs in any system had very few links.

The scientists went on to count how many hubs had at least two connections, then four, sixteen and so on, up to millions. They found that, in any small area they inspected, there was a regular pattern: every time the number of links doubled, the number of hubs having that many links declined by roughly five times. So, there might be five thousand hubs with two connections, but only about a thousand hubs with four connections, two hundred hubs with eight connections, and so on.

This is known as a *power law distribution*, where a few hubs hog nearly all the links. Power laws often follow an 80/20 pattern, where 80 per cent of phenomena or results belong to 20 per cent of people or causes. We might hypothesise, for example, that 80 per cent of society's wealth belongs to 20 per cent of citizens. And, indeed, the true figure is remarkably close to this: the richest 20 per cent of Americans own 86 per cent of America's wealth; and the richest 20 per cent of people in the world own 85 per cent of global capital. On the Web, Google is millions of times more connected to other sites and pages than the 'long tail' of almost all other sites – which are very poorly connected in comparison.

In other words, networks tend to *concentrate*, to have a few hubs that really matter, while most hubs hardly matter at all. Connectedness in networks, Barabási and Albert concluded, was not random or democratic, not spread about or widely shared. It was monopolistic.

The lopsided distribution of networks is completely different from the 'bell-curve' distribution that we are told is 'normal', where most observations are quite close to the average. Human height, for example, follows a normal distribution. Most men are only a few inches above or below the average height of five feet, eight inches, and there are no real extremes of height. You'll never find a hundred-foot giant in the normally distributed world of human height. But you might if height behaved as most hubs do.

With power law distributions, the typical pattern is one of extreme potential variation, where a few observations can be hundreds, thousands or even millions of times greater than the average. For instance, Bill Gates is a million times richer than the average American.

The dominant few can be so large that they change the shape of the whole system. With power laws, the top performers are so important to the total that the large majority is actually below average, below the 'arithmetic mean'. With human wealth, the 'average' net worth is distorted by the few billionaires and multi-millionaires, so the average is much higher than the median – that is, the level most people enjoy. Imagine ten people who have, on average, £50,000 in the bank – a total of £500,000. But if two of them own 80 per cent of the money, they account for £400,000, leaving just £100,000 for the other eight people – £12,500 apiece. So the average wealth might be £50,000, but eight of the ten people – 80 per cent – are a long way below that average. When this is the case, the concept of *average* stops making intuitive sense. This is what happens with money; and it is what happens with networks.

Barabási and Albert were stunned when they found the world of man and nature riddled with networks with this same power law distribution of links to hubs. A few hubs hogged nearly all the connections, so the 'average' hub scarcely got a look in. And this applied not just to Internet hubs, but seemingly to almost anything that was connected in a network – the US power grid, the neurons in a worm's brain, IBM computer chips, the distribution of book sales, the number of people's sexual partners, even the way actors are linked to co-stars during their movie careers.

Hollywood, for example, is a closely connected network. Tom London might have been in a movie with Rod Steiger, who might previously have acted with Christopher Lee, connecting London and Lee. But some actors have many more links than others. On average, every actor in Hollywood has twenty-seven links to other actors. But because this is a network, with a power law distribution of contacts, that average means little. For instance, Robert Mitchum didn't have 27 links – he had 2905, meaning that he played alongside that many different colleagues. John Carradine had four thousand links. Yet, more than 40 per cent of actors have fewer than ten links. Mitchum and Carradine were superconnectors, and a handful of others occupy that role today. Without them, Hollywood would not be a small world. One or two enormously connected hubs typically dwarf all the rest – the winner takes most, and sometimes almost all.

It should be said that not all hubs follow this pattern. For instance, with airports, the advantages of size, beyond a certain point, are outweighed by the time it takes to arrive at the airport or leave it. But the vast majority of human and other networks do mimic the Internet's pattern of hub connection – a few mega-hubs and masses of tiny ones.

Of course, these large hubs are superconnectors: they do the hard work in terms of linking their 'customers', the people who connect to them and therefore are connected to everyone else as a result. For whatever reason – ease or convenience, saving time or energy, superior information or experience – most people or other nodes link to the dominant hub. We don't stop to consider the thousands of search engines to which we *could* connect; without thinking, we plump for Google or Yahoo!

And when it comes to large and powerful hubs, there is a strong tendency for the big to grow, the rich to become even wealthier. They tend to concentrate further as time passes. The most connected hubs today are likely to be connected to an even greater extent tomorrow. For example, having taken the lead in the betting-exchange market, Betfair's market share keeps rising. Network scientists have explored how this might work in theory, and have even shown how wealth could become increasingly concentrated without the rich having any superior abilities. But we don't need computer simulations – the explanation is simple. In a network, everyone wants to connect to the hub to which everyone else connects – the network is more valuable simply because it is bigger. As long as it's a network – be it a restaurant, marketplace, social network, real or virtual sports league, computer system, mobile-phone network, business directory, or electronic exchange – popularity breeds popularity.

There is another explanation why markets concentrate, especially in network businesses. Back in 1973, Bruce Henderson made this rather papal pronouncement: 'The dominant producer in every business should increase its market share steadily.' Bruce's logic was that the market leader should have lower costs, and 'at least part of that superior cost position should be passed on to the customer in lower prices or better quality'. A virtuous cycle should therefore ensue – with a better deal for the customer, more customers should be attracted to the market leader, which in turn should give the top firm even more business and therefore even lower costs, leading to an even better price or higher-quality product for the customer. 'Failure of an industry to concentrate is failure to compete,' Henderson concluded, meaning that if the leader's market share didn't keep rising, that was an indictment of the firm's management.[71]

The network business provides the best possible justification for Bruce's theory. With a network business, the leader's cost position keeps improving, but so does the product, simply because more people are attracted to the network. Even if there are no new initiatives by the firm, the leader's product should keep improving over time. Smaller rivals should attract fewer new customers, or perhaps lose some of their existing ones. The rivals' products will not improve at the same rate as the leader's, and may even decline as customers fall out of the rival networks. We should therefore expect something close to what Bruce called 'benign monopoly' to arrive eventually. And if the leader in a network business does not increase its market share steadily, there is something wrong with the way the firm is being run.

So what we know about networks suggests that in an increasingly connected world, within most categories of product or service, we'll see an ever more concentrated world. This seems to work in business, where market shares of the leaders in network businesses – in most online categories, for example – tend to be higher than in markets which are not networks, such as most manufactured goods. But does it work in everyday life? Let's examine a few familiar aspects of our daily lives – language, money and cities – to see how pronounced concentration is, and whether it's increasing or declining over time.

First, language. It's one of the most basic ways people connect with each other. It's also easy to imagine the initial fragmentation of languages, how they might have multiplied over long periods of time as groups of people migrated across continents and then lived in relative isolation, separated by mountains or rivers.

Imagine, for instance, the bewildering profusion of tongues and dialects Meriwether Lewis and William Clark encountered on their epic voyage of discovery into the uncharted and sparsely populated American West in the early 1800s. They were the first white men to travel the length of the Missouri River in search of a route to the Pacific, and they came across a plethora of tribes and languages – Mandan, Cheyenne, Hidatsas, Sioux, Pawnees, Lakotas, Nez Perce, Cayuse, Blackfoot, Piegan, Wishram, Yakima, Wananpam, Shoshones and Salish.

What do you think happens to such isolated languages when contact between peoples increases rapidly, when it becomes an advantage to speak in a way that lets you connect to more people? Dr Michael Krauss, one of the first academics to investigate 'language death', has estimated that there were about fifteen thousand human languages ten thousand years ago. Today, there are only six thousand. He predicts that in another hundred years there will be only six hundred – nine out of ten will have disappeared, an average of one language perishing every week!

Language concentration, Krauss says, is accelerating geometrically. Why is this happening? The initial motive for language is communication between parent and child, so we might expect all languages to be preserved. But what happens when people learn other languages and they are translated into each other, when they are linked by travel, commerce and telecommunications? A speaker who wants to be understood outside her country will most likely learn a language that is already widely spoken. This naturally favours languages such as English, which are already popular as a second language. English, with about 375 million native speakers, is ranked a distant third in the world as a first language, well behind Mandarin Chinese (885 million) and Hindi (600 million), and is only just ahead of Spanish (350 million). But three times as many people speak English as a second or third language as speak it as their first, whereas there are far more native speakers of the other languages than there are foreign speakers. The demand for English as a superconnecting lingua franca and as the official language of science, aviation, seafaring and many international organisations propels it to a commanding lead when all speakers are aggregated: about 1.5 billion people speak English well enough to hold a conversation; no other language even approaches a billion. As many readers will know, teaching English as a foreign language is a growth business around the globe. So, whereas demographic growth might soon make Spanish the third most spoken native language and relegate English to fourth, English is expected to continue to increase its lead overall. Linguistics professor David Crystal predicts that globally English will both diverge *and* converge – local variants will grow, requiring a form of standard international English to emerge so that all English speakers can understand each other.[73] Simple international English, perhaps with easier phonetics and spelling rules, might then further increase the superconnecting value of the language and consolidate its global lead. It becomes increasingly easy and beneficial to be linked by the biggest hub – in this case, language – in the network; schools and adult learners will respond accordingly.

But whatever happens to the number of English or other-language speakers, we can think of language as a 'virtual' hub connecting everyone on the planet, starting with the connection between native speakers, then radiating out through connections made by those learning a foreign language. If everyone can speak a language – *any* language – that someone else around them can understand, humanity is connected in a new way, so the desire for communication naturally advances already-popular languages and relegates those that few people can understand. Picture all the people in the world joined by a line or lines to hubs denoting every language they speak, and we'd have a chart that looked suspiciously like the maps of the Internet drawn by Barabási and Albert. And that chart would probably become more lopsided, more dense in a few superconnecting places, over time.

Another great connecting invention – and another virtual hub – is money. It lifts commerce and trade above the constraints of barter by providing a medium for exchange and a store of value. Much like language, it's easy to see that a particular type of currency doesn't have much utility if only a few people use it; but if it is universally accepted, it becomes very useful indeed. Here's an understandable bigger-is-better dynamic, suggesting that the currencies of the world might well concentrate as time rolls on – a few superconnecting currencies will become more important, particularly for trade and international reserves, other currencies will disappear entirely, and most will fade in importance.

Again, recent history bears this out. Despite each country promoting and protecting its own currency, the US dollar is by far the most widely held international reserve currency, making up about two-thirds of all world foreign exchange reserves. In fact, over half of total US dollars in issue reside outside the United States, and several other countries use the greenback as their de facto currency.

The rise of the second most important currency in the world – the euro – is a story of even more dramatic and rapid concentration. Prior to 2002, twelve of the largest countries in Western Europe had their own currencies. All of these suddenly disappeared on 1 January 2002, and they are now just relics hoarded by numismatists and perhaps a few isolated peasants. Gone are some of the most redolent and proud currencies in the world, including the German mark, the Spanish peseta, the Italian lira, the French franc, the Dutch guilder and the Greek drachma, not to mention the Finnish markka and the Portuguese escudo. And the euro is still making converts. In 2007, the Slovenian tolar bit the dust; in 2008, the Cypriots and the Maltese abandoned their centuries-old pounds; and in 2009, the Slovak koruna followed them into the currency dustbin. The euro is also the sole currency of Montenegro, Kosovo, Andorra, the Vatican, Monaco, San Marino and five non-European states, and it is widely used in Cuba, North Korea and Syria. It now surpasses even the dollar in the value of cash in circulation, and, although still well behind the dollar as a reserve currency, it is gaining ground. In 1995, the US dollar and the (now defunct) German mark made up three-quarters of the world's currency reserves, with the hundreds of other currencies sharing the remaining quarter. Impressive concentration! But by 2008, the euro and the US dollar between them provided 91 per cent of all currency reserves, with only 9 per cent shared between the other currencies. Once again, very high concentration has led to even higher concentration – to the almost total dominance of two currencies in international reserves. If we add in the pound sterling (4 per cent of reserves) and the Japanese yen (3 per cent), just four currencies out of the hundreds in circulation constitute

98 per cent of reserves – it is a 98/2 rule, with 2 per cent of currencies comprising 98 per cent of reserves. These numbers are similar to the concentration patterns we see on the Internet: Google and Yahoo in search engines, Amazon in book retailing, Wikipedia in encyclopedia searches, eBay in auctions.

Our final everyday example of high and increasing connection and concentration is the city.

Cities have always been among humankind's greatest superconnecting machines, bringing people into contact with strangers and becoming ever more important magnets for trade, finance, government, production, learning, shopping and even leisure. In 1500, only about one person in a hundred around the globe lived in a city. By 1800, this had increased to three in a hundred. A hundred years later, the figure was fourteen in a hundred. Today, more people live in cities than outside them.

But in addition to urban concentration increasing over the past five hundred years, it has increased within the class of cities. Rather than cities becoming relatively dispersed, as many commentators predicted a generation ago, the big cities have become even bigger. And cities consistently seem to show the big-get-bigger pattern. The big cities of yesterday – New York, London, Tokyo, Peking and Bombay – are the even bigger cities of today, even if the last two have changed their names. Metropolitan Tokyo–Yokohama now has thirty-five million inhabitants, more than the whole of Canada.

Big cities appear to be practically indestructible. London was ravaged by bubonic plague in 1665. The following year, the Great Fire destroyed the homes of seventy thousand of the eighty thousand residents. Hitler tried hard to destroy the city in the Blitz of 1940–1, damaging or destroying more than a million homes. But throughout the centuries, London has just grown bigger and bigger – only the green belt around the city now limits further expansion, resulting in modest population growth but, over the decades, escalating house prices.

Compared to some cities, however, London has had a relatively easy time. Think of the tragedy of Hiroshima, which had a population of 420,000 in 1942. In August 1945, the American B-29 bomber *Enola Gay* dropped 'Little Boy', a nuclear weapon that immediately killed almost a fifth of the city's people and flattened 70 per cent of its buildings, leaving behind deadly radioactive contamination. By year's end, the city contained only a third of its former inhabitants. Yet, ten years later, Hiroshima had been rebuilt and its population had returned to pre-war levels. Today, the city has blossomed to three times that size.

Cities, currencies (especially reserve currencies) and languages are all communication devices, and all networks. And they each share three characteristic patterns of networks. First, they are concentrated, so a few of them are superconnectors while the majority are unimportant. Second, they are *increasingly* concentrated: the big cities grow; the more popular currencies and languages become more popular. Finally, without any master plan or deliberate encouragement, they are expanding spontaneously, driven by the human urge to connect and exchange, and, perhaps even more fundamentally, by the very nature of networks.

Do businesses exhibit these same inclinations to expand and concentrate? Many do, but some – network businesses – do so much more than others.

Greg was lucky enough to stumble into one such network star early in his career. It left him with the strong conviction that some businesses could be dominant, a belief that eventually led him to invest in Flutter and support its merger with Betfair. Here he explains what happened.

Toronto, my early twenties, new graduate from business school – not the foggiest idea how to start my career, but the desire to get my hands dirty. A few influential professors, and my father, a career lawyer who grew to like business more than law, had impressed on me the excitement of 'real business' and entrepreneurship. I joined a successful and entrepreneurial commercial real-estate firm founded by a fêted graduate of my business programme. It seemed a solid middle-class choice and everyone approved. Of course, I detested it with all my soul. I left after six months, and promptly did something that did not meet expectations: I went into used cars.

Bill Francis was the father of a friend. He owned a regional chain of photo-classified advertising magazines known as *Auto Trader* that helped people buy or sell used cars and other vehicles. My first visit made an impression. The company was located in a former belting factory in a light-industrial area of Toronto. Bill sat in the centre of it, in a large, round office created by cutting out the sides of a steel silo, a remnant of the building's industrial past. The foremost items on his desk were scissors and tape and piles of past editions of his myriad weekly and monthly titles. In an expansive mood, he'd light up a cigar and get busy with the scissors, snipping up old editions and pasting the strips together to mock-up new titles – *Recreational Vehicle Trader, Older Imported Car Trader, Snowmobile Trader, Heavy Equipment Trader*. These experimental front pages would be taped to the walls of his round room, joining dozens of others for smoky reflection.

The company bustled around him. There were telephone desks just within earshot that handled customer complaints and where photographers would set up meetings to take pictures of vehicles that customers wanted to sell. In the back there was a pre-press operation, and a humming newspaper-style press together with a bindery. And there was a staging area where delivery-route bundles for four thousand stores were assembled for forty drivers, typically itinerant musicians who prized this steady, one-day-a-week gig where they could pocket a few hundred bucks.

Bill was looking for someone to work with him on new magazines as well as initiatives to improve the existing business. That was me. I got to work with the boss who had built up this company from nothing. Founded twenty years earlier, it had an unbroken string of profits and growth. The outfit radiated a certain hard-to-explain buzz and confidence. It really took the full five years I worked there to understand just what a special business it was.

During my time, *Auto Trader* moved from about a 30 per cent share of automotive classified advertising to double that. The winning trend continued after I left, to the point where the company was really a local monopoly. It had beaten the large and powerful daily newspapers at their own game, stealing one of their most profitable sources of revenue. It also withstood more than one launch of a magazine copying its format at a lower price.

How did *Auto Trader* manage all this?

Well, it had the Holy Grail of competitive advantage. It started out with product advantages over a more expensive newspaper line ad – *Auto Trader* offered a photo and more words. Better information sold more cars. It also had cost advantages over the newspapers – unlike the papers, *Auto Trader* targeted only people who wanted to buy or sell vehicles, so it didn't have to pay for newsprint for ads that weren't read by most of its audience. And the scale economies of delivery, and of getting around the city to photograph customers' cars, improved as more magazines were sold and more people paid for pictures of their cars to be taken.

But the great advantage of *Auto Trader* was simply that the product improved as it garnered more customers, both buyers and sellers. Buyers wanted the greatest choice of cars, so they went to the publication that had the most ads. Sellers went where most buyers were looking. It was easy to mimic the *Auto Trader* photo-classified magazine format, but you couldn't match the usefulness of its product because you weren't starting with the same numbers of buyers and sellers. And it was impossible to attract them from scratch – even by offering a free service – because they already knew the best place to buy or sell used cars. Of course, they were not prepared to abandon that and go instead to a thin and illiquid market place.

*Auto Trader* was a great network, where the customers attracted each other, to the point where a near monopoly was created. Once created, such a network is a great asset for its owners, unless or until a new technology disrupts everything. *Auto Trader* is also a profound example of a network effect, where the collective action of users becomes part of the strength of the product or service itself. The customers sow the value, and the network owner reaps it.

Bill, with a newspaper and branded-goods background, was a stellar operator of this type of business. But when you examine the performance of *Auto Trader* in all its territories, the way they were managed may have had less influence on its success than you might expect. Bill held the Toronto franchise, but he had not invented the business. Stuart W. Arnold had the original idea, in Florida in the 1970s. The market for used cars is, of course, local, defined by region or large metropolitan area. Stuart didn't want to traipse all over North America, recreating a local *Auto Trader* business in each big city, so he sold about thirty franchises. The ticket price was $25,000. Stuart didn't care who the franchisees were, as long as they had the money. He sold franchises to his nephews, uncles, accountants, dentists, journalists, housepainters – you name it – as well as to established business people. In fact, most of his franchisees had no business training and some of them were manifestly unfit to run anything.

Now, you might assume that some of the franchises went to the wall while others prospered.

Wrong. No matter how unqualified the franchisee, not one franchise failed. They all became successful and worth at least a few million dollars; sometimes, as with Bill's franchise, a few hundred million. The network forces were so strong that once an *Auto Trader* franchise became established in any region, it was impossible for a competitor to overtake it. Managerial incompetence could make the franchise slightly less of a gold mine, but it would always remain the local market leader.

A British holiday-maker in Florida in 1975 also saw the potential of *Auto Trader*. When he went home, John Madejski started *Thames Valley Trader*, which sold houses, cars and much else besides. But the cars sold best of all, and soon Madejski renamed his title – wait for it – *Auto Trader*, focusing exclusively on vehicles. He sold the business in 1998 for £174 million. Since then, he has given a lot away – he was knighted in the UK Honours List in 2009 for his philanthropy – yet the *Sunday Times* reckons he is still the 222nd richest person in Britain.[74] Just like Anita Roddick and the Body Shop, John Madejski had linked up with a distant American idea that had already proved itself.

*Auto Trader*, in its various forms, had a clear thirty-year run, during which time several great fortunes were amassed. Then the playing field finally shifted – the Internet ended the dominance of the photo-classified print format and allowed other competitors, such as eBay Motors, to barge in. *Auto Trader* is still alive and well online, but it is no longer guaranteed to be the leader in every local market.

So what is it about network stars that makes them so much better than the plain vanilla star?

Network stars are the business world's beneficiaries of the phenomenon observed by Barabási and Albert – the inexorable concentration of networks. They outgun normal stars due to what we've come to term 'network effects' – instances where a product's value for any single user becomes correlated to the total number of users. The more users it has, the better the product. The consequence is a natural tendency to 'winner takes most' or 'winner takes all' end games, resulting from the insurmountable product advantages of the leading player. A network star can grow enormously, become the dominant player in its market, and sustain fat margins. The combination of growth, high profitability, dominance and sustainability results in an enormously attractive business, such as Betfair.

This logic is very different from the traditional view of why star businesses are attractive. BCG based its perspective on costs and economies of scale. For sure, a business with lower costs than its rivals has a strong hand. However, a determined challenger with a lower cost of capital, or with the willingness to invest heavily to gain market share, can match the leader simply by accepting lower profits. Cost advantage does not guarantee victory, because a rational rival can buy market share and hence overturn the leader's advantage in costs and experience. Cost advantage can be offset by throwing money at the problem or just by growing faster. When Raymond Ackerman started with four Pick 'n Pay supermarkets in Cape Town, Checkers was a much bigger chain; but Raymond knew that he had to become the biggest in South Africa to be able to buy groceries cheaper than his rivals, so he ploughed back in all his cash flow to open new stores faster than Checkers.

But network advantage is not so vulnerable to price cutters or expansion through heavy investment. Cost advantage does not explain why *Auto Trader*, Betfair, Google, Microsoft or Facebook has become so dominant. The most stunning market concentrations, and ensuing increases in wealth, are not driven by economies of scale. They come about because of product advantages created by networks that are fiendishly difficult for a competitor to duplicate. If Checkers had been in a strong network market – where the existence of many more stores made the groceries taste better – then Raymond wouldn't have stood a chance. But groceries, of course, do not work like that.

The more users a network has, the greater its value – and that of the product or service it proffers. The more buyers and sellers that use *Auto Trader*, the greater the choice, and the more likely you'll be to sell your car. The more people who congregate in cyberspace to bet through Betfair, the bigger the betting, the narrower the spreads, and the greater its value to all the gamblers. You can try to compete with a network star, but you don't have the best product until everyone switches to you. And why would they do that unless you had the best product? You can throw money at this problem, but you'll get nowhere.

This 'bigger is better' phenomenon applies to all networks.

Because the value of using a network keeps rising, the number of users increases alongside the extent to which each member uses it. Usage breeds usage. In the jargon used by network scientists, there are 'positive feedback loops' – every new participant on a betting exchange improves it for everyone else; and there are 'positive network externalities' – we all benefit from network growth without having to pay for it.

So once it starts growing fast, a network will continue to grow fast. This is great news for the network owners, but their good fortune doesn't stop there. Networks tend to favour one standard, one language, one supplier, one common system. In normal circumstances, the smaller network providers tend to drop away, while the biggest supplier makes ground hand over fist. Because it has the most users, the leading network has the most value – even if aspects of its product or service are not as good as those of a rival. The value of having the most users tilts the scales heavily in attracting new users.

Result: the winner takes at least most, and sometimes all.

In mainstream online social networking, Facebook and MySpace loom large over a host of rats and mice. There is one Microsoft. One eBay. One Google. One Wikipedia. One Yahoo! One Betfair. Yes, all of these have rivals, but they are tiny in comparison. Networks naturally tend to support the leader and make it dominant . . . unless and until new technology or some other unexpected change disrupts the established game.

Markets that are heavily networked – such as online services –

are more likely to see a dominant star emerge than less network-reliant markets, such as supermarkets. Paradoxically, in our increasingly networked world, it is easier to create a very valuable star business with network characteristics than it is to create a much less valuable non-network star.

You'll realise by now why network stars are so attractive. Their combination of growth, high profitability, dominance and sustainability results in a fantastic business. But while the network-star phenomenon is important from the perspective of understanding individual businesses, we should not miss its implications for industry, the economy and society in general. If you accept that increasing connection leads to increasing concentration, and acknowledge that our society and industry, aided by technology, are becoming increasingly, seamlessly connected, where does that lead us?

For commerce, it's becoming clearer. The more networked an industry is, the more its competitive structure will tend to concentrate around a few big, superconnecting companies. *Markets will become more monopolistic.* You'll find a single dominant network star in an increasing number of markets and niches. This is a pretty grand pronouncement, but look at what Eric Schmidt, Google's chief, has to say on the subject:

> I would like to tell you that the Internet has created such a level playing field that the long tail is absolutely the place to be – that there's so much differentiation, there's so much diversity, so many new voices. Unfortunately, that's not the case.
>
> What really happens is something called a power law, with the property that a small number of things are very highly concentrated and most other things have relatively little volume. Virtually all of the new network markets follow this law. So, while the tail is very interesting, the vast majority of revenue remains in the head. And this is a lesson that businesses have to

learn. While you can have a long tail strategy, you better have a head, because that's where all the revenue is.

And, in fact, it's probable that the Internet will lead to larger blockbusters and more concentration of brands. Which, again, doesn't make sense to most people, because it's a larger distribution medium. But when you get everybody together they still like to have one superstar. It's no longer a US superstar, it's a global superstar. So that means global brands, global businesses, global sports figures, global celebrities, global scandals, global politicians.[75]

This raises some thought-provoking questions. How 'free' are network markets if they always gravitate towards one mega-winner? Especially when it's the network itself, rather than the firm, that drives growth and profitability. Is the notion of anti-trust even relevant in a system that naturally, inevitably, ends in monopoly? Customers benefit from network effects – probably outweighing any disadvantage arising from the firm's monopoly power.[76] As Kevin Kelly, former editor of *Wired* magazine, says, 'Mono-sellers are actually desirable in a network economy . . . a large single pool is superior to many smaller pools.'[77]

Is the world really increasingly 'flat', as Thomas Friedman contends?[78] He argues that the challenge from low-cost suppliers in China, India or elsewhere means that competition is hotting up – there is a level playing field globally and nobody is safe. No doubt this is true in many markets – where one product is much like another and the one with the lowest price tag will win. But it is hard to argue the same thing for the star firms in network markets. Here the threat is not cheap labour, but new technology, stricter regulation or some other sea-change. Large parts of the competitive scenery may be flat, but there are some great hulking mountains as well. And that is where the serious money lies.

Do you find that a depressing prospect, with fewer and fewer players taking more and more of a market? Do networks, in this case, mean less opportunity? Well, yes and no. Networks lead to 'decentralised concentration' – the niche can be very concentrated, but it is often very specialised; and networks usually expand by splitting an existing market into two, and later fragmenting it again, with new ways of making a living and new types of customer. We used to have state monopolies of gambling, or else an oligarchy of a few big bookmakers. Then Internet gambling opened up other niches; and new players, different from the old ones, took the lead online. Then we had spread betting, then betting exchanges, each with their special innovators. Each expansion of a new niche tends to create a monopoly, but it is typically a new opportunity and a new monopolist. In Friedman's terms, the world starts out flat, then someone builds a mountain (Google); or takes an existing mountain, and erects a nice new hill alongside it (Betfair).

But that doesn't resolve all the issues with networks. In particular, what about the distribution of wealth? How will governments and societies respond to the immensely unbalanced split of wealth that will inevitably result when network markets concentrate? Not to mention the millions of dollars that flow to top executives who are in the right place at the right time. How should we guide and pay management in a business that is structurally slated to win? Who or what is responsible for its success? Really, the network itself is creating much of the value, far more than the individual. Yet a few individuals – skilled and shrewd, yes, but also often lucky – can capture extraordinary wealth, gaining more money at a faster rate than has ever been the case in human history.

Meg Whitman, when she ran eBay, famously said, 'Even a monkey could drive this train.' As with *Auto Trader*, as with Betfair, much of the spectacular growth has little to do with how they are managed, and much more to do with the initial idea, design and execution. Then the network takes over. This is not to say that there are no management challenges in these firms; there are. But shareholders and directors should understand that network stars benefit from a force denied to other businesses – the network tailwind that drives the firm forward. The network provides the growth; the executives just steer.

Executives and boards of firms must decide which markets to enter and invest in, and which to avoid. If our network view of markets had prevailed, would financial institutions have fallen over themselves, in their droves, to enter some areas of investment banking, which is an ultra-networked universe? There could only ever have been a few winners, and masses of losers. Of course, it is human nature to think that you'll defy the odds and succeed. But a full understanding of networks would have shown a legion of bankers just how slim their chances were.

What about the personal implications of network stars? If Greg and I had known what we know now at the start of our careers, neither of us would have bothered to work in any other type of firm.

So, not all businesses are equally attractive. Maybe 5 per cent of all businesses provide more than 95 per cent of all valuable new products and services, and probably a higher percentage of all new value creation to their owners. These most elegant businesses are all stars – the leading firm, preferably the overwhelming leader, in a market that grows fast for many years.

However, not all stars are equal. Some are predictably the most compelling, magnetic and seductive. Tapping the explosive energy of networks, new ventures can mushroom, bestriding their niches. The types of business that will take you furthest, and most likely give you enjoyment and freedom to widen your horizons, are the stars that happen to benefit from being the leader in a *powerful network*. Betfair and *Auto Trader* have not just been stars but *network stars*, where the network itself has created the growth and worked to produce a dominant leader.

In network markets, a small number of hubs, and usually just one, will predominate.

For anyone who works, there is no contest. It is immeasurably better to work in a young network star than anywhere else. The growth and cash created by these ventures give the early participants wonderful opportunities. And to *start* a new network star is even more rewarding. If you can identify one and set it up, success will be more likely than otherwise. Forget what you have been told – correctly – about the high failure rate of new ventures. New network stars go bust far less often if they are properly conceived. If the idea is good enough, if the new venture really taps the atomic energy of networks, it is much less likely to fail.

This, in short, is the business of hubs.

But there is more. There is the business of weak links.

## CHAPTER ELEVEN

# THE BUSINESS OF WEAK LINKS

*How firms can benefit from weak links*

A network-based social structure is a highly dynamic, open system, susceptible to innovating without threatening its balance.

*Manuel Castells*[79]

Weak ties provide the bridges over which innovations cross the boundaries of social groups.

*Mark Granovetter*[80]

Have you ever lived in an isolated small town? Everyone knows everyone else – or, indeed, is related to everyone else – and anonymity is impossible. Friendships can be strong; but so can feuds, dividing not just individuals but families and wider groupings. The classic example is Verona, the setting for *Romeo and Juliet*. If a small town is not growing – if there is no fresh blood flowing into it – then it can become incestuous, narrow-minded and intolerant. Even if these dangers are avoided, it will feel sleepy – at least to someone with wider horizons.

A small town with a stable population has this basic problem – there are too many strong links and too few weak links. Because family and friendship ties predominate, to the virtual exclusion of serendipitous new weak links, fresh information and initiatives find it hard to flourish.

Contrast that with a big city. Cities are huge incubators of weak links. We shouldn't be surprised, therefore, that they are also great centres of innovation.

Is it possible to look at our work and at firms in the same way? What is the relationship between weak links, strong links and innovation in the workplace? What facilitates innovation? What hinders it?

The knowledge we have of networks should lead us to believe that innovation and market growth would be greatest where there is a preponderance of weak links bridging different worlds – where, out of all links, the weak outnumber the strong.

Young firms fit this description, because most new firms rely heavily on external weak links. New ventures typically draw some of their most important ideas from external sources; and they are staffed, by definition, by people who haven't been in the new firm for long, and therefore retain links to their old firms. People in new ventures also tend to be more motley – drawn from a greater variety of companies and backgrounds – than the staffs of more mature firms, which usually develop established sources of hiring, both institutional and personal. There is less time for connections to formalise and harden into strong links and for established hier-archies to materialise. For all these reasons, new ventures generally have a higher proportion of weak links than more established firms. Of course, young firms may be more innovative for reasons unrelated to weak links – the people who start a firm have to break new ground in order to get going and survive. But we'd still expect the preponderance of weak links to help a great deal.

We would also expect small firms to have relatively more weak links than bigger firms. Small ventures are more likely to outsource some functions and less likely to rely on internal cen-tral services. A small firm will usually have less hierarchy, and be more exposed to random outside influences. And small firms have less volume, so jobs are less specialised and particular. Generalist or wide-ranging jobs are much more likely to have weak links than jobs in larger firms, where sub-division and automation are used to drive down unit costs. Think how few weak links an operator on a car assembly line has. Compare that with the manager of a small garage, who has to fix the car, deal with customers and suppliers, do the accounts, and so on. In small and growing firms there is also much less time for relationships to calcify because there is more change, more upheaval, more internal job redefinition and rotation, more fluidity.

We would also expect weak links to flourish where many different firms, some in different industries, are located in the same city or region, and where there is frequent job-hopping and social contact between the employees of different firms. Here we would predict that such cross-fertilisation of knowledge and skills would facilitate innovation and market growth. In a similar way, where there are frequent casual links between universities and firms, and between firms and non-academic incubators of innovation and sources of knowledge transfer – such as consultants – then innovation will flourish.

On the other hand, what we have said about strong links would suggest that when firms are introverted and secretive – relying on their own people rather than sharing with and learning from outsiders – innovation will be stultified. Such firms, one might reasonably expect, would tend to be large and confident in their own abilities – and therefore, if this is not too much of a paradox, historically successful.

Can we find hard evidence to support these suppositions? And, equally, are there any surprising or counter-intuitive patterns relating to strong and weak links?

Economists have long debated whether innovation is likely to be greatest in cities with lots of different industries and types of firms, or in those where all companies are in the same business.[81] Jane Jacobs (a great, intuitive expert on cities) plumps for the first view, claiming that many industries and cross-pollination between them stimulate innovation.[82] She illustrates this idea with a story about the invention of the bra in 1920s Manhattan. Ida Rosenthal made fine dresses for rich ladies but observed that her clothes often didn't hang well on her patrons. She reckoned the reason for this was poorly designed underwear – hence her innovation, the brassiere. She then gave up dressmaking and became an entrepreneur, making and selling bras. But how did someone with no experience of running a business manage to do this? She outsourced, and she found all her suppliers locally. In New York, she dealt with sewing-machine and textile suppliers, box makers, shippers, wholesalers and financiers. Without this diverse set of weak links all readily to hand, Ida and her bra might not have made it.

Harvard professor Michael Porter takes a different view.[83] He says that the most innovative cities have lots of companies in the same industry, which all learn from each other, drawing on a deep reservoir of specialised local experience. He cites winemaking, medical equipment and tailoring as industries which tend to be concentrated in cities or regions, where any minor improvement by one firm is seen and quickly copied by all the others.

In spite of their contrasting opinions, note that both Jacobs and Porter understand the importance of weak links in the transmission of ideas and innovation. Jacobs stresses the cross-fertilisation of ideas and practices from one industry to another; Porter emphasises the spread of myriad tiny improvements from one firm to another in the same industry. Strong links within the firms would not work the magic of innovation in either case. But Jacobs' view is more in the spirit of the small-world idea – weak links spanning more diverse industries should facilitate more radical innovation and growth.

So who is right? A group of economists led by Ed Glaeser examined data from 170 US cities over thirty years to find out.[84] The evidence clearly supported Jacobs – cities grew faster where there were several industries. Towns dependent on just one industry tended to contract.

It seems that a city which already boasts many different industries provides a hospitable home for new ones, and it can always shift its focus as some industries decline and others rise. Consider the fact that, outside the United States, most innovation and production in information technology tend to happen in the world's largest and oldest cities – Paris, Moscow and St Petersburg, Tokyo–Yokohama, Shanghai and Beijing, São Paulo–Campinas, Buenos Aires, Mexico City. The only non-US technology innovation centres that don't conform to this pattern are in the UK and Germany. But on closer inspection, even they cannot be said to go against the grain totally. In Britain, the main centres are the M4 'corridor', which starts just twenty miles west of London, and Cambridge, both of which draw on the capital's pool of talent and are relatively close to it. In Germany, Berlin was the country's technological power-house until 1945. It was only then, with Russian and American troops advancing on the devastated capital, that Siemens moved to the safer haven of Munich.

Innovation seems to thrive most wherever there is the greatest diversity – where weak links are plentiful relative to strong links. Glaeser's study also found that industry grew fastest in those cities with the greatest number of competing firms, and that small firms innovated more than large ones. His team's research also showed that cities with increasing proportions of people born outside the United States, such as Los Angeles and New York, were the most successful, with wages increasing fastest for all residents, irrespective of whether they were born in the USA or elsewhere. Diversity, the economists concluded, created wealth through innovation.

These findings suggest that innovation is easier where there are coincident networks than where there is one isolated firm. The real generator of invention is not the individual firm, nor even the network of competing firms and their suppliers, but rather a series of overlapping networks. The unit that really matters is the total commercial network in a particular place. The town with a few large companies, such as Detroit, may contract for want of diverse input, for lack of fresh weak links. By contrast, the 'sundry city' – large, miscellaneous and open to external influences, the incubator of weak links – will always be able to renew itself. Networks proliferate and cross-pollinate; individuals, firms and the city as a whole benefit.

Yet Michael Porter's view – that innovation comes from firms in the same industry being cheek-by-jowl – also works, in its own way. He formulated this idea after observation of regions and businesses that apparently benefited from specialisation in one industry. Santa Clara County – a half-rural enclave in northern California, better known as Silicon Valley – packs the world's heartland of electronics innovation into a very small region. The same is true of tailoring (New York, London), medical equipment and services (Boston), high fashion (Paris), fashion shoes (Milan), leather goods (northern Italy), pharmaceuticals (New Jersey), banking (New York, London, Frankfurt), diamond polishing (Antwerp), publishing (New York, London, Frankfurt), Islamic banking (Bahrain), aerospace (Toulouse), clean technology (Copenhagen), gambling (Las Vegas, London, Macao), racehorse training (Newmarket) and fine watchmaking (southern Switzerland). Firms that are located in these magically concentrated regions tend to do much better than firms elsewhere.

So why does Porter's analysis work, and yet diverse cities work even better? Part of the answer lies in perspective. From the viewpoint of an industry, regional concentration is good; but from the viewpoint of a city, industrial diversity is better. In both cases, we are talking about networks driven by face-to-face weak links.

It seems remarkable, given the alleged 'death of distance', that certain very profitable industries are still concentrated in very small geographical enclaves. In Silicon Valley, success is *local, physical, personal, contagious.* Four-fifths of the world's revenues and profits in financial services come from a few square miles in Manhattan, Frankfurt and the City of London. Half of all US breakthroughs in pharmaceuticals are made in New Jersey, which is home to only 3 per cent of Americans. In the UK, a large majority of the country's fine jewellers are found in a few short streets in Hatton Garden, London.

So why is this the case? Back in 1890, the British economist Alfred Marshall provided an answer that still rings true today:

> Great are the advantages which people following the same skilled trade get from near neighbourhood to one another. The mysteries of the trade become no mysteries, but are as it were in the air . . . Good work is rightly appreciated, inventions and improvements . . . have their merits promptly discussed: if one man starts a new idea, it is taken up by others and combined with suggestions of their own; and thus it becomes the source of further new ideas.[85]

Note: innovations are promptly 'discussed'. For all the faxes, emails, phone calls and videoconferencing we have today, the key element in the spread, amplification and adaptation of good new ideas is *face-to-face discussion*, just as it was a century ago. Knowledge is 'in the air'. This doesn't mean cyberspace; it means very local air. Anyone who has worked in Silicon Valley knows how apt Marshall's description is. People learn most from the other people they meet, and most of the time it's unconscious, natural and almost unavoidable – it happens at the gym, on the train, at the bar, in the back yard, in hundreds of casual encounters and conversations each week. It happens through weak links, through chance encounters, through meeting new contacts in other firms, because the local community is a hive of mutual learning and common aspiration. As Manuel Castells says, 'Silicon Valley kept churning out new firms, and practicing cross-fertilisation and knowledge diffusion by job-hopping and spin-offs. Late-evening conversations at the Walker's Wagon Wheel Bar and Grill in Mountain View did more for the diffusion of technological innovation than most seminars in Stanford.'[86]

But Silicon Valley was not America's original centre of high-tech excellence. That was the area along Route 128 outside Boston, where such firms as Digital Equipment, Apollo Computer, Prime Computer and Wang Computer set up shop. However, many of the Route 128 companies were acquired or went bust, and the area lost its pre-eminence in computer design and manufacturing as firms such as Intel, HP, Sun Micro Systems, 3Com, Silicon Graphics and Cisco all based themselves in Silicon Valley.

Harvard researcher Anna-Lee Saxenian investigated why this happened. She found that Silicon Valley developed a decentralised and experimental way of working characterised by collaboration and collective learning among webs of specialist companies and the engineers themselves. Route 128, by contrast, was dominated by a few self-sufficient firms that kept their expertise in-house, discouraging job-hopping or collaboration between different corporations. Competitive advantage in the Valley rested not with individual firms but with the whole region – there were far more frequent start-ups and exchanges of expertise, a kaleidoscope of ever-shifting alliances and experimentation, a mass of smaller firms rather than a few leviathans. This situation was remarkably similar to that described a century earlier by Alfred Marshall – improvements, new products and ideas did not remain within one firm, and innovation was continually lubricated by discussion assisted by various accomplices, such as head hunters, venture capitalists and universities.[87]

Route 128 was dominated by strong links and large firms, and the unit that mattered most was the firm; Silicon Valley was a hive of weak links and small firms, where the individual innovator and the network were crucial. The Valley is perhaps the most potent example of the power of weak links on the planet – on average, people stay in their jobs there only two years.

Network effects not only gave global leadership to the Valley, but made large fortunes for (mainly local) investors and many of the engineers themselves. This was a transformation not just of industrial practice, but of rewards and power. It was a new phase of capitalism, or possibly the birth of a totally new system: network society replacing corporatism.

Professor Henry Chesbrough of Harvard University has studied how America innovated in the twentieth century. The United States led the world in research and technology throughout that period, he says, but during the 1980s there was a dramatic change in the way industrial innovation began to operate. The golden age of internal research and development (R&D) was between 1940 and 1985 – real spending on research zoomed from $3 billion in 1940 to $102 billion in 1985. During those forty-five years, business applied a 'closed innovation' model – ideas were developed in secret, behind company walls, there was low labour mobility, little venture capital, the universities were generally unimportant, and there were few strong start-ups.

But by the 1980s, Chesbrough says, the model had begun to falter. The GI Bill, providing college or technical education for demobilised troops, and the expansion of universities created a huge pool of trained engineers, who were willing and able to surf from firm to firm. New ventures didn't have to spend a fortune on basic research; they could learn by hiring. Venture capital, which was unimportant until 1980, had grown fifty-one times by 2001, making start-ups possible for people with no money. External research and external suppliers became increasingly available, enabling small firms to create new products and markets. Individuals and small firms filed only 5 per cent of all patents in 1970; by 1992, they accounted for 20 per cent. Big firms – those with more than 25,000 employees – were responsible for 71 per cent of all spending on research in 1981; by 1999, that had dropped to 41 per cent.[88]

Many new companies, small and large – from garage shop operators to leading firms such as Amgen, Genetech, Genzyme, Intel, Microsoft, Oracle and Sun – do relatively modest basic research, preferring to take and adapt new ideas from wherever they arise, creating wonderful new products without massive R&D budgets. In the past thirty years, we have entered a new era of ever-faster innovation favouring creative individuals, small firms and venture capitalists, able to find and commercialise great ideas. The old corporate behemoths such as Xerox and IBM – once the exemplars of innovation and scientific excellence – have struggled to adapt and survive in the new terrain of open innovation. They may continue to do excellent (and expensive) deep research, but they are likely to miss the significance of the next 'new big thing'. Xerox invented the PC, Windows-type software, the mouse, laser printers, the paperless office and Ethernet. But it failed to introduce any of them to the market.

Firms outside the mainstream nearly always provide the next important innovation.[89] The three US leaders in electrical equipment – GE, RCA and Westinghouse – did not become America's electronics leaders. They were beaten by upstarts such as Fairchild Semiconductor and Intel, which never made vacuum tubes.

After IBM became the leader in mainframe computers in the late 1950s, it was challenged by some far bigger companies which invested heavily in R&D – GE, Xerox, RCA and Motorola. It saw off all of them, but later failed to repel much

smaller firms specialising in a raft of computer innovations –
Digital Equipment in minicomputers, Apple in home personal
computers, Silicon Graphics in 3-D workstations, Compaq in
portable business computers, and Dell in PCs sold directly. Every
important innovation in computers from the late 1970s came not
from the dominant industry leader, but from smaller firms.

Professor Clayton Christensen has provided a fascinating
explanation of why well-run leading firms find it so hard to
innovate. He calls it the 'innovator's dilemma': firms doing
everything right in their existing market are *especially* likely to fail
whenever a disruptive new technology emerges. His research in
a number of innovative industries – including disk drives, auto-
mobiles, computers, pharmaceuticals, retailing and steel – shows
that breakthrough innovations are initially resisted by the largest
and most profitable customers. The disruptive technologies are
therefore forced to find new networks of customers and suppliers – and it is nearly always new firms, founded by nimble
entrepreneurs, who catch the next wave of industry expansion.[90]
Time after time, the old, powerful companies, even when the
new innovation is laid bare for all to see and copy, just don't
move quickly enough, as if they were hamstrung. This pattern is
repeated across all industries, low tech as well as high tech.

Few companies are as well run, well connected and cash rich
as the Coca-Cola Corporation. Coca-Cola is still the world's
most valuable brand. Its distribution muscle and reach to con-
sumers around the world are legendary. Yet its only successful
new drinks in the twentieth century were Fanta – concocted,
incidentally, in Nazi Germany – and Tab/Diet Coke.
Meanwhile, new ventures innovated in several areas: Mountain
Dew in citrus drinks; Snapple in natural beverages; Red Bull in
energy drinks; and Gatorade in sports drinks. In spite of all its
resources, Coca-Cola's attempts to imitate rivals' innovative
brands have either failed utterly (Mellow Yellow, Fruitopia) or
become weak followers (KMX, Power-Ade).

McDonald's is the eighth most valuable brand in the world. Its innovation in fast-delivery hamburger restaurants went a very long way. The company built the world's first and best fast-food system and network, with unique advantages in real estate, franchising and quality control. Despite all these aces, however, McDonald's did not innovate in new fast-food categories or create any other fast-food brand. The gaps were filled by new players – Kentucky Fried Chicken, Arby's, Wienerschnitzel, Baskin-Robbins, Pizza Hut, Mrs Fields, Subway and Starbucks, to name just a few. McDonald's greatest strength – its devotion to the hamburger – was also its greatest weakness when it came to continued innovation.

What is it about the industry leader that makes it so vulnerable to innovative incursion? Christensen sets out the problem in an intriguing way:

> Simply put, when the best firms succeeded, they did so because they listened responsively to their customers and invested aggressively in the technology, products, and manufacturing capabilities that satisfied their customers' next-generation needs. But, paradoxically, when the best firms subsequently failed, it was for the same reasons – they listened responsively to their customers and invested aggressively in the technology, products, and manufacturing capabilities that satisfied their customers' next-generation needs.[91]

There is a strange duality to these industrial relationships: initially, they are the reason for a firm's success, but later the reason for its failure. So something must change over time.

Let's examine these relationships over the life cycle of an industry.

At the start, the market is typically fragmented – no firm has a high share of it, technologies are underdeveloped but stable, there is little disruptive innovation, market growth is low, as are returns on capital. Networks are undeveloped – there aren't many links, strong or weak. Then something different happens. Maybe an existing firm, a new entrepreneur or an innovator is able to concentrate the market – to gain market share by buying up rivals, providing a new product or cutting costs and prices. As this innovator succeeds, the market changes shape. It grows; more customer links are added, but principally to the innovating firm. It becomes a large hub – much larger than any of its rivals – and so reaps the benefits of volume production: lower unit costs, fatter margins, higher profits.

But the new leader also suffers side-effects from being bigger. It becomes more hierarchical, more confident, more set in its ways. Strong specialised and rigid links, together with specialised and capital-intensive assets, are formed to support automated, repetitive mass production. Strong links multiply, both internally and with its key customers and suppliers, as well as with regulators, local authorities and central government. The inside of the firm becomes bigger and more important relative to the outside world; because the firm is master of its technology and its market, outside threats and opportunities appear to recede. Weak links are downgraded – certainly relative to strong links – and may fall into disrepair. The people inside the firm become more alike; the corporate culture grows stronger and more uniform. The business becomes less like the ragbag of individuals who started it, more like a well-run army.

The leader was the innovator in its industry – think of Ford, IBM, Xerox, Texas Instruments, US Steel, Deutsche Bank, Philips, Unilever, Saint Gobain, Gestetner, Encyclopaedia Britannica, Fairchild Semiconductor, Kodak, Wang Computer. But second time around, it's probably going to be a different story. The rigidities of strong links – their very success: the tight and warm relationships that are enjoyed with key customers, the efficiencies of production, the beautifully orchestrated harmony of the whole distribution system, the mastery of the existing technology, the confident conformist mindset instilled throughout the firm – ensure high profits today. But what of tomorrow? Tomorrow will be fine, and the day after . . . but then suddenly . . .

It might be disruptive technology. Or it might be another business model, a new entrepreneur with a bright idea, a fresh way of delivering better value to some or all existing customers, a refugee firm from a part of the market that seemed far away but suddenly is close, as the firm starts to invade the leader's domain from an unexpected and undefended direction.

The leader is typically in a good position to pick up the new ideas and run with them. It has the resources, the market intelligence, the distribution system, the firepower, the expertise. Yet it nearly always passes up the new idea, even when its significance is apparent to independent observers. It is hard for the leader to break or rearrange its existing strong links, to write-down its huge fixed investments in dedicated equipment, to slash its prices, to turn its back on its traditional markets and its biggest customers, or to do something new.

The innovation typically involves individuals and firms from outside the mainstream. A small hub emerges, the synthesis hub, comprising eclectic weak links between individuals, firms and new customers. Ideas and people come from the periphery, a motley crew, often with no previous experience in the industry, assembled from scratch to form the vehicle for innovation. They bring new perspectives and, even more important, are free of old ones. Consequently, everything is worked out from first principles. This means it is usually a shambles, but no matter. If the new technology or new business idea is sufficiently strong, it will win through. The vehicle will eventually become roadworthy. Sometimes the new firm will challenge the incumbent head-on. More likely, it will carve out a new market, consisting partly of the existing one and partly or mainly of new customers.

Let's assume the new market grows fast and becomes significant. The start-up attracts rivals, there is no clear leader, and market shares ebb and flow. Inevitably, though, a leader emerges – perhaps the original innovator, perhaps one of its rivals. If the market has strong economies of scale, or marked network effects, it will concentrate. Volumes grow. Specialisation increases. Relationships are cemented. Strong links form. We now have a dominant firm. A big hub. A success. Even more strong links. Just as before. The wheel has come full circle.

Then, sooner or later, it all happens again.

The cycle seems to be that firms with a greater balance of weak rather than strong links are better at innovating – Apple, for example – while those with a preponderance of strong links, such as IBM, are better at efficient production. Successful firms can fail if the world outside – the market or technology – changes. When the environment shifts, it is usually another firm – smaller and more entrepreneurial, more in tune with the outside world through its variety of weak links – which steps forward to accommodate the change. Of course, a firm does have some control over the balance and effect of its weak and strong links. These are not preordained by its maturity and success. But changing the mix of links usually means changing people – enriching the firm's gene pool – which almost always goes against a firm's deepest instincts and inclinations.

We found three organisations that understand this point.

## Boston, Massachusetts, late 1990s–early 2000s

The partners of management consultants Bain & Company knew they had a problem – not the usual sort of problem, but a problem flowing from success. One of those partners explains the firm's dilemma:

> We knew we had an intense and effective culture. We have incredible shared identity and values. Any partner will go to

the ends of the earth, quite literally if necessary, to help any other partner. But we knew we had a weakness. Yes, we knew each other and we knew our clients and we knew our clients' affairs inside out – but there was quite a lot of stuff going on in the outside world that we suspected we didn't have a handle on. So we decided to do something different. We've always had a policy of promoting from within and this has been a great strength. But not since the very early days had we hired in many senior people from the outside. We decided it was time to try this. And not just any excellent partner from another consulting firm. No, we wanted people *who were not like us*. We wanted people who had spent a long time working in industry, preferably entrepreneurs; people with a lot of external contacts that we didn't have.

Then we thought some more about it and we realised that one or two partners would get swamped if they just joined the regular practice. So we looked for people around whom we could build new units, where they could have a degree of autonomy and keep their external contacts, while not interfering with our culture or being too bothered by it. Then, gradually, we could draw the new partners fully into our way of doing things.

The first external partner we hired had most recently worked as chief executive of an industrial company; before that, he had started his own successful venture; and he was not American. He was brought in to head a new specialist unit outside our normal consulting practice. And it worked brilliantly. He brought it a lot of profitable business and the unit grew to be huge. Then we hired more and more people like him. They were all great. The fallout rate has been minimal.

It all sounded a little too good to be true, so we tracked down the first 'dissident' partner. Did everything really go as smoothly as our original interviewee described? The new partner tells a somewhat different story:

It's true that Bain has a fantastic culture and collaboration, and it's also true that it's been a great commercial success. But it was hard in the early days. You see, Bain has a policy of not consulting for competitors – if Bain works for Hertz, it can't work for Avis. Never. But my unit had different needs.

In my business, there are only a few big global clients, and they often collaborate with each other on deals. We get no confidential information about our clients; we just work on the deals. So the traditional Bain policy of not working for competitors doesn't apply. Yet many partners in Bain's traditional consulting practice were hostile when they found out that we wanted to work for 'competitors'.

It took me three years to persuade the partners to allow a multi-bidder policy. But eventually they did, and I grew to admire Bain tremendously. I think it's the best consulting firm in the world, by a mile.

Many Bain partners – probably a majority – didn't like the policy of hiring hot-shot new partners from outside. But it gave the firm a powerful network of weak links that otherwise they would have continued to lack. By now, of course, most of the 'external' partners are thoroughly dyed in the Bain wool. So the price of being externally connected is eternal hiring.

## London, England, 2009

What would you expect a global firm specialising in gathering legitimate intelligence for commercial firms to be like? A highly disciplined, homogeneous group, discreet and highly secretive, a kind of private sector FBI or MI5?

If so, you might be surprised. Greg recently talked to the senior partner of a very successful one of these 'business intelligence' firms in London, one that provides confidential and unbiased information for corporate decision-making and due diligence on deals. The first surprise was the variety of staff floating around the office: ex-spooks, as expected, but also former senior industrialists, bankers, diplomats and politicians. In addition to the forty or so permanent staff in London, there are 'a few hundred operatives' on modest retainers scattered around the globe, and another three thousand contacts who are used on a freelance basis. The partner explains:

> The money is never a key factor in getting and keeping our operatives. They are all senior people and they do it for a taste of the cut and thrust. They like to engage at a level where they can demonstrate their judgement and knowledge, and their connections. The way we gather information is to be discreet but completely open internally. All information is triangulated to build a composite picture and to avoid being misled by a few pieces of rogue data. There is no 'need to know' policy here. The only hanging offence is if someone hoards information – the bankers in particular take some time to adjust to this. It's company policy that every email communication with an operative or external contact is sent to management here as an automatic blind copy. Although few of these are read thoroughly, and many not at all, it turns all private conversations into public ones, within these walls.

It may seem a paradox that an intelligence firm believes in openness and heterogeneity, but it seems to work very well, and it fits with the idea that better information comes from weak links bridging different worlds.

At the end of the interview, the partner gives a further insight into how he and the rest of the firm's staff work:

> I'm on my way to talk to the mergers and acquisitions department of a big company. I talk for free for fifteen minutes on a

topical issue, open up the discussion, then I start my serious work. I listen very carefully. They feel I've done them a favour, but I always come away with much more information than I've given.

## New York City, 1980

Sociologist Judith Blau is studying the Bronx Children's Center, a psychiatric hospital that cares for mentally impaired children. Most similar hospitals are blighted by low staff morale and high turnover. But this hospital seems to have high morale. Judith learns that it deliberately fosters weak ties between the two hundred staff, so they all know each other on first-name terms. There are no cliques and information is shared between disciplines (such as psychology and nursing) and departments (residential units, clinical teams, arts and recreation programmes).

Judith attributes the overwhelming predominance of weak ties to two policies: project teams comprising a small number of staff from various departments are formed; and the hospital refuses to employ two or more staff who have 'a sexual or family alliance'. Although this sounds draconian, Judith says, 'In a complex structure . . . extensive weak networks can remain viable only when close ties are prohibited.' The absence of strong friendship and family ties, and departmental loyalties, weakens 'in-group solidarity', which in turns makes it possible for the entire staff to share information.[92]

The stories of Bain & Company, the intelligence and the Bronx Children's Center provide some guidance to executives of successful organisations who want to maximise weak links and minimise the dangers of strong ones. To stimulate weak links, flat structures and project teams appear to be important, as do informal opportunities for people who rarely see each other to meet and socialise; diverse hiring; rotating staff through different departments, functions and locations; semi-structured cooperation with other organisations, including exchange programmes; and encouraging employees to cultivate links with people outside the firm. Hiring superconnectors is clearly desirable, as is being in the industry's 'world capital'.

Minimising the dangers of success and strong links requires being alert to their downsides; being paranoid about upstart competition, however small; having a senior executive act as 'devil's advocate' towards your strategy, and reviewing it whenever anyone sniffs potential peril; being willing to do U-turns, or cannibalise your most profitable products by latching on to lower-cost technologies or ways of doing business as soon as these become feasible or a potential rival starts to use them; ferreting out new types of customer, and pursuing small markets, at least on an experimental basis; and bringing 'dissident' executives with a foreign mindset into the highest levels.

These remedies may sound simple, and indeed they are. But to put them into practice – against the grain of success, the requirements of volume production and a firm's culture – requires vision, determination and studied pessimism. That is why the prescriptions, although obvious, are so rarely tried.

Such is the tension of networks, the tension between strong and weak links, the resolution in favour of one, then the other. Weak links find better things to do; strong links find ways to do things better. Weak links are most adept at *creating* new value, jump-starting a new market; strong links are crafty at *capturing* and maximising value. (Value capture is distinct from value creation. For example, great scientists such as Charles Darwin and Albert Einstein created enormous value, but they didn't capture much of it. The same is true of the creators of Wikipedia. But it is emphatically not true of Bill Gates, who created a lot of value but also managed to capture a large proportion of it.)

For individuals in business and small firms, however, there is no contest between strong and weak links. Weak links are the way to innovation, and possibly to a jackpot.

And, as we move through the twenty-first century, weak links are becoming more important. There are more hubs and strong links, but even more weak links, and the latter are becoming relatively more influential. As the world shrinks, as the six or seven billion individuals on the planet connect to each other more and more, the number of permutations, the proliferation of weak links, continues to multiply. Power and wealth follow this track. A few individuals – the superconnectors, the super-innovators – are making fortunes and beginning to challenge corporations and governments, and their earlier near monopoly of power and philanthropy. Power and wealth may be concentrated, but the concentration is decentralised, split into narrow niches that often did not exist before. The identity of the winners, over a generation or more, is fragile.

The saving grace of the network world – its human face, its unpredictability, its ultimate bias in favour of individuals, even within the densest networks – is weak links, which counterbalance the reliable, ordered and sometimes oppressive domain of strong hubs and strong links. Weak links bring us into concert with unlikely bedfellows and exotic ideas. Weak links allow free will and new creations to triumph. And, as we are about to see, if weak links are not allowed to form, human life becomes nasty, brutish and short.

CHAPTER TWELVE

# POVERTY, URBAN RENEWAL AND GANGSTERS

*Can networks reduce poverty?*

The lower one's class stratum, the greater the frequency of strong links.

*Mark Granovetter*

## Gazipur, Bangladesh, 2002

Icy water, clouded grey with silt, tumbles from the Himalayas into the tributaries of the Ganges. The river widens and the water slows, in time joining the Jamuna and Meghna rivers in a great delta. The sediment settles in a rich alluvial plain, comprising a large part of the country of Bangladesh. One hundred and forty million people live here, half of them on less than a dollar a day. Toiling on small rural landholdings, two-thirds of Bangladeshis work on farms. Despite this great effort and the fertile earth, the country cannot feed itself. Bangladesh is over-populated, suffers damaging monsoons and has inadequate infrastructure and public services.

Two hours from the capital, Dhaka, at the back of a pharmacy in the town of Gazipur, past crooked shelves stacked with medicines, soaps, condoms and household sundries, sits Jamirun Nesa. She is the village superconnector. She's used a loan from the Grameen Bank to create a simple connection business that lets Gazipur reach the rest of the world, which in turn places her at a busy crossroads. Using a mobile phone purchased for something approaching the average annual income, a TV-aerial-like contraption at the top of a bamboo pole to improve reception, and a car battery for back-up electricity when the mains supply fails, she runs the village phone booth.

People line up to talk to friends and relatives, make and receive simple mobile payments, and place texts and calls that could make or break their finances for that year. Before the arrival of Jamirun's phone, farmers had no idea where the market was for their produce. They would often have to transport it to distant places without knowing the price they would be paid, or if there was a price at all. Warning of a storm would come with mercilessly little time, if any, to protect their harvest or prepare shelter. And it was hard to find out which were the best crops to grow, or what to do if a harvest was struggling or blighted. Time was wasted, and food spoiled, until the weak links radiating from the back of the pharmacy helped change it all.[93]

Jeffrey Sachs, a professor of economics at Columbia University and director of the Earth Institute, predicted in his 2005 book *The End of Poverty* that extreme privation could be ended by the year 2025.[94] Information technologies can connect us in markets and social networks, helping us to share our knowledge and cooperate to solve our problems. Jamirun needs no convincing. In 2002, she earned close to a thousand US dollars running her connection business – about three times the country's GDP per capita. But the economic benefit that distant links have brought to her region is many times greater – time saved for productive tasks, harvests sold for better prices, the introduction of high-value cash crops, less spoilage and storm damage. Jamirun's status has also risen markedly. 'Before, people in the community wouldn't talk to me, but they do now,' she says. 'I get more respect from my husband and family.' And while this vibrant little business will not last for ever, as mobile phones start to become more commonplace, Jamirun will have a new house and a chicken farm before the party's over.

## Bangladesh, 2009

Seven years on, one in three Bangladeshis owns a mobile phone. In other developing countries, penetration of phones is roughly similar. Almost none of the world's foremost telecommunications analysts saw this coming fifteen years ago, even though cellular telephony was all the rage in the developed world at the time. After all, how many phones were you going to sell when they cost half a year's wages? People in rich countries neither understood nor predicted just how compelling the economic benefits of weak links, via mobile telephony, would be for the developing world.

Bangladesh is now making major strides towards meeting its food needs.

Can the poor find their own route out of their situation, or does guidance have to come from outside? And, either way, is there really a general solution to poverty? Some conservative writers claim that the 'underclass' in rich societies has little or no chance of bettering itself without what amounts to moral reformation – kicking drug habits, embracing two-parent families, a sense of personal responsibility. In his closely reasoned and highly praised book *Wealth and Poverty*, originally published in 1981, George Gilder says:

The only dependable route from poverty is always work, family, and faith . . . the effect of marriage . . . is to increase the work effort of men by about half . . . it is manifest that the maintenance of families is the key factor in reducing poverty . . . The key to lower-class life in contemporary America is that unrelated individuals [single people] . . . are so numerous and conspicuous that they set the tone for the entire community. Their congregation in ghettos, moreover, magnifies greatly their impact on the black poor . . . The short-sighted outlook of poverty stems largely from the breakdown of family responsibilities among fathers. The lives of the poor, too often, are governed by the rhythms of tension and release that characterize the sexual experience of young single men.[95]

Liberal commentators, on the other hand, blame society or the welfare system for locking the poor into a life without hope. Back in the 1970s, sociologist Carol Stack did pioneering fieldwork in one of the poorest communities in the US Midwest, spending most of her time with the residents in their homes and on their streets. She concluded that the ascent from poverty was virtually impossible: '[Mere] reform of existing [welfare] programs', she wrote, 'can never be expected to eliminate an impoverished class in America. The effect of such programs is that they maintain the existence of . . . a sizable but docile impoverished class.'[96]

Poverty, it seems, has too many explanations and too many causes, but too few solutions. This is an endless, inconclusive and depressing debate. Gilder and Stack seem to agree on only one thing: poverty will remain intractable. 'There will be poverty in America for centuries to come,' Gilder states flatly.[97]

But is it possible that the network perspective of strong links, weak links and hubs can help identify a solution to poverty in both the West and the developing world?

## Boston, Massachusetts, 1950s

Two Boston working-class community groups – the North
End and the West End – are under threat of 'urban renewal'.
The North Enders successfully campaign against the development plans and defeat them, keeping their homes. Across the
city, the West End plan is particularly offensive – the compul-
sory purchase of 7000 people's homes in order to build 2400
luxury apartments which will sell at prices way beyond the
budgets of current West Enders. More noxious still, and a
powder-keg in the hands of a journalist, the developer has links
with the mayor, who stands to profit at the expense of the
evicted community.

Surely such unfair proposals will be defeated? Yet the protests
of the West Enders are totally ineffective. In 1958, the City takes
title to the land and the stunned West Enders, still not believing
their fate, start to move out.

Why did this happen? Herbert J. Gans wrote a sympathetic
account of the West Enders' failure in which he explained that
a protest committee was set up, but

> The Committee received little overt support from the rest of
> the West Enders, and its opposition did not significantly inter-
> rupt the city's planning . . . West Enders, who knew much less
> about the process, and could not call city officials to get the
> facts, [believed that the City would not proceed with the
> plans] . . . the West Enders [were unable] to organise in their
> own behalf . . . The leaders were also hampered by lack of
> information . . . Nor did the West End have other attributes
> of power such as those displayed by the neighboring North
> End, which had successfully repulsed efforts towards its own
> redevelopment. This area . . . had a much larger business com-
> munity – some of it politically influential.[98]

The West Enders lacked information and support; by contrast, the North Enders had information and links to middle-class business supporters, a few of whom lived or worked in the North End. The West Enders' network was internally focused; they had very few weak links to more knowledgeable and influential people outside the community. The North Enders' network was varied and effective.

Mark Granovetter says: 'The lower one's class stratum, the greater the frequency of strong ties.'[99] That is, the poorer people are, and the more insecure they feel, the more likely they are to seek the protection of strong ties to family, neighbours and powerful employers. A study in Philadelphia confirms this picture – people who are young, poorly educated or black rely much more on strong rather than weak ties than the rest of the community.[100] When disgruntled working-class youths want to break away, they may find it difficult to escape the boundaries of their own community. Lacking weak links to better worlds of opportunity, they sometimes fall into the gang culture (or fundamentalist cults) on their doorstep, which may be the 'best offer' for social and economic gratification available within their bounded world.

In his 2008 book *Gang Leader for a Day*, sociologist Sudhir Venkatesh tells a fascinating story about crack dealers in Chicago at the height of the crack boom in the 1990s and early 2000s.[101] His intrepid research revealed that most of the crack dealers lived in the neighbourhoods where they grew up, and many still lived at home with their mums.

Venkatesh relates how one of the gang deputy leaders, T-Bone, arranged to meet him surreptitiously and turned over notebooks recording the gang's revenues and expenses for the last four years:

Perhaps the most surprising thing in T-Bone's ledgers was the incredibly low wage paid to the young members who did the dirtiest and most dangerous work: selling drugs on the street. According to T-Bone's records, they barely earned minimum wage . . . Now I knew why some of the younger . . . [gang] members supplemented their income by working legit jobs at McDonald's or a car wash.[102]

The foot soldiers' average pay was only $3.30 an hour. Why would anyone want to work for wages like that, enduring terrible working conditions – standing around on the street dealing with crazy addicts, risking imprisonment, and having a one-in-four chance of being shot dead? One reason was their inability to escape from the area. 'It's a war out here,' one dealer told Venkatesh. 'I mean, every day people struggling to survive, so you know, we just do what we can. We ain't got no choice, and if that means getting killed, well shit, it's what niggers do around here to feed their family.'[103]

Mark Granovetter implies that dependence on strong ties is a trap. His research shows that people who found jobs through strong ties had longer periods of unemployment than those whose jobs came through weak ties: 'The heavy concentration of social energy in strong ties fragments communities of the poor into encapsulated units with poor connections between these units . . . one more reason why poverty is self-perpetuating.'[104]

## The Flats, Jackson Harbor, Midwest USA, 1970s

Carol Stack's research shows how the poor naturally become reliant on strong ties, to the exclusion of any other relationships. In the 1970s, she studied the people of a poor Midwest ghetto she disguised as 'The Flats' in 'Jackson Harbor' – the real city is on a major rail line connecting Chicago with the Deep South. She worked much as an anthropologist would: spending most of her waking hours there and befriending the inhabitants, especially the women.

The residents, she says, fall back on a circle of friends and kin-folk in order to survive. They expand their actual circle of relatives by, for example, taking in their children's father's kin as members of their family, thereby extending the group who are obliged to look after each other. Whatever they have – food, stamps, a television, a hat, milk, grits, a cigarette here, a nickel there – is shared within the group. Welfare benefits barely pro-vide enough for shelter and food, and any wages or windfalls are also made available to the kin group, according to need.

Although such strong ties help the poor cope day to day, we can also see from Stack's account that reliance on strong ties blocks two possible escape routes from poverty. One is to marry and move out of the community, in the hope of gaining a job elsewhere and so beginning the slow ascent from poverty as a nuclear family, free of community responsibilities. But the com-munity resists such a move:

> Marriage and its accompanying expectations of a home, a job, and a family built around the husband and wife have come to stand for an individual's desire to break out of poverty. It implies the willingness of an individual to remove himself from the daily obligations of his kin network . . . one cannot simultaneously meet kin expectations and the expectations of a spouse.[105]

Stark recounts the case of Ruby Banks who said:

> If I ever marry, I ain't listening to what nobody say. I just listen to what he say. You have to get along the best way you know how, and forget about your people. If I got married they would talk, like they are doing now, saying 'He ain't no good, he's been creeping on you. I told you once not to marry him. You'll end up right back on ADC [welfare].' If I ever get mar-ried, I'm leaving town![106]

The other route out of poverty is to save or receive an inheritance and buy a house or some other marketable property. Saving is conspicuous by its absence in Stack's account; it appears unthinkable to her interviewees, since they have no surplus to save. She recounts a telling story about Magnolia and Calvin Waters. Magnolia's uncle in Mississippi died and left them $1500 (equivalent to about $20,000 today). It was the first savings they'd ever had, and they planned to use the money as a deposit to buy a home. But their kin in the community had other ideas. Three days after Magnolia and Calvin had received the cheque, word spread. One niece borrowed twenty-five dollars from Magnolia to avoid getting her phone cut off. Another uncle in the South became seriously ill, and Magnolia bought round-trip tickets for herself and a sister to visit him. Then an elderly 'father' in the community died and nobody else could pay for a grave. Then another 'sister' needed two months' rent to avoid being evicted. Winter was cold and Magnolia bought the whole family decent coats and shoes. To make matters worse, the welfare officer cut off payments to Magnolia's family.

'Within a month and a half,' Stack reports, 'all of the money was gone. The money was channeled into the hands of the same individuals who ordinarily participate in daily domestic exchanges, but the premiums were temporarily higher. All of the money was quickly spent for necessary, compelling reasons.'[107]


## Harlem, New York City, 1932

We may contrast the devastating effects of relying solely on strong ties with a solution tried at a time of even greater economic deprivation, the Great Depression. In 1932, a charismatic black preacher calling himself Father Divine (his real name was George Baker) moved to Harlem. He inspired thousands of followers to start a small business or at least work in one. There were hundreds of ventures in Father Divine's network, funded by him with money from his adherents – cheap hotels and boarding houses (he became Harlem's biggest landlord), budget restaurants and clothes shops, grocery stores, dry cleaners, a coal delivery business shuttling between Pennsylvania and New York, and mobile vendors of fruit, vegetables and fish.

People who needed work were sent by Father Divine to one of his ventures. His people also set up employment agencies placing black nannies and cooks – 'angels' – with white families, and ran kitchens providing free meals to near-starving blacks. Faithful Mary, one of the Divine's lieutenants, ran a kitchen in Newark that fed 96,000 hungry people in one year alone. In the 1940s and early 1950s, Divine's empire diversified into building and decorating firms, furriers, tailors, photographic studios and garages.

Father Divine was an odd figure – part cult guru, part community leader, part entrepreneur, and part sexual adventurer and conman. Yet he gave economic independence to thousands and a job and self-respect to many more. Anyone could become a follower or entrepreneur, and ventures were founded and run through a large variety of weak links, including volunteers and paid workers, politicians and journalists, cutting across several communities – New York, Baltimore, Bridgeport, Newark, Jersey City and Philadelphia. Most importantly, Divine was able to get capital from donors and later financiers, black and white – his micro-ventures made money and he had assets he could pledge as security.

## Jobra, near Chittagong, Bangladesh, 1976

The link to capital providers outside the poor community is also a key plank of one of the most successful recent initiatives against poverty. In 1976, the head of economics at Chittagong

University, Dr Muhammad Yunus, began wandering around nearby villages, observing poverty and the efforts of poor people to surmount it. Whereas Carol Stack was a professional sociologist exploring how society was oppressing the poor, which she found in the iniquities of the welfare system, Yunus was a banker and economist, looking for solutions to poverty, for hopeful signs of entrepreneurial behaviour among the poor themselves. He found them in the village of Jobra, where forty or fifty women were making furniture from bamboo. They should have been making a substantial profit on the chairs they made, but nearly all of it was disappearing in the high rates of interest they paid to money-lenders for the cash they needed to buy the bamboo. Yunus calculated that they were paying between 50 and 100 per cent interest per annum. What, he wondered, would happen if the women could ply their trade while paying a reasonable rate of interest?

He took the equivalent of twenty-seven dollars of his own cash and loaned it to forty-two village women. He returned a few weeks later to find them jubilant. They had made a new batch of furniture. After repaying him, they'd made a profit of eighty-eight cents, many times what they had ever made before. Yunus, touched by the difference his small loan had made, pondered whether his actions could be repeated on a larger scale.

With backing from the state bank, he tried to find out. He grouped his micro-entrepreneurs into 'solidarity groups', generally women from the same village but different families, who took individual and collective responsibility for the debt. Consequently, bad debts were rare. By 1982, the bank was making loans to 28,000 villagers – 95 per cent of whom were women.

In 1983, Yunus turned his project into a proper micro-lending institution, the Grameen Bank. By 2007, it had touched the lives of more than seven million poor entrepreneurs. The bank has also developed a series of other entrepreneurial ventures, including fisheries, software and phone companies, bringing cell phones to more than a quarter of a million poor villagers through loans to people like Jamirun Nesa.

The networks formed by Muhammad Yunus comprised a few strong ties, many weak ones, and a new series of hubs – the village solidarity groups, the bank and its spin-off ventures.

Yunus is an altogether more reputable and admirable character than Father Divine – he received the Nobel Peace Prize in 2006 – but there are still strong similarities between what the two men did, cutting across generations and half the globe, to rescue the poorest of the poor. Both solutions were community based, reaching well beyond families, using a series of weak ties within the locality and beyond, especially to capital providers. In both cases, poor people formed micro-ventures; and their profits lifted many of them out of poverty altogether.

It's also telling that only a slight stimulus was needed to release the entrepreneurial abilities of mainly uneducated, wretched people. Could the bootstrapping micro-business – primed by cheap and available money, guaranteed by joint responsibility of the poor – be a more cost-effective solution to poverty than top-down education and infrastructure projects?

Pioneering research by Hernando de Soto, a Peruvian social reformer, supports the enterprise thesis.[108] He reminds us that widespread prosperity did not come to Western countries until there was access to property, and therefore capital, for most of the population. To break out of poverty, the poor need to claim undisputed ownership of a substantial asset, usually their home. This process takes time – most of the Americans who 'went west' during the nineteenth century started out as squatters, but once they eventually acquired undisputed ownership, their homes fulfilled a double role: as somewhere to live; and as 'capital', collateral for a loan that would enable them to start a business.

De Soto says that the world's poor people collectively own trillions of dollars of assets – the value of all those shacks in

shanty-towns adds up. But they generally lack proper legal title
to those assets; they are excluded from the magical world of capital, where assets can fulfil a dual function.

In America and other Western countries, legal property title
turned some poor and often undirected people into motivated
individuals. They now had a chance to generate surplus value
from what they owned:

> People no longer needed to rely on neighbourhood relation-
> ships . . . the lack of legal property thus explains why citizens
> in developing and former communist nations cannot make
> profitable contracts with strangers, cannot get credit, insurance
> or utility services: they have nothing to lose . . . trapped in the
> grubby basement of the pre-capitalist world . . .
>
> A legal structure that prevents enterprising people from
> negotiating with strangers defeats the division of labour and
> fastens would-be entrepreneurs to small circles . . . and low
> productivity . . . like computer networks, which had existed
> for years before anyone thought to link them, property sys-
> tems become tremendously powerful only when . . .
> interconnected in a larger network.[109]

In network language, poor people are excluded from forming
weak links with strangers or casual acquaintances that could help
them make money. The economy from which the poor are
excluded is an intricate web of weak links that arise spontaneously and easily when enterprise is established. This can
happen only when people own property or other capital, and
can rely upon a framework of law to make their assets work for
them. Without such links, people are utterly dependent on
strong links – friends, family and the immediate community.
Without proper legal title to assets, such commercial transactions
as there are must take place within the poor community, and
even then they can be enforced only by goodwill or violence.

If poverty is to be escaped, the networks of the poor must be enlarged through the injection of a few weak links that connect to capital and enterprise.

Provided there are links outside a community, it also seems that the common identity afforded by a struggling group can be a great help. Examples include Dr Yunus's village-solidarity groups, black communities in the north-eastern USA, and previously poor or oppressed groups – the *Mayflower* pilgrims; later waves of immigrants to the United States, including Irish, Italians, Russians, Poles, Ukrainians and Hispanics; and Scottish and Jewish communities throughout the world. Most helping hands came from within the community but *outside* immediate circles of family and close friends. For instance, most Irish or Italian families landing at Ellis Island in the late nineteenth and early twentieth centuries were met on the quayside by compatriots who were weak links – friends of friends, more tenuous family or occupational acquaintances, even strangers wanting to do a good turn (or make a quick buck renting a room or hiring cheap labour).

Community, then, appears to be most valuable where common identity coexists with a large and scattered group that has links to other worlds or to the mainstream. We may see, for example, the Irish community in Boston or New York as a bridge for Irish immigrants fresh off the boat to the wider American society. What is the celebrated American 'melting pot' – really a succession of melting pots for each ethnic group – but a series of weak links writ large?

What of the widely mooted idea, then, that poor communities may be a curse – that escaping from poverty may require escaping from the community itself? George Gilder cites the negative effect of single young men setting the tone in many ghettos. Carol Stack shows how 'the sisterhood' in the Flats discouraged the only possible escapes from poverty – marriage, leaving the community or buying property. Sudhir Venkatesh recounts how the Robert Taylor Homes project on Chicago's South Side – both a series of dismal and dispiriting high-rise buildings and a genuine, if largely extra-legal, community – was eventually razed to the ground by President Clinton, scattering the Black Kings drug gang and ending much of the associated extortion and money-laundering.

Malcolm Gladwell says:

> When we're faced with an eighteen-year-old high-school dropout whose only career option is making $5.50 an hour in front of the deep fryer at Burger King, we usually talk about the importance of rebuilding inner-city communities, attracting new jobs to depressed areas, and re-investing in neglected neighborhoods. We want to give that kid the option of another, better-paying, job right down the street. But does that really solve his problem? Surely what that eighteen-year-old really needs is not another marginal inducement to stay in his neighborhood but a way to get out of it altogether. He needs a school system that provides him the skills to compete for jobs with middle-class kids. He needs a mass-transit system to take him to the suburbs, where the real employment opportunities are. And, most of all, he needs to know someone who knows someone who knows where all those good jobs are.[100]

Economists talk about 'failed cities'. They're easy to identify – houses are dirt cheap. In thriving cities, the cost of a house comes more from the cost of the land than the building. But in downtown Detroit, for example, the land appears to have zero or even negative value – the average price of a house is $60,000, but its building costs alone are at least $80,000, meaning that the land is worth *minus* $20,000. You can see the evidence by visiting the Masonic Temple in central Detroit. It's surrounded by acre upon

acre of abandoned land and buildings. Nobody can build anything there and sell it for the cost of building.[111]

It's the same sad story in St Louis or New Orleans – old housing stock, low prices, and people attracted to the city, if at all,
only by the low price of housing. Generally such people are
retired or have few skills. The absence of lively networks within
the city diminishes opportunity and leads to a vicious circle –
skilled or ambitious people leave; there are fewer newcomers and
they have less to offer.

After Hurricane Katrina in 2005, the federal government allocated two hundred billion dollars to rebuild New Orleans.
Economists reckoned it was money down the drain – rebuilding
a trap, baiting the hurricane victims to return to poverty. Far
better, they said, to spend the money on grants to the people
rather than the place, so they could improve their lives, in New
Orleans or elsewhere. One writer calculated that each family of
four could have been given eight hundred thousand dollars that
way!

But the economists ignore the unfortunate network effects
that would probably have kicked in had their approach been
adopted. Given a pile of cash, New Orleans residents who were
the most enterprising, or had links beyond the local community,
might well have left town in large numbers. And once residents
who stayed in New Orleans had spent the cash, the problem of
isolation and lack of skills or links to any viable economic network would have been even worse. The examples of Father
Divine and Muhammad Yunus and the theories of Hernando do
Soto suggest that there might be a better solution, based on stim-
ulating a large number of tiny enterprises – primed by outside
capital, but using the complementary skills of the community to
make profits and build fresh capital.

Jane Jacobs discusses other important community issues in *The
Death and Life of Great American Cities*.[112] She was the first person
to claim that, while successful neighbourhoods protect us from

crime by facilitating 'eyes on the street', tower blocks, especially in poor communities, cannot fulfil this role. Tall buildings take people away from the street. As we've seen, Jacobs was also the first to claim that cultural diversity makes cities more productive and innovative through cross-pollination – ideas leap from firm to firm and from industry to industry, and sometimes even create new industries, when there are many different types of commerce in the same place. She also says that thriving cities and neighbourhoods require a *mixture* of different activities on top of each other – residences *and* businesses *and* places to shop and relax: restaurants, cafés, green spaces, markets, all cheek by jowl. Economists have since validated these theories.[113]

The real problem, then, may not lie so much with poor communities per se, or even with the reliance on friends and family within those communities, but rather with people's *exclusive* or nearly exclusive reliance on the community and its strong ties. The problem occurs when poor communities are monolithic, isolated from broader society and especially from capital providers.

The antidote, perhaps, is the addition of bridging weak ties, of diversity, of links beyond the shanty town, the ghetto or the isolated rural village.

Three economists – Ed Glaeser, David Cutler and Jacob Vigdor – conducted careful research and proved that ghettos do indeed stop poor people getting jobs or doing well in school. But they also found that certain players do well out of ghettos, and not just the drug dealers. The main winners are those who build bridges between the ghetto and the outside world – what we would call superconnectors. These people live *near* the ghetto, belong to the same ethnic group, and are typically entrepreneurs, often selling into the ghetto and providing jobs outside it to the inhabitants. The number of ethnic superconnectors is growing quite fast, but only expanding cities – Austin, Phoenix, Los Angeles – have seen burgeoning weak links between the poor and mainstream communities. Once again, Detroit and New Orleans have missed out, not because of anything specific in the poor areas, but because there is little to connect to locally, no dynamic economy, no new jobs.[114]

So what can be done? Plainly, new ventures near poor areas are crucial – but these are developing naturally anyway, and it is hard to stimulate them in any other way. Better transport systems linking poor and rich areas are also important, and eminently feasible when there is money for infrastructure projects. But often the poor areas, lacking political clout and campaigning skill, lose out. In Johannesburg, for example, one of the most divided and dangerous places on earth, there is very little public transport. Now huge funds are being spent on a swish new local train service – but it will link the airport with the rich suburbs and business areas, bypassing the nearby black settlements.

However, some diverse worlds have been linked in ways that enhance economic wellbeing. Take the recent enlargement of the European Union, which has allowed millions of people from Eastern Europe to settle in richer North and West European areas, especially Britain and Scandinavia. While mass immigration is always controversial, particularly in times of high or rising unemployment, no other phenomenon generates such an increase in diverse weak and strong links. Economists also say that immigration boosts host-nation economic performance.

Sometimes all it takes is one or two individuals, armed with a powerful conviction and a commitment to spreading it, to generate a large number of links and lift millions out of poverty. Such was the case when Americans Joseph Juran, an electrical engineer, and W. Edwards Deming, a statistician, moved to Japan in the early 1950s. In 1951, Juran, who had been born in Romania, published the first edition of his *Quality Control Handbook*, the Bible of the nascent quality-improvement movement. Few Americans were very interested in Juran's ideas, so when a lecture tour in Japan sparked a wave of interest there, he moved and began to consult with Japanese firms. At the time, Japanese industry was notorious for churning out cheap, shoddy imitations of Western products. By the 1970s, leading Japanese consumer electronics firms such as Sharp, Canon and Hitachi were producing higher-quality goods than their US and European rivals. Only then did Western industry begin to take an interest in ideas that had originated in America decades before.

Many of the most cost-effective philanthropic initiatives use well-off volunteers to educate poor people, forming links between rich and poor hubs. In South Africa, a company in which I'm a director encourages its employees to help local schools by donating computers and showing the kids how to use them. In London, 'Debate Mate' sends successful university debaters into schools in poor areas, where they help set up debating clubs. According to astonished teachers, debating engages and encourages previously unmotivated pupils in ways they never thought possible.

There are no easy ways to tackle poverty, but one direction seems clear – facilitate and multiply the weak links, especially financial and commercial, that can improve the networks of poor people.

Poverty displays similar characteristics all around the world – in Harlem and New Orleans, in Peru and rural Bangladesh, in Paris and London, in Johannesburg and Detroit. Moreover, the effects of poverty were much the same in the pre-industrial world, in early America and in the Great Depression as they are today. And they are similar in inner cities, remote villages, ghettos and shanty towns. Being poor is about being confined to limited enclaves, unable to break free, unable to climb up to even the lowest level of property and capital formation. Poverty is about the absence of varied networks, of connections to people who are economically and socially active.

It therefore seems likely that poverty could be reduced, and perhaps eventually eliminated, by connecting poor people to mainstream communities, by facilitating weak links to people with money. So we must identify and remove the barriers to the spontaneous and rich flowering of weak links. Given a fair chance, the poor themselves will do the rest.

## CHAPTER THIRTEEN

# A NETWORK SOCIETY

*Networks, past, present and future*

The network is the least structured organisation
that can be said to have any structure at all.
*Kevin Kelly[115]*

## Berlin, Germany, 1932–45

Around 1930, Germany was a highly decentralised and sophisticated society, with many centres of power and influence. Its regions and cities had strong local authority, a legacy of its formation only sixty years earlier out of many smaller states. It also had trade unions, an army that jealously guarded its independence from the state, Catholic and Protestant churches and schools, local and big business, a wide array of regional and national political parties, a large number of ancient and independent universities, and numerous cultural and civil institutions. After Italy, China and Japan, no country in the world had such a rich cultural heritage. After the United States, no country had such widespread and effective industry and technology. Possibly no country on the planet had such a profusion and variety of hubs and weak links.

In the 1932 elections, Adolf Hitler's National Socialist (Nazi)

Party won more seats than any other party, although it was still well short of an absolute majority. However, through a deal with the German National People's Party (the 'Nationalists'), the Nazis gained a slim working majority and Hitler became Chancellor in January 1933. Having come to power constitutionally, he proceeded to abolish civil rights and the constitution. Six months after taking office, he declared a one-party state. In January 1934, local government was abolished and all power centralised. In June 1934, Hitler ended the competition between his two paramilitary forces, the SA and the SS, by killing the leaders of the former, disbanding it and consolidating all power in the brutal hands of the SS.

By doing all this, Hitler greatly simplified the network map of Germany. He closed a huge number of the country's social and political hubs and weak links, and reduced the country to one centre of power and propaganda. By the late 1930s, gone from German society were the communists, socialists, anarchists, social democrats, conservatives, nationalists, Catholics and all other non-Nazi politicians. Gone were the trade unions. Gone were independent mayors and regional parliaments. Gone were independent intellectuals, certainly every Jewish one, including such luminaries as Albert Einstein. Gone were the scientists who were to give America, rather than Germany (or the Soviet Union), the first atomic bomb. Gone, to concentration camps, were millions of Jews, socialists, anarchists, communists, Freemasons, Jehovah's Witnesses, gays, gypsies and anyone who dared criticise the regime. Gone was intellectual, political or social debate. And if, to the outside observer, the churches, army and big business operated largely as before, the tacit bargain was their acceptance of Nazi tyranny.

All governments that aspire to total control shut down free networks. Many hubs are rubbed out or consolidated into state-controlled mega-hubs. Spontaneous weak links are discouraged or crushed. Stalin, Mao Zedong and Pol Pot all did the same.

Dictators multiply the number of degrees of separation between citizens, isolating them from random contact and corralling them into just a few institutions that are either part of the state apparatus or approved by it.

Now, imagine that God is standing at the beginning of time, trying to decide how to organise human society. One way would be to impose a heavy, rigid structure on the population: a monolithic, hierarchical, centralised society; at the extreme, a slave or military society. The great advantage of this society, from God's point of view, would be that it requires only a few people – possibly just one person – to be smart enough to direct everyone else. In a world where humans are battling with nature to survive, where wealth and education are limited, the highly structured society has clear practical appeal.

At the other extreme, imagine that God is a social scientist, experimenting with a completely 'flat', decentralised society, where there are no structures to tell people what to do. He might well wonder: 'How is anything going to work without structure when everyone is the equal of everyone else?'

Then God has a brainwave, perhaps inspired by reading a book on political freedom written far in the future, and proceeds to invent networks. Because God, in this scenario, is a Trinitarian, networks are composed of three constituent elements – strong links, weak links and hubs. And society is not completely unstructured, because networks do have some sort of structure, but since God has been converted to the cause of democracy by reading Thomas Paine, he decides that the networks must be spontaneously generated by the people themselves, rather than imposed on them by, well, God or other humans. God also understands that network hubs can exert gravity on their members, causing them to stay longer than they should or to revert to primitive deference to authority. To minimise these potentially harmful effects, God writes a line of computer code automatically blowing up all hubs after they have been in existence for fifteen years. The best-placed competing hub then takes over for its maximum of fifteen years of fame.

For this decentralised, relatively unstructured society to work, everyone must be able to earn a decent living based on their own skills and initiative. So God invents markets, education and rock music, to endow everyone in society with, respectively, wealth, knowledge and attitude. And God reckons the result is not too bad.

Would you expect a less structured society to be more or less connected than a highly structured one? Common sense might suggest that the less structured society would be less connected. One might expect there to be a price to pay, in terms of absence of connections, for the benefit of autonomy for individuals. But the surprise of the network society, as we have seen, is that the less structured a country or the world becomes, the *more connected* it becomes. Most people would prefer autonomy to slavery; and most would prefer to live in a united rather than a divided world.

Hitler proved that a move away from network society produces more structure, but less connection. This was not a peculiarity of the Third Reich – greater hierarchy *always* produces greater isolation. That is why totalitarian regimes strive to manufacture, through propaganda, a sense of identity between citizens who are cut off from one another by their society's structures.

Imagine standing still and in formation with hundreds of thousands of fellow-devotees, all wearing the same smart uniform, in a huge stadium, cheering an inspirational speech by The Leader. You appear to be connected, but you cannot talk to your neighbour or step out of line. You are being choreographed. The connection is impersonal, synthetic and ultimately fraudulent. No new information is exchanged as a result of such 'contact', because there is absolutely no authentic or spontaneous communication.

The delight of network society – relative to a highly structured, hierarchical society – is that it offers the best of both: greater autonomy *and* greater connection. This happy outcome is entirely due to the superconnectors, the hubs and people that connect diverse groups and individuals. Without superconnectors, network society would not be so attractive, and might not work at all. Viewed this way, the rewards that pass to superconnectors seem entirely reasonable. We may think of Nelson Mandela, who more than anyone else was responsible for breaking down the highly structured, hierarchical, oppressive apartheid regime and replacing it with an open, liberal, democratic society. After he became the first black president of South Africa in 1994, Mandela went out of his way to bring together black and white South Africans. One seminal moment was when the Springboks – the South African rugby team, associated with white machismo and hated by many blacks – won a thrilling final in the 1995 World Cup, beating the favourites New Zealand. Mandela presented the trophy to the Springbok captain, Afrikaner Francois Pienaar, wearing a shirt with Pienaar's number 6 on the back, and grinning so widely that he might have been the team's sponsor.

Now we can ask the question: if the two extremes of society are highly structured and poorly connected, on the one hand, and loosely structured and well connected, on the other, is there any trend in history from one type of society to the other or is there just a random interplay between them?

One way of answering this question is to look at the history of human connection. The facilitating mechanisms were language, the alphabet and writing, and eventually printed books; stories, myths, music and architecture; and perhaps the most important single device for communication with strangers throughout human history, the city, which attracted people from the countryside, strange lands and eventually anywhere else in the world. For several thousand years, cities were the most important hubs in facilitating human connection, as well as the most fertile incubators of weak links. Civilisation and communication were, and still are, largely urban phenomena. Cities have grown ever larger, and, as we've seen, a greater proportion of people now live in them than at any time in human history.

Also, in the last six centuries, other communication devices have proliferated. Humanity has become sewn together by connecting technologies which are constantly being invented and reinvented, becoming ever more widespread and influential. In Chapter Six, we saw the massive psychological and practical impact of the printing press, invented around 1450 – how private reading, printed books and popular journals triggered an explosion of learning, which circulated ideas ever faster, connecting individuals to useful knowledge; and stimulated trade, industry and further inventions; and allowed people to think for themselves and plan for a future where they could do more than simply take orders from superiors.

In 1492, Christopher Columbus reached the Caribbean. Less than a hundred years later, other explorers had circumnavigated the earth, shrinking the world into one single place. The eighteenth century saw the extension of road and canal networks; the nineteenth, railways, the penny post, the telegraph, steamships and the motor-car. Then came aircraft, telephones, radio, television, computers, microchips, high-speed trains, cheap international travel, fax machines, overnight courier delivery across and even between continents, connected computer systems, mobile phones, videoconferencing, fibre-optic cables, the Internet, and Internet-based communication applications and services – all of them network phenomena, all connecting more and more people, in more and more ways, to increasingly high-quality standards at ever-lower cost. These technologies have progressively linked remote people, reduced distance barriers and immeasurably boosted trade, making the world smaller, richer and less divided.

Over time, and despite long setbacks such as the Dark Ages and the rise of totalitarian states, society has increasingly resembled a network more than a hierarchy, and this seems to have gone hand-in-hand with innovation. Does innovation lead to network society, or network society lead to innovation? It is probably a two-way process, which would account for the exponential increase in networks and innovation. For instance, there would be much less use for a network if there were no innovation – less need to communicate, less chance to profit through trade. In just the same way, an innovation without a network becomes an isolated secret that has no chance of improving the world. Take the case of the steam engine. Industrialisation was triggered above all by its invention, with engines used for the first time in eighteenth-century England to power cotton mills and other factories, and later railways, ships and motor-cars. But historians of technology have puzzled over the fact that the Romans invented steam-driven mechanical action almost two thousand years earlier. They also had gears that could have been used in clocks, knew about leverage and stress, and built very impressive buildings, sewer systems and aqueducts. So why didn't steam transform the world much earlier? Simply because Roman steam wasn't supported by a free network.

As the Roman orator Seneca (54 BC–AD 39) pointed out, most inventions were the work of slaves, many of whom were Greeks or had received a Greek education.[116] Now slaves, of course, could not network freely – their communications were generally constrained to dealings with their masters and their families. Slaves – and therefore inventors – could not network widely with other slaves, or with free men who might bankroll the commercial exploitation of their inventions.

Hierarchical and closed societies are probably much less prone to innovation than network societies; and innovation is likely to be greatest when, as today, there are global networks of ideas and enterprise.

The shift from hierarchies to networks in the past forty or fifty years is also apparent in the world of enterprise. To his enormous credit, possibly the first person to spot the trend was the Canadian philosopher and educator Marshall McLuhan. In 1962, he wrote:

> In our electronic age the specialist and pyramidal forms of structure, which achieved vogue in the sixteenth century and later, are not any longer practical . . . pyramidal organizational structures, with many layers of supervision, and with functions divided by specialty, simply did not work [any more]. The communication chain between top scientific or engineering leadership and work centers was too long for either the scientific or managerial message to be communicated . . . [Industry needs] groups of researchers with different competences . . . cutting across organizational lines.[117]

Indeed so. Since around 1970, firms around the world have been giving up hierarchies and adopting network structures, because they work better, both inside and outside the firms.

Internally, mass production is giving way to flexible production. The nineteenth-century notion of 'scientific management' through a hierarchy that minutely controls what each worker does, leading to extreme worker specialisation and job demarcation, is inappropriate now that customer needs change rapidly, workers are more educated, and technology can be used to inform workers and allow them a much greater degree of autonomy. The assembly line is being complemented and often replaced by the network, where workers are organised into small teams that connect with other small teams and often directly with customers, cutting out swathes of supervisory 'middle management'.

Businesses are increasingly setting up 'project teams' – comprising staff from different functions or locations – to deal with new initiatives or improve performance. Each team operates as a network connected to its various members' parts of the firm. When the team is disbanded, and the members return to their normal jobs, they retain a new network of personal contacts, which is helpful to their own careers and to the firm.

Firms are also increasingly focusing on their 'core competencies', a rather grand piece of jargon meaning 'what they do best'. This typically leads firms to give up activities in which they are merely competent (or incompetent), clearing the way for specialists – often small or medium-size firms – to take charge of particular products or activities (for example, cleaning, security, catering, or the supply of raw materials and components).

Vertical integration – where, for example, an oil firm might explore for oil, produce it in a refinery, market it to customers, and have its own petrol stations – is being reduced, so that each stage of the 'value chain' (exploration, production, marketing, retailing) is handled by a specialist firm. The coordination between stages is no longer hierarchical, but based on a network of cooperating firms. Firms are becoming increasingly 'virtual'. For instance, British Airways does not own all of its planes; and it is perfectly possible that the pilots and cabin crew, although wearing British Airways livery, might in fact be employed by another firm, leaving BA to focus on its brand management and customer relations. Similarly, cleaning and the provision of food might be undertaken by third parties. Through this outsourcing of everything except the 'core competencies', networks are substituting for hierarchies.

Licensing, subcontracting, outsourcing, the sale of 'non-core' divisions, and the increasing trend of breaking up conglomerates or dividing large firms into two or three new companies result in the average size of firms decreasing. Structures naturally become flatter internally; and external links are also increased. Flexible networks replace rigid hierarchies. In Silicon Valley, for example, engineers typically change firms every two years. Their employers are much less important than the personal connections they have with other individuals – head hunters, venture capitalists, suppliers, subcontractors, ex-colleagues and all kinds of acquaintances. The boundaries between firms become increasingly porous, penetrated by numerous networks. As two writers from the Boston Consulting Group comment:

> Individual firms come and go – temporary alliances of people pursuing specific, narrowly defined projects. The more permanent reality is the fluid business 'ecosystem' within which those firms compete. In some ways, Silicon Valley performs as a large, decentralized corporation. The Valley, not its constituent firms, owns the labor pool. The Valley, through its venture capital community, starts projects, terminates them, and allocates capital among them. The Valley, not its constituent firms, is the real locus of core competencies.[118]

Another way of looking at Silicon Valley is to recognise that individual executives are gaining power and wealth – personal networks drive the system more than corporate hierarchies.

Though the Valley is in some ways unique – a leading indicator, perhaps, of what is going to happen throughout Anglo-Saxon business – cultural expressions of network power are evident everywhere. In Valencia, Spain, networks of independent firms cooperate to produce footwear, textiles and toys. Benetton sources knitwear from small firms and home producers in Italy, Turkey and other Mediterranean countries, then sells it through a network of five thousand franchisee stores throughout the world.

In Hong Kong, exports of manufactured goods, which mushroomed from the late 1950s, came predominantly from small family firms in China: 'networks of production and distribution formed, disappeared, and reformed on the basis of variations in the world market'.[119] Most Japanese firms are organised into networks with overlapping ownership, the most popular form being *keiretsu* – vertical networks – centred on a large firm such as Hitachi, Matsushita or Toyota and embracing hundreds or thousands of small suppliers. Korean networks of firms – *chaebol* – are typically owned and controlled by a powerful individual or family. In China, most business is conducted through a fluid kaleidoscope of family firms, a decentralised and fast-changing network usually involving substantial subcontracting, often connected to the personal networks of senior army or Communist Party officials. And, of course, many firms in developing countries are parts of a network of supply orchestrated by leading brands in America and Europe.

Everywhere there are overlapping networks – producer networks, supplier networks, retail networks, customer networks, employee networks, consultant networks, technology cooperation networks, venture capital and banking networks, networks of friends and acquaintances cutting across firms, ex-colleague networks, online networks and computer information networks.

The expansion of hubs and weak links has opened up a new dimension of work, a different way of working. The business world used to divide neatly into a few entrepreneurs and a mass of passive employees. Now it is not so clear cut. There are many more entrepreneurs; but the really important change is that ordinary employees can behave like entrepreneurs, either in preparation for becoming one, or as an alternative.

By expanding our personal network and using weak links, our jobs can become more interesting and self-directed, and we can become more valuable. We may still work in somebody else's firm, but we strive to control our own destiny, based on the unique networks each of us creates. Instead of work being starkly divided into owners and wage-slaves, we increasingly see a spectrum, a continuum ranging from total dependence on an organisation to ownership of it, with most people positioned between the extremes, yet gradually moving towards greater independence. Within each firm there are *embryo entrepreneurs*, poised to break out. Alternatively, we may choose to gain many of the benefits of running our own business – through making our value clear to our employers – without the risk or bother of setting up a new firm.

The more people who think of themselves as autonomous hubs with a useful network in tow – a unique and personal set of valuable weak links – the more society and the economy will change. For sure, power and wealth still reside in many long-established hubs, notably in government bureaucracies and the giant corporations listed on the stock exchange. Slowly but surely, however, innovation, wealth creation and therefore influence and independence are moving towards newer firms, entrepreneurs and the semi-autonomous individuals within all firms, away from the hubs themselves and towards the links within the hubs and outside them. These links may lead to new hubs, which for a time might become powerful, but they are usually the vehicles of individuals and groups of individuals. And hubs, old or new, will always be challenged by innovators whose main weapons, at least initially, are usually their weak links to other individuals and their ideas.

The links are personal alliances – easily formed, constantly shifting, nearly always non-contractual – based on casual friendship, empathy and millions of unrecorded favours granted and reciprocated. The network economy allows some lucky or creative individuals to capture unprecedented fortunes. Yet the source of wealth is not organizational – it is *personal*, a huge extended chain of information and insight where no money changes hands, a collage of favours freely given with only the vaguest sense that they will be paid back somewhere in the chain at some undetermined future time. In this new form of capitalism, competition has not been abolished or abated a whit, but the human instinct for cooperation has become a parallel force driving the economy and society forward, increasing wealth and autonomy at the same time.

Whether at work, as citizens or in our leisure pursuits, we used to be connected primarily by organisations – firms, trade unions, holiday camps, clubs and societies, travel firms. Increasingly, we are now also connected by individual initiatives, online links and spontaneous offline meetings, personal networking and chance meetings with acquaintances, friends of friends, and strangers. Whenever individuals take the initiative and organise their own lives, independent of existing institutions or by forming their own informal groupings – such as Burning Man – society becomes more fluid, unpredictable, open ended, uncontrolled, organic and personal. Hierarchy ebbs; personality flows. Networks are individualised, and individuals networked.

So, we are not only shifting from hierarchies to networks, but also seeing a shift from the more hierarchical and inflexible networks towards the least structured and most personal kind of network – weak links. People who maintain a wide array of diverse weak links make use of network power in its purest and most spontaneous form – social, personal and based on intelligence in the broadest possible sense: superior information and insight that are transformed into something useful through collaboration.

We started this book with two contrasting views of the world: Charlie Chaplin as victim; and James Dean as iconoclast and forerunner of the 'me-generation'. We have argued that there is a third way between the extremes of hierarchy and individualism, and that networks provide a better model in two senses – a more accurate map of the modern world and a better way of organising society.

The idea of the lone individual against the world has a mythical, romantic attraction for many of us; but it provides no map of social reality. If we do not realise the importance of choosing our hubs carefully, of moving on from them when we do not want or plan to do so, and of noticing the beautiful and intricate intertwining web of weak links around us – any apparently inconsequential one of which might move our life up to a new level – then we will be unlikely to fulfil our individual potential. Actually, networks thrive on individuality, because new networks are always created and expanded by innovators. They thrive on the differences between people, on the insights that come from pulling together good ideas from diverse worlds. Networks facilitate communication; communication facilitates networks. For communication to have content, there has to be an exchange of information, some element of surprise, some news or insight.

History reveals a pattern whereby humans have become increasingly specialised, yet increasingly connected. The world has never been bigger: more people; more land occupied; more countries; more cities and gathering places, even unto cyberspace; more wealth; more ideas and inventions; more hubs of all kinds, organisations devoted to business, government, education, culture, mutual help, strange specialties. But the world has also never been smaller: we can travel, use the phone, meet online and use weak links that will take us from one acquaintance to another in a marvellous, unending chain of human existence stretching right around the planet.

The fact that the big world is also a small world is due entirely to the growth of networks and the decline of hierarchies, to the victory of communication over regimentation, and to the triumph of individualism. A small minority of people have superconnected, and the rest of us have responded, albeit imperfectly, to the opportunities that new networks have bestowed.

Of course, social, religious and ideological barriers remain. Huge numbers are still trapped in oppressive regimes; or in poverty and isolation, exclusively reliant on friends, family and employers, without the vital weak links into a broader community. But most of us in developed countries are lucky enough to be able to roam free, not as reckless individuals, but as collaborators who can connect intelligently to a large number of people – our own unique set of contacts and information – many of whom are far removed from the constraints that our social background, location and training used to place on us.

We are all acutely aware of the dark side of life – of death and decay, of insecurity and depression, of tottering economies and hard times, of addiction and indifference, and of the cruelty that humans, almost uniquely as a species, visit upon one another. For the moment, we have triumphed over nature and material need, but suffering continues shamefully and nature may still take its revenge.

Yet there is also a truly bright side to human evolution. We have created networks that allow society to develop increased wealth and welfare, variety and cohesion, freedom and responsibility for one another's wellbeing, individuality and sociability. That is no mean feat. It has been achieved because, as time has passed, humans have been able to pay increasing attention to personal and social considerations, less to the need for survival and the requirements of bare subsistence, and more to the deployment of individual talents and cooperation, in a tight but light web of mutual dependence.

Viewing life through the simple prism of hubs, strong links and weak links, our vital personal and business decisions become clearer, less fraught, less frenetic, less bounded. Every few years we choose a new career hub or add a social context that has the potential to propel us to a new world. Every day we notice unexpected links with interesting people, links that can enrich our lives in small or big ways. Unlike Charlie Chaplin the hapless screen victim, we choose increasingly congenial yet challenging hubs, as Chaplin himself did in real life. Unlike the adolescent James Dean, we are not alienated from mainstream society. Yet we become individuals to the highest possible degree.

We are full, active and engaged members of a truly connected society; of that mysterious but no longer elusive entity – the human race. Our individuality and distinctiveness make deep communication possible, binding us all together in history's greatest paradox – the ever closer, tighter, freer and richer fabric of humanity.

# Acknowledgements

*Superconnect* took ages to write, and although we enjoyed the process, releasing the book is a cause for great joy.

And also much gratitude.

First, we'd like to thank all the scholars who have toiled in the field of network science and its antecedents. We've been inspired most by Mark Granovetter, our favourite sociologist, the late Stanley Milgram, Albert-László Barabási, Réka Albert, Steven Strogatz and Duncan J. Watts. We are also grateful to many philosophers and authors who have made us think and have contributed to ideas found here – the great John Stuart Mill, Vilfredo Pareto, Frigyes Karinthy, Bruce Henderson and the much-missed Jane Jacobs; William Gibson, Malcolm Gladwell, Daniel Goleman, Marshall McLuhan and Steven Pinker; and three economists – Thomas Schelling, Paul Krugman and Tim Harford – all of whom are very much alive.

Plaudits are also due to the sixty or so people, from all walks of life and many different countries, whom we interviewed for this book. Many of them are identified by name in the text, so there is no need for a long list here; but we are profoundly grateful for their insights and time, not just in being interviewed, but in checking the transcripts of their interviews and providing additional thoughts. We are also thankful for the many other distinguished people who were interviewed and preferred to remain anonymous, but similarly took great trouble with their stories and comments. Further thanks to everyone who connected us with their own contacts, nominating interesting interviewees – Jim Lawrence, Rick Haller, André Plisnier, Sally Holloway and John Hewitt were particularly helpful here.

Thank you to the many friends who read drafts of the manuscript – oh, so many drafts! – and provided valuable and critical feedback, even if it was not fully appreciated at the time. Some people even managed to provide inspiration and feedback over lunch, without ever seeing the drafts! Those who spring to mind as we write this are Andrin Bachmann, Eric Benedict, Neil Chalmers, Helen Clark, Chris Eyles, Robin Field, Matthew Grimsdale, Stuart Heather, John Hewitt, Charles Hutchinson, Jim Lawrence, Iain MacMillan, Martin Nye, Jamie Reeve, Anthony Rice and Mary Saxe-Falstein.

In a category all her own is our agent, Sally Holloway, whose work cannot be praised too highly, and without whom this book would not exist. Our agent in America, Zoe Pagnamenta, has also been a great light in our lives, and her enthusiasm for the book has been very encouraging.

Our publishers, Angela Vonderlippe at W. W. Norton, and Tim Whiting at Little, Brown, have been tremendously helpful and a pleasure to work with. And their respective colleagues, Erica Stern and Iain Hunt, have been splendid, too.

Richard would like to pay tribute to his extremely pleasant and efficient new assistant, Francisco Martins, as well as his neighbours in Portugal – Susan, Paul, Uli and Horst; the people and dogs of Butoque for their daily inspiration; and Bernhard and Irene Strathmann, who not only designed and commissioned the wonderful house where much of this book was written, but sold it to Richard – they have played a large part in making the last year highly enjoyable and productive. Richard's greatest thanks, however, go to Matthew and Tocker, who have done more than they know to make this book possible.

Greg would like to thank his colleagues, particularly Andrin and Helen, for their generous encouragement in his book-writing. Finally, he is most grateful to Christina, who, against all his instincts, got him to buy a house on a hill in the middle of nowhere. It has turned out to be a place in the middle of somewhere very special indeed, and a perfect place to write. And to his six-year-old daughter Zoe, who has taught him more than anyone else about human nature.

# Endnotes

## CHAPTER ONE

1 Jean-Philippe Bouchard and Marc Mézard (2000) 'Wealth Condensation in a Simple Model of the Economy', *Physica A* 282, page 536. See also Richard Koch (1997) *The 80/20 Principle*, Nicholas Brealey, London.

## CHAPTER TWO

2 Jane Jacobs (1961) *The Death and Life of Great American Cities*, Random House, New York.

3 Stanley Milgram (1967), 'The Small-World Problem', *Psychology Today* 1, pages 61–7.

4 Jeffrey Travers and Stanley Milgram (1969) 'An Experimental Study of the Small World Problem', *Sociometry* 32 (4) (December), pages 425–3; quotation page 426.

5 Judith S. Kleinfeld (2002) 'The Small-World Problem', *Society* 39 (2), pages 61–6.

6 Peter Sheridan Dodds, Roby Muhamad and Duncan J. Watts (2003) 'An Experimental Study of Search in Global Social Networks', *Science* 301 (8 August), pages 827–9.

7 After Watts adjusted mathematically for incomplete chains. We think Judith Kleinfeld exaggerates both how scanty Milgram's data were and how difficult it was to see his workings. In 1969 Jeffrey Travers and Stanley Milgram published their results quite clearly in the academic

journal *Sociometry* (see note 3 above). Table 2 breaks down the three different samples, described as 'Nebraska Random', 'Nebraska Stockholders' and 'Boston Random', showing for each the number of completed chains, and the range and average chain length for each sample. In the Nebraska Random sample, there were 18 completed chains and the mean chain length was 5.7; in the Nebraska Stockholders, 24 completed chains and a mean length of 5.4. The difference between the two samples' number of intermediaries – perhaps surprisingly, given that one would expect the investors to be considerably more successful – was not statistically significant. The investor group was chosen not to rig the results but specifically to test whether it would have more success compared with a random group – and it didn't. Therefore, we can aggregate these samples, producing forty-two completed chains. Although the Boston Random group had a shorter average chain length than the Nebraska Random group (4.4 and 5.7 intermediaries, respectively), it is surprising that the difference wasn't greater, considering that the folders travelling from Nebraska had to cross 1300 miles while those from the Boston area had to go fewer than 25 miles.

## CHAPTER THREE

8  John Stuart Mill (1848) *The Principles of Political Economy*, reissued as *Principles of Political Economy and Chapters on Socialism* (2008), Oxford World's Classics, Oxford Paperbacks, Oxford. See book V, chapter 17, section 3.

9  Mark S. Granovetter (1973) 'The Strength of Weak Ties', *American Journal of Sociology* 78 (6) (May), pages 1360–80.

10  The quotations in this paragraph are taken from Granovetter's second major paper on weak ties: Mark Granovetter (1983) 'The Strength of Weak Ties: A Network Theory Revisited', *Sociological Theory* 1, pages 201–33; all quotations from page 202.

11  Mark S. Granovetter (1973) 'The Strength of Weak Ties', *American Journal of Sociology* 78 (6) (May), page 1366.

12  Mark Granovetter (1974, 1995) *Getting a Job: A Study of Contacts and Careers* (2nd edition), University of Chicago Press, Chicago, page 22.

13  Granovetter (1973), op. cit., pages 1371–2.

14 Quoted in Emanuel Rosen (2000) *The Anatomy of Buzz: Creating Word of Mouth Marketing*, HarperCollins, London, page 73.

15 Gary Fine and Sherryl Kleinman (1981) 'Rethinking Subculture: An Interactionist Analysis', *American Journal of Sociology* 85 (1), pages 1–20. Quotation from page 9.

16 Gabriel Weimann (1980) 'Conversation Networks as Communication Networks', abstract of Ph.D. dissertation, University of Haifa, Israel.

17 Rose Coser (1975) 'The Complexity of Roles as a Seedbed of Individual Autonomy', in L. Coser (editor) *The Idea of Social Structure: Essays in Honor of Robert Merton*, Harcourt Brace Jovanovich, New York. Quotations from pages 241–2, 256–8.

18 For example, a 1978 study in the Tri-City area of the eastern United States replicated Milgram's small-world experiments but paid particular attention to whether booklets reached their target more easily through strong or weak links. The researchers found that 'participants in the successful chains tended to utilize fewer strong links . . . [Those who reached the targets] dramatically showed that they had weak links with the targets.' See Nan Lin, Paul Dayton and Peter Greenwald (1978) 'Analyzing the Instrumental Use of Relations in the Context of Social Structure', *Sociological Methods and Research* 7 (2), pages 149–66. The same conclusion was reached in Duncan Watts' email experiment: 'successful chains in comparison with incomplete chains disproportionately involved professional [weak] ties rather than friendship and familial relationships' (Dodds *et al.*, op. cit., page 163).

19 E. O. Wilson (2002) *The Future of Life*, Knopf, New York.

20 D. J. Watts and S. H. Strogatz (1998) 'Collective dynamics of "small-world" networks', *Nature* 393, pages 440–2. See also Duncan J. Watts (1999) *Small Worlds: The Dynamics of Networks between Order and Randomness,* Princeton University Press, Princeton NJ. The best short explanation of the Watts/Strogatz model is in Mark Buchanan (2002) *Nexus: Small Worlds and the Groundbreaking Science of Networks*, W. W. Norton, New York, pages 51–5.

21 Note that connecting 1000 points in a circle to each of the 10 neighbouring points, 5 to the left and 5 to the right, does not result in 10,000 links, but only 5,000. This is because each link serves as two connections – from point A to point B, and from point B to point

A. As a simple proof imagine a circle of ten points with each point connected to its two immediate neighbours. The number of connections needed is not 10 points × 2 neighbours. Only 10 connections are needed to achieve this.

## CHAPTER FOUR

22 Milgram (1967), op. cit., page 66.
23 Malcolm Gladwell, 'Six Degrees of Lois Weisberg', *New Yorker*, 11 January 1999.
24 Alan Zakon (1992) 'Remembrances of Bruce Doolin Henderson', unpublished memorial service document at the Memorial Church, Harvard University, 11 December. Dr Zakon went on to become chief executive and chairman of BCG. Later comments by Seymour Tilles, George Stalk and John Clarkeson were made at the same service.
25 Thomas Schelling (1978) *Micromotives and Macrobehavior*, W. W. Norton, New York.
26 I've found it easiest to use a chessboard and two packs of cards to conduct the random scrambling. Take sixty-four of the cards, ignore what's printed on them, and write in the position on the chessboard that each card represents (for example 3, 1 for the third row and first column). Shuffle the sixty-four cards. Deal twenty of them at random. These represent the twenty chess pieces to be taken off the board. Shuffle these twenty cards and deal five of them. Replace five of the twenty chess men, picked at random, on to the spaces represented by the five cards. Repeat the whole process as many times as necessary to convince yourself that Schelling's pattern of segregation from integration is typical.

## CHAPTER FIVE

27 Paul Seabright, 'Darwin and the Terrible Games of Homo Sapiens', *Financial Times*, 2 January 2009.
28 Robert Alexrod (1984) *The Evolution of Cooperation*, Basic Books, New York, chapter 4.

29 Richard D. Horan, Erwin Bulte and Jason F. Shogren (2005) 'How Trade Saved Humanity from Biological Exclusion: An Economic Theory of Neanderthal Extinction', *Journal of Economic Behavior and Organisation* 58 (1) (September), pages 1–29.

30 Interview by Steve Paulson, 'Proud Atheists', 15 October 2007, www.salon.com.

31 Daniel Goleman (2007) *Social Intelligence: The New Science of Human Relationships*, Bloomsbury, London.

32 Broadcast for WLS Radio, a Chicago station.

33 Daniel Goleman (2007) op. cit., page 49.

34 Barry Schwartz (2004) *The Paradox of Choice: Why More Is Less*, HarperCollins, New York.

35 'Japan's Killer Work Ethic', *Wall Street Journal*, 8 June 2008.

36 Thomas J. Johnson (2004) 'The Rehabilitation of Richard Nixon', in Harry P. Jeffrey and Thomas Maxwell-Long (editors) *Watergate and the Resignation of Richard Nixon: Impact of a Constitutional Crisis*, CQ Press, Washington, DC.

37 Stanley Milgram (1974) *Obedience to Authority*, HarperCollins, New York.

38 Jut Meininger (1973) *Success through Transactional Analysis*, Signet, New York, pages 127–8.

39 In 2009, Microsoft sold Razorfish to giant advertising agency Publicis in exchange for a 3 per cent share in the latter.

40 Quoted in Steven L. McShane and Mary Ann Von Glinow (1999) *Organizational Behavior: Emerging Realities for the Workplace Revolution*, McGraw-Hill College, New York.

41 J. Useem, 'Welcome to the New Company Town', *Fortune*, 10 January 2000, pages 62–70.

42 Dave Arnott (1999) *Corporate Cults: The Insidious Lure of the All-Consuming Organization*, Amacom, New York.

## CHAPTER SIX

43 William Gibson in an interview with CNN, 26 August 1997.

44 William Gibson (1984) *Neuromancer*, Ace Books, New York, page 51.

45 Marshall McLuhan (1964, 1993) *Understanding Media: The Extensions of Man*, Routledge, London.

46 IDC (2008) *US Consumer Online Behavior Survey Results 2007*, 19 February.

47 Written in 1948, published in 1949.

48 Published in 1956, a surprise bestseller railing against the conformity of middle management.

49 A number-one hit around the world in 1963, written the previous year by Malvina Reynolds after driving around Daly City, California, and seeing identical houses blotting the hillside: 'they're all made out of ticky tacky and they all look just the same'.

50 Sir James George Frazer (1890, 1993) *The Golden Bough*, Wordsworth Editions, London.

51 Randall Stross, 'Why Television Still Shines in a World of Screens', *New York Times*, 7 February 2009.


## CHAPTER SEVEN

52 Julian Fellowes (2004) *Snobs*, Weidenfeld & Nicolson, London, page 57.

53 See Tim Jackson (1994) *Virgin King: Inside Richard Branson's Business Empire*, HarperCollins, London, page 7. According to Jackson, Branson's acolytes carry identical black notebooks in imitation of the great man.

54 Ray Oldenburg (1999) *The Great Good Place: Cafes, Coffee Shops, Bookstores, Bars, Hair Salons and Other Hangouts at the Heart of a Community*, Marlowe & Company, New York.


## CHAPTER EIGHT

55 Mark Granovetter (1974, 1995), op. cit.

56 Mark Granovetter (1974, 1995) op. cit., page 89.

57 Charles Handy (2001) *The Elephant and the Flea: Looking Backwards to the Future*, Random House, London.

## CHAPTER NINE

58 James Champy (1994) *Reengineering Management: The Mandate for New Leadership*, HarperCollins, New York.

59 This is the traditional account as outlined in the Acts of the Apostles (9: 2) by Luke, who writes that Saul was authorised by Jerusalem's high priest to barge into the synagogues of Damascus, arrest any followers of the Way, and 'bring them bound to Jerusalem'. However, it is highly unlikely that this version, written thirty or forty years after the events it purports to describe, is accurate. Damascus was not in Judaea, the Jewish authorities in Jerusalem had no jurisdiction there, it is implausible that they would go in for kidnapping and rendition, and there is no independent evidence (beyond the New Testament) that Jews ever persecuted anyone for their religious views. Paul's own account in his letter to the Galatians does not square with Luke's, although Paul does claim that he was 'violently persecuting the church of God'.

60 Galatians 1: 11–17

61 '[T]hrough Jesus, God will bring with him those who have died . . . we who are alive, who are left until the coming of the Lord, will by no means precede those who have died . . . the dead in Christ will rise first. Then we who are alive, who are left, will be caught up in the clouds together with them to meet the Lord in the air; and so we will be with the Lord for ever.' This was written by Paul around AD 50–1 in the first letter of his that has survived (1 Thessalonians 4: 13–18).

62 'He [God] does not deal with us according to our sins . . . so great is his steadfast love towards those who fear him; as far as the East is from the West, he removes our transgressions from us' (Psalms 103: 10–12).

63 Galatians 3: 28.

64 See Andrew Welburn (1991) *The Beginnings of Christianity: Essence Mystery and Christian Vision*, Floris Books, Edinburgh, and Keith Hopkins (1999) *A World Full of Gods: Pagans, Jews and Christians in the Roman Empire*, Orion, London.

65 Quoted in Francis Wheen (1999) *Karl Marx*, Fourth Estate, London, page 313.

66  Karl Marx and Friedrich Engels (1848, 1967) *The Communist Manifesto*, Penguin Classics, London, page 87.

67  As a proportion of the population in America and Europe, industrial workers reached their peak around 1950 (more broadly, between 1920 and 1970) and then began to decline as the number of white-collar 'knowledge' workers grew rapidly. See Manuel Castells (1996) *The Rise of the Network Society*, Blackwell, Massachusetts, chapter 4.

68  As a leading historian writes: 'Only Lenin could have galvanized the Bolsheviks to his goal of seizing power . . . no Lenin, no Stalin . . . And also no Russian Civil War? No famines, including the half-intentional one of forcing the peasantry into collectivized agriculture? And no murderous purges . . . ? Almost certainly not . . . The purges and the Great Patriotic War, as Moscow called its death struggle with Nazi Germany, claimed some forty million Soviet lives. It's hard to imagine a fraction of that loss without Lenin's obsession and legacy . . . there would almost as certainly have been no Cold War either . . . No draining of measureless effort, money, and resources by "defense" on virtually every continent.' (George Feifer (2001) 'No Finland Station', in Robert Cowley (editor) *More What If? Eminent Historians Imagine What Might Have Been*, Penguin Putnam, New York, pages 233-4)

69  Macintyre, James (11 September 2007) 'Anita Roddick, Capitalist With a Conscience, Dies at 64', *Independent*, http://www.independent.co.uk/news/uk/this-britain/anita-roddick-capitalist-with-a-conscience-dies-at-64-402014.html. Retrieved 25 September 2009.

70  Jim Collins (2001) *Good to Great: Why Some Companies Make the Leap . . . and Others Don't*, Random House, New York.

## CHAPTER TEN

71  Albert-László Barabási and Réka Albert (1999) *Emergence of Scaling in Random Networks*, Science 286: 509–12.

72  Bruce D. Henderson (1973) 'Failure to Compete', *BCG Perspective*.

73  David Crystal (2002) *The English Language: A Guided Tour of the Language*, Penguin, London.

74  *The Sunday Times Rich List*, 26 April 2009, page 42.

75  Interview with Eric Schmidt, *McKinsey Quarterly*, September 2008.

76  A network star enjoying a virtual monopoly may exploit its customers by raising prices. But − with the possible exception of Microsoft − most network stars don't price higher than their few competitors, or at a level customers find unacceptable. They don't need to. And if they rile their customers, they may eventually lose their coveted position and end up with nothing.

77  Kevin Kelly (1998) *New Rules for the New Economy: 10 Ways the Network Economy is Changing Everything*, Viking Penguin, New York.

78  Thomas L. Friedman (2005) *The World Is Flat,* Farrar, Strauss and Giroux, New York.

## CHAPTER ELEVEN

79  Castells, op. cit., page 470.

80  Granovetter (1983), op. cit., page 219.

81  Tim Harford (2008) *The Logic of Life: Uncovering the New Economics of Everything*, Little, Brown, London.

82  Jane Jacobs (1969) *The Economy of Cities*, Random House, New York.

83  Michael Porter (1998) 'Clusters and the New Economics of Competition', *Harvard Business Review* 76 (6) (November–December) pages 77–90.

84  Edward L. Glaeser, Hedi D. Kallal, Jose A. Scheinkman and Andrei Shleifer (1992) 'Growth in Cities', *Journal of Political Economy* 100 (6) (December), pages 1126–52.

85  Alfred Marshall (1890, 1920) *Principles of Economics*, Macmillan, London, book IV, chapter 10, quoted in Harford, op. cit., pages 169–70.

86  Castells, op. cit., page 55.

87  Anna-Lee Saxenian (1994) *Regional Advantage: Culture and Competition in Silicon Valley and Route 128*, Harvard University Press, Cambridge, MA.

88  Henry W. Chesbrough (2003) *Open Innovation: The New Imperative for Creating and Profiting from Technology*, Harvard Business School Press, Cambridge, MA.

89  Al Ries and Laura Ries (2004) *The Origin of Brands: Discover the*

*Natural Laws of Product Innovation and Business Survival*, HarperCollins, New York.

90 Clayton Christensen (1997) *The Innovator's Dilemma: When New Technologies Cause Great Firms to Fail*, Harvard Business School Press, Cambridge, MA.

91 Ibid., page 4.

92 Judith Blau (1980) 'When Weak Ties Are Structured', unpublished manuscript, Department of Sociology, State University of New York, Albany.


## CHAPTER TWELVE

93 Based on 'Mobile Money Spinner for Women', *BBC News*, 8 October 2002.

94 Jeffrey D. Sachs (2005) *The End of Poverty, Economic Possibilities for our Time*, Penguin, New York.

95 George Gilder (1981) *Wealth and Poverty*, Basic Books, New York, pages 68–70.

96 Carol Stack (1974) *All Our Kin*, Basic Books, New York, page 128.

97 George Gilder, op. cit., page 67.

98 Herbert J. Gans (1962) *The Urban Villagers: Group and Class in the Life of Italian-Americans*, The Free Press, New York, page 283–98.

99 Granovetter (1983), op. cit., page 210.

100 Peter Blau (1974) 'Parameters of Social Structure', *American Sociological Review* 39 (5), pages 615–35.

101 Sudhir Venkatesh (2008) *Gang Leader for a Day: A Rogue Sociologist Crosses the Line*, Penguin, New York.

102 Ibid., page 256.

103 Quoted in Steven D. Levitt and Stephen J. Dubner (2005) *Freakonomics: A Rogue Economist Explores the Hidden Side of Everything*, William Morrow, New York, page 97.

104 Granovetter (1983), op. cit., page 213.

105 Stack, op. cit., pages 113–14.

106 Ibid., page 115.

107 Ibid., page 107.

108 Hernando de Soto (2001) *The Mystery of Capital: Why Capitalism Works in the West and Fails Everywhere Else*, Black Swan, London.

109 Ibid., page 53.

110 Malcolm Gladwell, op. cit.

111 See Harford, op. cit., pages 187ff. See also Ed Glaeser and Janet Kohlhase (2003) 'Cities, Regions, and the Decline of Transport Costs', Harvard Institute of Economic Research, Working Paper No. 2004; and 'Don't Refloat: The Case against Rebuilding the Sunken City of New Orleans', *Slate*, 7 September 2005, available at: www.slate.com/id/2125810.

112 Jane Jacobs (1964, reprinted 1992) *The Death and Life of Great American Cities*, Vintage, New York.

113 See Harford, op. cit, pages 133–5 and 185–7.

114 Jacob Vigdor (2006) 'When Are Ghettos Bad? Lessons from Immigrant Segregation in the United States', working paper, quoted in Harford, op. cit., pages 164f.

## CHAPTER THIRTEEN

115 Kevin Kelly (1995) *Out of Control: The Rise of Neo-biological Civilization*, Addison-Wesley, Menlo Park, pages 26–7.

116 Seneca (2005) *Dialogues and Letters*, Penguin Classics, London.

117 Marshall McLuhan (1962) *The Gutenberg Galaxy*, University of Toronto Press, Toronto.

118 Philip Evans and Thomas S. Wurster (2000) *Blown to Bits: How the New Economics of Information Transforms Strategy*, Harvard Business School Press, Boston, page 211.

119 Castells, op. cit., page 161.

# Index